SHOPPING
for GOD

HOW CHRISTIANITY WENT FROM
IN YOUR HEART TO *IN YOUR FACE*

JAMES B. TWITCHELL

Simon & Schuster
NEW YORK • LONDON • TORONTO • SYDNEY

SIMON & SCHUSTER
Rockefeller Center
1230 Avenue of the Americas
New York, NY 10020

First Simon & Schuster hardcover edition September 2007

SIMON & SCHUSTER and colophon are registered trademarks
of Simon & Schuster, Inc.

For information about special discounts for bulk purchases,
please contact Simon & Schuster Special Sales at 1-800-456-6798
or business@simonandschuster.com.

Text designed by Paul Dippolito

Manufactured in the United States of America

1   3   5   7   9   10   8   6   4   2

Library of Congress Cataloging-in-Publication Data

Twitchell, James B., 1943–
    Shopping for God : how Christianity went from in your
heart to in your face / James B. Twitchell
        p.   cm.
    Includes bibliographical references and index.
    1. Church marketing. 2. Religious institutions—Marketing.
    3. Consumption (Economics)—Religious aspects—
Christianity.
    BV652.23 .T85   2007
    254'.4—dc22   2007017621

ISBN-13: 978-0-7432-9288-7

For Stella

Contents

SHOPPING
for GOD

CHAPTER ONE

Oh Lord, Why U.S.? An Overview of the Spiritual Marketplace

This is not a book about God. Turn back now if that's what you're after. Save your time, money, and perhaps your temper. This book is not about belief, or spirituality, or the yearning for transcendence. Don't get me wrong: those are truly important matters. Rather, *Shopping for God* is about how some humans—modern-day Christians, to be exact—go about the process of consuming—of buying and selling, if you will—the religious experience. This book is about what happens when there is a free market in religious products, more commonly called *beliefs*. Essentially, how are the sensations of these beliefs generated, marketed, and consumed? Who pays? How much? And how come the markets are so roiled up right now in the United States? Or have they always been that way?

By extension, why are the markets so docile in Western Europe? In 1900 almost everyone in Europe was Christian. Now three out of four Europeans identify themselves as Christians. At the same time, the percentage who say they are nonreligious has soared from less than 1 percent of the population to 15 percent. According to the Center for the Study of Global Christianity, another 3 percent say they don't believe in God at all. Churches in Europe are in free fall, plenty of sellers but no new buyers. According to the World Values Survey in 2000, in twelve major European countries, 38 percent of the population say they never or practically never attend church. France's 60 percent nonattendance rate is the highest in that group. Here in the U.S., only 16 percent say they rarely go to church.

No wonder Europeans look at us and think we're nuts. Are we? We're consuming the stuff in bulk 24-7. Religion here is perpetually ripe. Are we—a nation disparaged as shallow materialists—more deeply concerned about the eternal verities than our high-minded European cousins? That is doubtful. So what gives?

One answer is that we're doing a better job of selling religion. Or to put it in the lingo of Econ 101, we are doing a robust business in supplying valuable religious experiences for shoppers at reasonable prices. But, if so, how so? And do I really mean to suggest that the marketplace is not just a metaphor, but a reality? Does the small church on the corner operate like the gas station? What about the megachurch out there by the interstate—is it like a big-box store? How come the church downtown with exactly the same product is in shambles? And, while we're on this vulgar subject, how do churches sell? How do they compete for customers, called *believers* and *parishioners* in some venues and *seekers* in others, if indeed they do? They say they don't compete. At least they say this in public.

Are the religion dealers, if I may call them that, in any way like the car dealers on the edge of town? And what of the denominations that they represent—do *they* compete? How similar is their behavior to what happens when General Motors goes up against Ford or Chrysler? And what happens when foreign lower-cost suppliers (like Honda) and higher-end suppliers (like Mercedes-Benz) enter the market? And how about home-grown low-cost discounters (like Costco) or web-based services (like Autobytel.com) that often sell cars almost entirely on price? The analogy is blasphemous, yes, but it may help us understand not just the spiritual marketplace but the current state of American culture.

If denominations don't compete for consumers (and they say they are interested only in new believers or lapsed believers, not in brand switchers, or what they call *transfer growth*), why are almost all of them spending millions of parishioners' dollars on advertising campaigns? Why are they hiring so many marketing consultants? We will look at some of these denominational campaigns because it's clear that they are poaching other flocks. There is an entire new business model called the Church Growth Movement to help them along.

Essentially, this book is about how religious sensation is currently being manufactured, branded, packaged, shipped out, and consumed. The competition is fierce. Some old-line suppliers (think Episcopal, Methodist, Lutheran) are losing market share at an alarming rate. Some of them are barely able to fund their pensions without dipping into investment capital. For them, things are going to get worse, a lot worse. They can't change their product fast enough. For them, *doing church* is a two-hour Sunday affair, but for an increasing number of super-efficient big-box churches, it can last for days, even the whole week.

These new churches, megachurches, are run by a very market-savvy class of speculators whom I will call *pastorpreneurs.* By clever use of marketing techniques, they have been able to create what are essentially city-states of believers. They are the low-cost discounters of rapture that promise to shift the entire industry away from top-down denominationalism toward stand-alone communities. Small case in point: in the last few years, we all have learned a new common language. We use *born-again, inerrancy, rapture, left behind, megachurch,* and *evangelical* in ways that our parents never did. Some of us even use the word *crusade.*

Religion Goes Pop

Religion has become a major source of pop culture. You can see this in the role of celebrity. The old-style celeb kept his religion to himself. Now he's in your face. In a way, however, this represents a return to the original definition of *celebrity,* namely, the one who

Religion as fashion statement or fashion statement as religion?

celebrates the religious event. Nothing is more revered in American popcult than the renown of being well-known.

So we all know of Mel Gibson's evangelical Catholicism and Tom Cruise's Scientology. And what of Madonna and kabbalah, Richard Gere and Buddhism, Muhammad Ali and Islam? I think it's safe to say that a generation ago, most entertainers did not wear their religiosity on their sleeves, or anywhere else for that matter. Madison Avenue and the film studios saw to that. Now, just the reverse. You wear your belief on your sleeves, right next to your religious bling.

Since the religious experience is moved through media, through delivery systems (of which the church itself is becoming less important), let's have a quick look at the transformations being wrought in film, television, radio, the internet, and even dusty old book publishing. What we'll see is how transformative the new version of Christianity has become on the very vehicles that move it around.

MOVIES

If, as the saying goes, the religion of Hollywood is money, then the returns of Christiantainment have proven a God-send. Back in the

1950s, as television was stealing the movies' thunder, there was a spate of big-budget, big-screen, big-star, little-religion movies called "Sword & Sandal" epics. Some are still cycling through late night television: *The Robe, The Ten Commandments,* and *Ben-Hur.* The Bible was invoked more for Sturm und Drang, *son et lumière,* and, let's face it, really steamy love scenes than for any presentation of dogma.

It was in the marketing of one of these movies, incidentally, that the faux Ten Commandments tablet first appeared in a public space. In many ways its exploitation neatly condenses the theme of this book. As Cecil B. DeMille readied his costly Paramount production of *The Ten Commandments* for release, he happened on an ingenious publicity scheme. In partnership with the Fraternal Order of Eagles, a nationwide association of civic-minded clubs founded by theater owners, he sponsored the construction of several thousand Ten Commandments monuments throughout the country. DeMille, a Jew, was interested in plugging the film, not Christianity.

A generation later, two of these DeMille-inspired granite monuments, first in Alabama and then on the grounds of the Texas capital in Austin, became the focus of the *Ten Commandments* case before the U.S. Supreme Court. What was essentially an advertisement for an entertainment had become a deadly serious pronouncement of in-your-face faith.

The modern biblical epic is nothing if not drenched in the blood of Calvary. *Adios,* Samson and Delilah, David and Bathsheba, Demetrius, and all those gladiatorial interludes with the smarmy and wonderfully named Victor Mature. Golgotha, usually glimpsed only as the curtain falls in the Sword & Sandal epic, is now stage center. The modern version, viz. Mel Gibson's *The Passion of the Christ,* is nothing if not a total rearrangement of the genre. This film revels in small budget, no star, no love scenes. *Shhh,* please, this is a serious re-creation of *what really happened.*

Nothing in film history compares with Gibson's film. It is truly sui generis. And as such, it's a condensation of broader changes. First, it is unflaggingly serious. The language is Aramaic, for goodness' sake. If not literally true, then why use the real language? Next, it was released in a totally un-Hollywood way. The movie was initially shown in a venue aptly suited and wired for this experience: the megachurch. After all, when your projection and sound equipment rivals that of the local cineplex, why not use it to showcase film? And since the megachurch is open 24-7, you can schedule multiple viewings. And there are stadium seats and amphitheater architecture. This place was ordained for film.

The marketing of *The Passion* was still more revelatory of cultural shifts. The initial advertising did not go from studio-to-you, but from studio-to-minister-to-you. If you ever wanted to see the much-ballyhooed targeted entertainment, here it is. And finally, *The Passion* was what the earlier attempts only dreamed of: it became a legitimate blockbuster. Not only did it gross some $400 million in the U.S., not only did it revolutionize how movies are taken to market, but it also had what is called a huge *back end*.

The big money in movies is not just in theatrical display but in this aftermarket. Here is the new way that many movies will be seen, not out of the house and in the theater, but out of the house and in the church. Like King Gillette and the disposable razor, with some products you can give the thing away (the razor, the movie) and make up for it in the aftermarket (the blades, the accessories). The big money is not at the box office gross but in the, say, ten million DVDs that come after the show. People want to own this "text," to add it to their video *library*. In earlier days, a family had a going-to-church Bible and a stay-at-home family Bible. The family Bible now sits next to *The Passion* DVD.

So too the merchandise that travels with the experience, as the crucifixion nails (licensed by Mr. Gibson) worn around the neck to announce that you've not just seen the movie, you've suffered the experience. You can buy this memorial merchandise at the store inside your megachurch.

How powerful was *The Passion* as a marketing event? An online poll on Beliefnet.com, answered by about twelve thousand people, found that 62 percent were reading the Bible more often after seeing the film. The poll also found that 41 percent had a more positive view of the Bible after the movie. But that's not the count that really counted. Show me the money. In Hollywood there is a new term to describe the receipts from such events; they are now being called *Passion dollars.*

In the parting of the revenue seas are coming the never-ending Left Behind series of novels based on apocalyptic themes, as well as *The Chronicles of Narnia, The Gospel,* and countless other Christian stories. When the movie version of *The End Is Near* opened in 2005, it put in a cameo at the Bijou, then went straight to video and then straight to the family library. *Left Behind: World at War,* for instance, was the first film ever to open only in churches, not theaters. The movie premiered, on a late-October weekend, on 3,200 screens, largely in churches. You could buy the DVD and other mementos at the display table on your way out.

The struggle to find *Passion* dollars has become so wonderfully crazed that 20th Century Fox, a minor subsidiary of News Corp., has announced an upcoming movie based on John Milton's epic poem *Paradise Lost.* Its producer, Vincent Newman, has pledged to keep the script faithful to the original 1667 text. Not that the story of Satan's rebellion and expulsion from heaven and his subsequent role in the fall of man is not a rollicking good tale, but if the 1667 text is followed, it will indeed show how devout faith can be. English professors at least are on pins and needles.

What does this marketing portend? Instead of renting or buying all the seats in a theater, as did many churches with Mel Gibson's *The Passion of the Christ,* congregations themselves will debut the film in their sanctuary after paying a nominal licensing fee. The revolutionary film-release strategy seems like a no-brainer. Here's why: There are more than two hundred thousand churches in America compared to five thousand theaters, and many of these churches already have state-of-the-art projection equipment. But the real marketing genius is to realize that the audience does not regard this as *mere* entertainment but as something to own and treasure on DVD. See the film. Now buy a copy. From the producers' point of view, that's real rapture.

TELEVISION

While the upper tiers of cable television have been populated by the pant-blow preaching and money-grubbing chicanery of Oral Roberts, Jimmy Swaggart, Jim Bakker, and Peter Popoff, along with the deliciously wacky Jerry Falwell and Pat Robertson (who said of liberal professors on *The 700 Club* [March 21, 2006]: "They are racists, murderers, sexual deviants, and supporters of Al Qaeda—and they could be teaching your kids!"), the next step in religious programming is already happening. It's moving downtown, into daytime programming on network channels, away from the Christian Broadcasting Network (CBN) ghetto.

So, on one hand, individual churches are buying airtime not in the Sunday morning slot or the late-night wasteland but all through the day on what are essentially local channels. A megachurch like Lakewood in Houston produces Joel Osteen's show and then essentially cobbles together an ad hoc network. By waiting until the last minute, as well as buying time at the beginning of the season, they are lowering their cost per thousand and, better yet, shifting demographics to the "unchurched."

This is especially savvy because as cable stations may become unbundled from the various tiers, subscribers will have a choice of which channels they want. Currently, the religious networks *pay* the cable carriers to be included in the various tiers, the same way the shopping channels do. A la carte selection is anathema to religious begathon channels. After all, not many people would opt to pay for the privilege of having Pastor Benny Hinn come into your late-night airwaves to save your soul and drain your pocketbook.

But if dedicated all-religion-all-the-time channels are at risk, the networks are picking up some of the slack. Network television stations are also tuning in to the Christian market, a market they once avoided like the biblical plagues. So, increasingly on prime-time television we have characters who converse directly with a higher power, from *Joan of Arcadia* to Jaye on *Wonderfalls*. Meanwhile the

Armageddon-fueled worldview of the Left Behind books has resurfaced in an NBC prime-time miniseries of gimmickry, *Revelations*, sold with the captivating slogan "The End Is Near." The End is *dear* might be more appropriate.

Programmers may not know much, but they knew that *Touched by an Angel* was the second most watched television program in 1997. And the Nielsen numbers show its appeal cut across all religious boundaries. Advertisers loved the fact that the program mixed evangelical Christian and New Spirituality themes, giving it an aura of spiritual excitement and anticipation, but absolutely no content.

I find NBC's *The Book of Daniel* interesting, for here we had what looked to be the diametric opposite of in-your-face religion. We had in-your-face religious subversion. Or, better said, the subversion of the old-style religion; in this case, the religion the new Christianity is trying to get away from—hoary old Episcopalianism.

Here's a bit of it: Daniel, an Episcopal priest in an affluent New York City suburb, has a relationship with the real Jesus—well, the Warner Sallman Jesus with the flowing blond hair of Presentation Bibles. Daniel also has a gay son, another son bedding the teenage daughter of an influential parishioner, a daughter busted for dealing pot, a mother with Alzheimer's, and a boss, a female bishop, who's doing the dirty deed with his own father, another bishop. Little wonder that Daniel has been turning not only to Jesus, who rides shotgun as the pastor is out doing his chores, but also to the Vicodin pills stashed in the glove compartment.

Get the point? OK, this is a parody. But mark well that in almost every scene we are told that Daniel is Episcopalian. Again and again we cut to the moss-covered stone church that reeks of old money. It is simply inconceivable that Daniel would be pastor of a megachurch or an evangelical of any stripe. The show drew the immediate ire of the American Family Association (AFA), a conservative cultural watchdog group, which charged that it "mocks Christianity." True enough. But what I found so intriguing is that *The Book of Daniel* was all about old Christianity, the stumbling, bumbling Christianity that is full of fussbudgets. And there is no doubt, not for a nanosecond, which denomination best represents this kind of Christianity. It's those Episcopalians!

If the old Christianity prizes concepts of blood, heritage, taste, proper accents, clubbiness, Ivy League schools, and gentle chucks under the chin at the club supper, then the new Christianity is nothing but pious, loud, and a tad puritanical. The Episcopal Church used to rule the roost, and now it's in free fall. The word Episcopalians themselves would use is "dysfunctional family."

As we will see in later chapters, this Episcopal dysfunction exists for a number of reasons (ordination of the wrong people, supporter of the wrong causes, and invoker of irony at the wrong times), but *The Book of Daniel* is an apt condensation of what's happened in the religious markets. The subtle and admittedly woebegone have been replaced by the dynamic and aggressive. The so-called mainstream and mainline have sunk in their own contented sloth. The cocktail hour of American religion is over. *The Book of Daniel* was cancelled after only a few airings, but not because the Episcopal Church of America objected. The audience was too small, and most of them probably were . . . Episcopalians.

Far more interesting in terms of television content is that the network *news* divisions are the ones churning out religious-themed specials, and they are clearly informed by believers, not skeptics. From *Dateline NBC*'s "The Last Days of Jesus" to ABC News's ambitious three-hour special on Jesus and Paul, the networks are realizing what their Hollywood counterparts are finding out: the community of believers is one of the few audiences that will sit quietly and watch. The demographics may not be great, skewed toward middle age, but at least someone is not hitting the remote during commercials or TiVo-ing the program.

So when Barbara Walters did an ABC news special on the afterlife, she covered all the bases: a Catholic cardinal, the Dalai Lama, Richard Gere, suicide bombers, and evangelical impresario Ted Haggard. Before cavorting with sin, Mr. Haggard was the president of the National Association of Evangelicals, the largest evangelical group in America, and pastorpreneur of a 14,000-member megachurch called the New Life Church, in Colorado. That is, until he was caught up in scandal and forced to resign those positions. The news show was called "Heaven: Where Is It? How Do We Get There?" It was not called "Heaven: Does It Exist? How Did It Recently Become So Important?" ABC is a subsidiary of the Walt Disney Company. If there's one thing the corporate suits know it's where their audience is located. And Procter & Gamble, sponsor of the show, knows too.

RADIO

If you've turned on your radio recently, you'll hear what has happened, especially on the AM dial. It's become the voice of salvation. The FM band now carries most of the old-time content, both musical and news. AM radio is being further distanced from mainstream listeners by subscription services like Sirius or XM Radio, which are moving listeners farther away into niches. Chances are that if you now get into your car, turn on your radio to the AM dial, and hit "search," you will find only a few orphan stations, and the content will be either Rush Limbaugh or one of the more than 150 syndicated evangelical programs. Check www.christianradio.com and you will see the national coverage, almost all of it coming from small independently owned and often local-church-supported stations. Christian broadcasters now control more than 10 percent of U.S. broadcast licenses.

One of the unintended consequences of the opening up of the airwaves by the Reagan administration was not just that televangelism could colonize the upper channels of the television spectrum, but that AM radio would become overwhelmingly evangelical. Say what you want about the free market in media transmission; it opened gaps soon filled with highly concentrated religious programming.

In a peculiar way, the AM dial is returning radio to its early days, when "Church of the Air" was one of the standard shows on Sunday morning. Except that this church of the air has turned hot and breathy. The content from the 1930s to the 1980s was lukewarm, in part because the middle-of-the-road National Council of Churches denomination's controlled content. Until the explosion in FM band-width and a new Federal Communications Commission, the voice of Christianity was the dulcet tones of Fulton J. Sheen or Norman Vincent Peale. Tune in today, it's passionate and proselytizing.

Interestingly, the great transformation of radio content from highcult to popcult happened in the mid-twentieth century, and was not because of words but because of music. Rock and roll made radio the first truly popular medium, and it was a medium supported by advertising. Every year the audience dropped in age and sophistica-tion as receivers became cheaper. Programming moved to the most common denominator: kids. What was once promised as the great intellectual and unifying force (educational radio went along with "Church of the Air") turned out to be Dance Party of the Air.

Top 40 ruled. It soon colonized the AM dial. Christian music, first gospel, then country, went along for the ride and was also transformed, in part thanks to radio. What was once part of a musi-cal tradition from the Gregorian chants to oratorio to hymns has now cross-pollinated with other forms, even rap, and has moved over to FM.

This interpenetration of genres is the context of one of the hottest new musical forms, radio-based Christian rock. Christian rock reg-ularly earns more broadcast time than country, Latin, or classical music. The devil no longer has the best tunes. Completely assimi-lated into mainstream pop would be the band U2 and lead singer Bono, who often sings about matters of personal faith, but consider groups like 12 Stones, MercyMe, Audio Adrenaline, and Newsboys. They now rival mainstream rock groups on the FM airwaves. The band Casting Crowns has sold more than one million CDs without a mainstream hit by targeting church groups to promote such songs as "If We Are the Body," "Love Them like Jesus, and "Father, Spirit, Jesus." The cross-pollination of religion and rock and roll music also has produced a subset of Christian metal called "screamo," in which the religious lyrics are simply yelled. There's also a weird mutation of Christian rap called "extreme prayer," a ravelike exhilaration in which the participants pray all night, fueling themselves not on Ecstasy the drug, but on ecstasy the Word.

Music is crucial to religion because it is so emotional and resolutely nonintellectual. You can't explain a piece of music, you can only feel it. That's one reason why it is so appealing to adolescents. When you go into megachurches, you invariably hear an excellent band—93 percent of which use electric guitars and lots of percussion. There's even an ideal acoustic level—98 to 108 decibels. You invariably see a band room for the boys. It's filled with all kinds of expensive musical equipment, the likes of which mom and dad could never afford at home and the local school is too financially strapped to provide. When I was at Willow Creek (the ur-megachurch outside Chicago) doing research for this book, during some of the sermons the audio and video feed would come from the band room onto the JumboTron screens, and we'd look around at one another and be truly thankful for walls lined with acoustic tile. I realized not just the power of music to get in your face (albeit via the ears) but its power to attract the most recalcitrant churchgoers of all: teenage boys.

INTERNET

Right behind viewing porn, the next most popular use of the internet is for religious purposes. A recent survey by the Pew Research Center found that 64 percent of the nation's 128 million internet users say they use the web for religious or spiritual purposes. Here are the four most common words involved in generating passwords: *God. Love. Sex. Money.*

And what is it that people who use *God* as part of their password are looking for? If the object of their searches is like most other ones, they are not after a coherent compendium but a collection of tidbits, a ménage of factoids and partial conversations about things that matter. As denominations have become less important, or at least more in flux, people are cobbling together their own personalized spiritual plans. They are logging on to blogs, listening to Godcasts, interacting in chat rooms, and, in a sense, creating a highly personal just-for-me-religion that connects with a panoply of other beliefs. Do-it-yourself religion.

There are millions of religious-themed websites, of which the largest is Beliefnet. Beliefnet is gargantuan. It attracts 2.5 million visitors per month. More than 4.2 million people subscribe to Beliefnet's daily email newsletters, which send spiritual wisdom in various flavors all around the world. Generic "good words" is most popular (2.4 million), but right behind that is Bible-based "inspiration" (1.6 million). This service is like those telephone messages telling you how important you are to them each time you call. It's like the greeting card industry gone haywire. And it's very popular and doubtless important in making religion part of the rhythms of everyday life.

Beliefnet also runs Soulmatch, a faith-oriented online dating service, offers spiritual content to cell phone users, and publishes a series of Beliefnet guides with old-line publisher Doubleday. Additionally, Beliefnet regularly partners with ABC *World News Tonight* on its religion and spirituality coverage. What's telling about the current surge in religiosity is that Beliefnet is not affiliated with a particular religion or spiritual movement. Beliefnet Inc. is a privately held company funded by employees, individual investors, and Soft-Bank Capital and Blue Chip Venture Company. While it services the worshiper, it also worships the gods of profit and loss.

All the major denominations have sophisticated sites allowing believers access not just to a smidgen of doctrine and counseling but, more important, information about close-at-hand churches. Needless to say, almost every thriving church in the country has a website (some, as we shall see, are quite complex, especially those of the megachurches). Nearly 6 out of every 10 Protestant churches now have a dedicated website. Since 2000, the greatest increase in the use of church websites is evident among mainline Protestant churches (up 79 percent, to 70 percent of mainline congregations); ministries in the South (increased by 87 percent, up to 56 percent), and churches pastored by baby boomers (doubled, with websites now in

65 percent of the churches they pastor). If your church is interested in growth, the first thing you get is a marquee sign out front for clever sayings; the second is a website; the third is a bus.

In churning religious culture and making it increasingly central to modern life, nothing compares to the blogs. We may well look back at them as we now do to the 95 theses posted by Martin Luther that launched the Protestant Reformation. Blogs are stirring an already churned market. These personal vehicles range from intense explorations of particular questions to a simple daily expression of opinion on everything that comes into the writer's head. Bloggers tend to be both writers and readers, linking their blogs together and emailing back and forth. The daily give-and-take winds up connecting people across great distances. There are no scientific studies on the religious attitudes popping up among the world's more than ten million blogs, but the general bias is clearly evangelical. After all, those are the people with something to say. And they want *you* to hear it.

But content is not the power. Community is. The mechanism that makes blogs work is the ease with which they can call attention to one another through links—a single click, and you can be redirected halfway around the world; another click, and you return, all for free. There is no friction on the web. Blogs thrive through the process of linking to one another, thereby simultaneously defining the community with which they identify and increasing their traffic—and their claims to influence. Such "blogrolls," or lists of links to "Sites We Like," are usually found in the left or right rail.

Why is this so important for religion? Because religion is a voluntary interaction among consenting believers. Religion doesn't come installed at birth. You pick it up along the way. It's organic, a process, viral. Blogging is like what social scientists call *collaborative filtering,* itself very much like forming and unforming beliefs. Blogging and linking to other blogs becomes an exercise in collective belief making; you're designing and crafting your faith. This linking has the effect of identifying a handful of favorites and then amplifying their influence until they become the favorites of a much larger group.

Naturally the hot-button issues—abortion, homosexuality, assisted suicide, and intelligent design—get foregrounded while religious oppression, poverty, and world hunger get left behind.

This process of blog-transformed belief has become so pronounced that the American Academy of Religion, a professional association of scholars and teachers in the field of religion, has established a panel called the New Religions Group to study new faiths generated outside the religious mainstream and the way they interact with already established faiths. As typical of academia, there has to be a journal to make it scholarly (and tenure accruing)—hence *Nova Religio: The Journal of Alternative and Emergent Religions.*

For our purposes, some of the most interesting blogs are those dealing with How to Market Your Church, like the amazingly named but really sophisticated site churchmarketingsucks.com. Here the casual visitor can get a sense of how clergy attempt to position their product in a highly competitive market. They even link you to shipoffools.com, which encourages readers to submit their most offensive religious jokes.

BOOK PUBLISHING

If you want to see how Christianity went from arm's length to the end of your nose, compare the best-seller lists of the 1950s and today. What you'll see is not just an exponential increase in religious fervor, but an entirely new approach. Two generations ago, in and around fiction by the likes of Hemingway, Hersey, Wouk, Marquand, Steinbeck, du Maurier, O'Hara, and Michener, was midcult work like *The Cardinal* by Henry Morton Robinson, *Moses* by Sholem Asch, *The Silver Chalice* by Thomas B. Costain, or *Exodus* by Leon Uris. Such fiction was more reportorial than reverential, never disturbing. To be sure, serious religious fiction existed—works by the likes of Anthony Burgess, Robert Graves, Nikos Kazantzakis, D. H. Lawrence, Norman Mailer, José Saramago, and Gore Vidal—but it was usually in the service of the Big Theme. The category of nonfiction—religious self-help—simply didn't exist.

No longer. In 2004, books about religious subjects accounted for 7 percent of all book sales, with $1.95 billion in net revenues. Consumers spent $3.7 billion on "religious books," a category that includes Christian books as well as print paraphernalia like calendars, mementos, and knickknacks. By 2009, industry experts expect the religious books segment to account for $2.91 billion, almost a 50 percent increase from 2004. The category also includes the intriguing subset called "other religious." These books encompass thrillers, mysteries, general fiction, and a burgeoning romance category—no bodice rippers, however, but obvious links to Harlequin Romances in the sense of formulaic fiction.

If you want to see the distribution channel, go out to the strip mall and observe the mushroom-after-rain appearance of the Christian bookstore. It's had an amazing increase of nearly 285 percent since 1983. The only time like it in American economic history was the book market in the seventeenth century. Recall that the first book printed in what now is the United States was a 1640 Puritan psalter titled *The Bay Psalms Book,* but it was the almost furious printing of the Bible itself that started the entire publishing industry.

No one doubts that one of the reasons for this jump in interest in things religious is the rise of evangelical Christianity, perhaps helped by general anxiety over terrorism. Christian bookstores enjoy a special relationship with customers in many respects analogous to AM radio. They're local, and they are believers dealing with believers. The stores tend to blend a bit of ministry with retailing. If you visit, you'll see that both venue and inventory reflect a much more aggressive approach to selling not just books, but vision.

We'll look at some of the best sellers from megachurch pastorpreneurs later (Rick Warren's *The Purpose Driven® Life,* Joel Osteen's *Your Best Life Now,* and others), but suffice it to say that New York publishing houses have taken notice. An imprint of the publisher of the book you are currently reading signed a contract with Mr. Osteen for a book that according to some reports may net him some $13 million (approximately $12,950,000 more than this book will earn). The big-box stores and book chains, which consider books just so many stock-keeping units and hence are the most sensitive cultural barometer of modern life, are also aware of what's happening. Target, Costco, and Wal-Mart started increasing floor space for the religious category in 2002, and it looks to me as if at least a quarter of their book space is allocated to this genre. Amazon has an entire category called "Christian Living."

There are some pitfalls that publishers must be aware of. Here is an example: Zondervan is an old-time religion publisher; in fact, the largest Bible publisher. Now owned by HarperCollins, a subsidiary of Rupert Murdoch's News Corp, Zondervan is trying to introduce a new franchise product—*Today's New International Version of the Bible (TNIV)*. This is a modern English translation featuring updated language and scholarship.

As part of an advertising campaign, one of the ads shows a serious young man apparently pondering the problems of modern life. The text touts the *TNIV* as a source for "real truth" in a world of "endless media noise and political spin." A blue Bible peeks up from the corner of the ad. *The Onion,* the weekly satirical magazine, carried a similar ad, and even *Modern Bride* featured an ad of a woman in bridal white promoting *True Identity,* the women's study version of the *TNIV.* More ads were booked for websites, and for cable channels VH1 and MTV. God isn't mentioned in any of these ads, only in ads placed in Christian media such as *Relevant,* a Christian monthly magazine aimed at hip twentysomethings. But every ad carries this slogan: "Timeless truth; today's language."

That assertion of "truth" evidently triggered a rebuff from *Rolling Stone* magazine, which refused to carry the spot. But this was only the beginning of Zondervan's problems. If there was concern about "timeless truth," it was nothing compared to "today's language." *TNIV* is in gender-neutral language. Some American fundamentalist Protestants claimed that the publication of a gender-inclusive Bible was a travesty to the inerrant word of God. Of course, the word of God has always been up for grabs, as translators have been shifting grammar and language for generations. Only Homer Simpson's pal Ned Flanders believes otherwise.

In any case, Zondervan felt the pressure as a number of prominent evangelical leaders like James Dobson, Pat Robertson, and Jerry Falwell openly voiced their rejection of the *TNIV.* Additionally, the Southern Baptist Convention passed resolutions denouncing the translation. In a way, reminiscent of how important translations used to be when just the act of translation was heresy or publishing the wrong translation meant death, the open and vociferous response not to errors in belief but to relatively esoteric matters in the gender wars is symptomatic of how intense these finger-wagging concerns can become.

But in the book-publishing community, the big news in recent years was the reception of Dan Brown's *The Da Vinci Code.* As we all know, whether or not we've read the book, this is a theological whodunit with an entirely new spin on Jesus and Mary Magdalene. Not only does it shows traditional Christian followers as a little strange (such as "the hulking albino named Silas" limping through Paris, spiked band jabbing his thigh, thinking, "Pain is good," while whipping himself bloody with a scourge), but it makes a free-for-all of old-style Catholicism itself. If *The Book of Daniel* is parody, *The Da Vinci Code* is travesty.

What is also extraordinary about *The Da Vinci Code* is the number of readers who are convinced it is true. Some fans, mostly Americans, even make pilgrimages to sites mentioned in the book, including the Louvre, the Château de Villette in France, and Westminster Abbey in Britain. Could this be because the religious climate has become so fecund that belief itself is sprung loose of historical rigor and has become a matter of over-the-top enthusiastic taste?

As in Brown's other religious-themed best seller, *Angels & Demons,* there is a sense that decorum is no longer necessary. Let 'er rip. Believe what you want, especially if it flies in the face of old-line denominationalism. This book as well has become the print part of an industry spawning not just the predictable movie but fusty commentary—most of it wishing for the days of the 1950s when certain subjects (the Catholic League and Opus Dei, for instance) were treated at arm's length. The Catholic Church, which has complained that no Protestant denomination has been so pilloried in popular culture, has a point.

The Da Vinci Code was published by an imprint of a mainstream publisher, Random House, which, by the way, owns its own religious imprint, Waterbrook Press. Little wonder that Anne Rice, after stupendous sales for her tales of vampires, witches, and just plain lust, has turned to Jesus—personally and literarily. Her innovative novel *Christ the Lord: Out of Egypt,* published by high-cult Knopf, depicts Jesus as a seven-year-old lad, speaking in his own words as the holy family moves from Egyptian exile to Nazareth. She, as well as her publisher, intends a series of chronicles like the one she hatched with the now long-of-tooth Vampire Lestat. When Farrar, Straus & Giroux gets on this bandwagon, I predict, the market will hit a top.

The Free Market in Faith: The American Religious Enterprise

One reason why the American religious enterprise is so explosive is because it is just that: an *enterprise.* There is a famous quote, so on-point that it has lost its specific source:

> In the beginning the church was a fellowship of men and women centering on the living Christ. Then the church moved to Greece, where it became a philosophy. Then it moved to Rome, where it became an institution. Next, it moved to Europe, where it became a culture. And, finally, it moved to America, where it became an enterprise.
>
> (ATTRIBUTED TO RICHARD HALVERSON, FORMER CHAPLAIN
> OF THE UNITED STATES SENATE)

The religious enterprise in the United States is perpetually "in play." Here's why: at the macro level, roughly equal minorities of the American population, say 35 percent to 40 percent, hold contrasting and ultimately irreconcilable convictions on the purpose of life. That's what makes a market.

One group, composed overwhelmingly of those who adhere to the basics of Christian Revelation, is God- and faith-centered. Members of this group believe they have the right and duty to participate freely in American politics and culture to influence laws and customs in ways that reflect the sovereignty of Christ the King. I call them "hot Christians." They are also called Dominionists or Christianists. They tend to drive cars with "Christ Is Lord over [your town's name goes here]" bumper stickers.

The second group consists, for the most part, of people who, while they may acknowledge the existence of God in minimalist fashion, base their lives in the mundane. They are not focused on the afterlife. They are believers, but mainly on Sunday morning. They are *lukewarm* Christians, and so, as you might imagine, the hot variety like to quote a little Revelation 3:15–16. Lukewarms support what Thomas Jefferson called "public religion." It's out there, yes, but not in your face. These two groups endlessly jockey for position and, in a sense, are dependent on each other for sustenance.

Divided by God

And they've been at it for a while. Both sides know how to play their roles. No cue cards are necessary. There are certain times in our history when the religious marketplace tips in favor of the true believers, and then times when it tips the other way. One might predict this has to do with threats to well-being like war or terrorism and what we have come to call "Islamic extremism," but I suspect otherwise. I think our current religiosity has more to do with shifts in marketing, in supply chains, in brand extensions, in packaging, and in consumption communities. Don't get me wrong. Megareligions compete. But the most fierce competition goes on in the cultural bedroom, so to speak, between churches.

We are in one of those periods of competitive spatting that old-style historians called "awakenings." The believers are holding forth. I suspect that by the time you read this the forces of contraction will have taken hold, and cultural enthusiasm will have waned a bit. But because this subject is so unwieldy, and because we are still in the middle of the market burst, let me just hint at the perplexities by stringing together some statistics.

The numbers are coming at you in an undifferentiated bunch, not because they make sense when joined, but just the opposite. They often contradict themselves. But they show the depth and breadth and complexity of what has been happening in the American religious marketplace in the past generation. They show an active market. They may also show that you can't trust people to tell you the truth about religion.

(The data are gleaned from reputable sources: the Gallup Organization, Barna Research Group, Beliefnet, *Newsweek,* Center for the Study of Global Christianity, *The Economist* magazine, Pew Research Center, Harris Interactive, and American National Election Studies. True, you can lie with statistics, but if you can get enough of them, complete with variations, the lies become cushioned with some truth—or at least some entertaining oxymorons.)

In order to get to a potpourri of data in three main categories—belief, Bible, and church attendance—we are bypassing the indubitable fact that the United States is the most religious nation in the developed world. Detractors love to point out that we also have some of the highest rates of murder, infant mortality, teen abortion, and teen sexually transmitted disease in that same world. Religious fervor does not seem to have made us a better world citizen, but that melancholy, thankfully, is not the subject of this book.

Belief: Just about every American—96 percent, in one poll—believes in God. Eighty-five percent of Americans identify themselves as Christians. Sixty percent of the two billion Christians in the world think of themselves as *evangelical.* In the United States, being *born-again* is now a self-described condition of about eighty-eight million people. In the 1980s two-fifths of American Protestants described themselves as born-again. The percentage has climbed to more than half. Born-again Christians now make up 39 percent of America's adult population. Further, 4 out of 5 Americans say they have "experienced God's presence or a spiritual force," and 46 percent maintain it happens to them often. A larger fraction of American adults now believe in life after death than did a generation ago. The belief has been so powerful that Jews and persons with no religious affiliation have become more likely to believe in an afterlife. Well over half of Americans believe in miracles, the devil, and angels. Sixty-seven percent of Americans believe in the virgin birth of Jesus, and 82 percent believe Jesus is the Son of God. Three times as many Americans believe in the virgin birth as in evolution. And almost half of the U.S. population—45 percent—believes that human beings did not evolve, but instead were created by God, as stated in the Bible, about ten thousand years ago.

Bible: Ninety-two percent of American households own a Bible; 59 percent say they read it at least occasionally; 37 percent say they read it at least once a week; 14 percent say they belong to a Bible study group or something similar; 60 percent say it is totally accurate in all its teachings; 50 percent of adults interviewed nationwide could name any of the four Gospels of the New Testament; 37 percent could name all four Gospels; 58 percent cannot name five of the Ten Commandments; fewer than half know that Genesis is the first book of the Bible; 12 percent believe Noah's wife was Joan of Arc; 87 percent say the universe was originally created by God; 81 percent say angels exist and influence people's lives; 35 percent of Americans deem the Bible the "inerrant word of the Creator."

Church attendance: Sixty percent of Americans say religion is very important in their lives; 41 percent say they have attended church or synagogue in the last seven days, but various weekly attendance records indicate that the real number is closer to 20 percent. Since 1970 the number of Americans who said they attended church every week has dropped from 38 percent to 25 percent, while the number of Americans who say they never attend church has risen from 12 percent in 1970 to 32 percent in 2002. Sixty-four percent of Americans say they pray every day and attend church (43 percent reportedly attend a service once a week or more), but only 20 percent report reading a sacred text every day (36 percent more read texts monthly or weekly).

Scramble Competition

Can we agree on just one fact? American religion is a wonderful free-for-all that has been studiously overlooked by all except a few die-hard economists and marketing scholars. It deserves more. What makes it unique is that it allows new suppliers into the market with little more than a prayer. Consider: In 1900 there were 330 different religious groups; now there are over 2,000. This happens only in America. And it is not hard to explain. We have learned how to buy and sell almost anything: hospital care, art, education, philanthropy; you name it, and you'll soon find a market trading it. Everything in this culture goes to market. Why should religion be any different?

Pretending otherwise is exactly what distinguishes this market. What a nifty irony that some Christian denominations don't care for the Darwinian model when applied to biology or social engineering, yet they themselves have to hustle, innovate, adapt, mutate, grow new appendages, or become the lunch of those who do. Before "scramble competition" became an economic term, it was a biological one. Now it's a religious one.

How come there's so much scrambling in our religion marketplace? Easy. What makes us unique is that our religious markets are protected *to make sure* Darwinian scrambling happens. The explanation is to be found in the First Amendment to our Constitution. Consider the amazing separation clause: "Congress shall make no law respecting an establishment of religion, or prohibiting the free exercise thereof. . . ." Not only does the Constitution prohibit a state religion, the law goes on to protect all suppliers from one another as well as from the state. Essentially this mandates two freedoms: the freedom to believe, and the freedom to act so as to get others to believe.

Oddly enough, we didn't start off this way. The Protestant pilgrims, after all, were fleeing religious persecution by Anglicans who, themselves, not many years later were fleeing for their lives when things turned nasty under Oliver Cromwell and his Roundheads. But the Puritans wanted religious domination, a theocracy. As the old saying goes, they fled tolerant Holland so that they could come to the New World and be intolerant. By the eighteenth century, we had learned our lesson. Puritans are no fun, and theocracies stink.

The First Amendment, written just a few years after the publication of Adam Smith's *The Wealth of Nations,* essentially mandated an open market, a scramble market, in the salvation of souls. Left without the guarantees offered by state monopolies, congregations would live or die by their own efforts in recruiting members, getting their money, and kindling their enthusiasm. Churches would have to hustle, or they'd be hustled out of business. And they have.

To understand our spiritual market, imagine that the soap aisle down at the supermarket was mandated to carry not just the barely differentiated products from Procter & Gamble and Unilever but also every product from Tom's of Maine to Bill's of Duluth. From a marketing point of view, this means there will not be a monopoly supplier, no "Church of America." In such a market, extremes are not just welcomed—they are encouraged. Well, up to a point, as David Koresh, Joseph Smith, Bhagwan Shree Rajneesh, John Humphrey Noyes, and some others have found out. In such an aisle, the competition for eye-level placement is furious, packaging is paramount, and price matters. You don't get bought unless you make noise.

American religions have been noisy from the time the constitutional ink was dry. By the time Alexis de Tocqueville, patron saint of cultural historians, arrived on these shores in the 1830s, the pattern was set. The charismatic off-the-wall preacher, the bewildering variety of new denominations, the determination to innovate, and the across-town and across-the-street cutthroat competition were good to go. Ironically, the farther religion was kept from state control *but* under state protection, the more frantic the competition.

If you want to see what a scramble market looks like, check out this 1879 cartoon from *Puck* magazine. There they are—a few of the suppliers we still recognize—lined up at the carnival of culture, each jostling for a piece of the action. Written on the fringe over the various booths: "U.S. Faith." "Take Your Choice." Lower right under a banner reading "Rapid Transit to Heaven" is a cardinal of the Roman Catholic Church taking in money for selling indulgences. In the next stall is a smugly satisfied Henry Ward Beecher selling white souls, at least according to his placard. A buck-naked Baptist is offering soap-free hot or cold immersion in his water drum—for a price, of course. Up top on the roof is a charlatan conducting a spirit show for the mingling crowd. An elderly gent is promoting polygamy as "the only sure & pleasant road to salvation," an Episcopal priest is touting the

The religious *Vanity Fair*: "Shopping for God," circa 1879. (SOURCE: *PUCK MAGAZINE*, OCTOBER 22, 1879, PP. 526–27.)

rewards of ritual, while to his right is a pedo-Baptist claiming the "foot of salvation." In the center is a toy monkey presumably held together by wobbly pins like the synods in the Presbyterian church. He is waving a guarantee of salvation. Over by the stairs is the Jew brandishing a huge knife, probably a reference to circumcision or to "blood libel," a common belief that Jews required the blood of Christians, mostly newborns, for use in rituals. Meanwhile, at the foot of the heavenly stairs, sprawls a cupidlike baby in top hat and tails holding a scroll that reads, "The best route, *integer vitae scelerisque purus* [unimpaired by life and clean of wickedness], clean hands and a pure heart" implying that this marketplace is indeed the religious *Vanity Fair. Plus ça change . . .*

Separation of Church and State Creates This Carnival

While individual suppliers go at it hammer and tongs on one side of American culture, religion is kept at arm's length by that half of the population who tremble at the sight of the true believers. Thanks to them—the lukewarm Christians—there are more legal obstacles to religion in American *public* life than there are in almost any other important country except China. Both sides duke it out, confident that religion really matters.

Just consider schools, for instance. Kids in state schools are not allowed to say a short prayer together before a football game. We endlessly nitpick over who can or cannot be in the school Christmas crèche—a reindeer yes, a baby Jesus no. In fact, it now looks as if nativity scenes are forbidden from all public schools no matter who's in the manger. Some loony school district is always trying to ban some work like Goethe's *Faust* (the devil), Miller's *The Crucible* (witches), or Rowling's *Harry Potter* (magic) on religious reasons. And they almost always manage to find a tone-deaf judge to go along for a while.

And let's not even discuss the argument over intelligent design, which has been roiling both the religion and school markets. Who cares that this cockamamy scheme undermines not only science but religion itself. (If you found an Intel chip on a deserted beach, would you infer that God created it or some Silicon Valley whiz kid?) It's great in-your-face marketing, however, and it annoys the hell out of the lukewarms. Ironically, by ensuring that religion is a private and protected matter, nonbelievers have never let it suffer the debilitating infections of education. American secularists have ensured that religion not only flourishes but that the most innovative and sometimes the noisiest versions triumph.

Or take politics. Hot Christianity, because it depends on shared faith in something essentially unprovable to promise a better future, has much in common with organized politics. When it becomes political, however, religion invariably weakens. Kept apart, religious groups continually energize one another with competitive promises. Observe cultures where church and state have been close, and you see that they both become complacent, blaming each other for failures of vision. European religions like French Catholicism, English Anglicanism, and Scandinavian Lutheranism show the problem of inclusion. Religion suffers when it takes on the failures of the state.

Theocracies in the West, as John Calvin and Oliver Cromwell found out, are potent but short-lived. That's because sooner or later the state invariably screws up. It gets into the wrong war, or it forgets to take out the garbage, or it just horses around too much with taxpayer monies. The man behind the curtain shows the lipstick on his clerical collar. The key to religious suppliers is that they be, at least while making the sale, infallible and deadly serious. To make the sale, they have to argue that, yes, there is one God and many religions, but only *this* religion, my religion, is the true one.

Politics is flypaper to religion. Observe Sweden and the Lutheran Church. For generations, everyone born in Sweden became a member of the church. The church was supported by state taxes. In 2000 the church was separated from the state as part of the country's secular trend. Swedes could write to their local parish, telling the vicar they no longer wish to be members and opt not to pay taxes to the church, which range from 2 percent to 3 percent of their income. They did. Although some 85 percent of Swedes are church members, only 11 percent of women and 7 percent of men go to church. American fundamentalists may rue the day they flew into the arms of the Republican party. But Republicans will suffer more.

Here's the take-away. A secular government that enforces religious tolerance often ends up fostering more furious religiosity than does the pious state that enforces intolerance. More specific, the free market in religious choice has increased the levels of *religiosity.* That's because in highly competitive markets suppliers have to stay on their toes, be innovative, be resilient, and always be selling. Coke sells more going up against Pepsi. McDonald's needs Burger King.

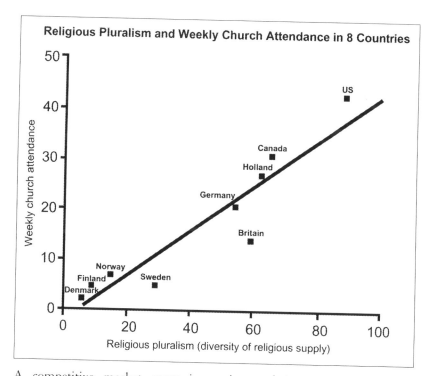

A competitive market spurs innovation and increases consumption. (SOURCE: EVA HAMBERG AND THORLEIF PETTERSSON, "RELIGIOUS MARKETS: SUPPLY, DEMAND, AND RATIONAL CHOICES," IN TED G. JELEN, ED., *SACRED MARKETS, SACRED COMPANIES*, P. 109.)

When markets are supplying interchangeable products, selling can become frantic. Brand war! The complacent get killed. Think anemic Dr Pepper or almost kaput Royal Crown Cola. Remember Burger Chef. The suppliers who increase market share really do have to "get in your face." Hustle, baby, hustle.

How I Came to This Subject

I am often asked how an English teacher ever got interested in this subject. Here's how: When I'm doing my day job, I'm talking about stories. I teach romantic literature: Blake, Wordsworth, Coleridge, Shelley, and, well, you know the rest from high-school English. These stories are part of literature, and stories get into this category by being a little complex. My job is to explicate them.

In addition, these stories are often quite powerful. They get power by delivering a specific sensation. Sometimes we group them by that sensation. So you can have a course in comedy (stories that make you laugh); horror (stories that make you shiver); melodrama (stories that make you cry); or tragedy (which, as Aristotle first said, are stories that make you feel pity and terror).

About twenty years ago I became intrigued by how we were attaching stories to consumer products. This process is called *branding*. What separates Evian bottled water from tap water is that it comes with a story that delivers a feeling. Ditto Coke and Pepsi. Or, say, the General Motors Cadillac Escalade and the Lexus GX 470. If I were to blindfold you and drive you around, could you tell me which car you were in? But the minute you see the nameplate (story), you know how you feel. The taste separation is in your imagination, not in the product. That's because machine-made products are essentially fungible, interchangeable, but the brands (stories) are not. As they say on Madison Avenue, you drink the advertising, not the beer. In other words, the story is what is sold; the product is thrown in free.

I started to write about this storytelling-on-the-take and ended up dealing with a special group of products called "luxury goods." If you go into stores such as Gucci, Prada, Louis Vuitton, or Fendi, you see much the same inventory, but the logos (again, stories) are all different, and so are the consumers' responses. Often the products are the same, made on the same machines, of the same fabrics and textures. The sensations are very potent and come to us not from the product but from the marketing. Luxury is a sensation, and it can be attached via branding (you know what that means) to such things as bottled water, scarves, vodka, ties, works of art, shoes, handbags, schools, wine, automobile tires, and then retailed for a higher than seemingly rational price.

In the chapters that follow, I look to see whether the same condition exists in church markets, most specifically in the Protestant markets. Here's the central question: are there doctrinal/ingredient differences among and between Protestant denominations that generate value for the consumer? Or are the denominations separated more by other factors, like marketing, competitive amenities, packaging, a better selection of friends? There used to be an old saying that paid tribute to this lack of doctrinal distinction: A Baptist is a Christian who has learned to wash; a Methodist is a Baptist who has learned to read; a Presbyterian is a Methodist who has gone to college; and an Episcopalian is a Presbyterian whose investments have turned out well.

If I blindfolded you and put you into a Presbyterian, Methodist, or Episcopal church, could you tell me where you were? And if the separation is not in doctrine but in the marketing, how does that happen? Once we get a grip on branding, will it help to explain why merged churches and churches in the middle are failing? Or help to explain why some extreme (luxury, in a way) churches that demand high sacrifice (high prices) are growing like Topsy?

Is Confession Good for the Soul?

One more matter before we begin. In the last few years, I've read a lot of books on religion. At the beginning, the author invariably tells us how important religion has been to him (and usually it's a *him* writing about this subject). He's been a member of the blankety-blank denomination, even though perhaps he's grown in faith a bit over the years. Or he was a believer, viz Richard Dawkins (*The God Delusion*) and Sam Harris (*The End of Faith*), and has now found a new passion. When the critics get hold of the book, just like clock-work they will say, "Hey, whaddaya expect from a blankety blank."

So here are my bona fide blankety blanks. On religious subjects I'm a blank, not just a tabula rasa but a tabula *Teflon*. A lot has been applied; alas, not much stuck. I'm one of those who don't go to church. Or at least I *didn't*. In the last few years I have gone to church a lot. In fact, I often take long trips just to go to church. I like going to church. I like singing. I like the sense of community. I especially like observing the people around me. What are they feeling? I like looking at what's on the walls, and I really like a good sermon, a stem-winder.

I should confess that I have trouble reading the Bible, especially the King James Version. I've certainly tried, but it's tough going for me even though I'm supposed to be a professional reader. I must not be the only one, as the publication of such "trots" as *The Light Speed Bible* and *The Bible in 90 Days* attests. Sometimes I think the Bible is toted around in public rather the way graduate students of a generation ago used to lug around *Finnegans Wake*. You didn't have to really read it; you only had to look as if you'd like to. It's comforting to hold, perhaps a bit of a fetish.

I do like to hear Bible stories explained. I often think that I would explain them differently. So for me, doing church is a bit of a busman's holiday. After all, the pastor is usually doing almost exactly what I do. He calls it exegesis. I call it close reading. We should be cultural cousins. After all, we come from the same place historically and only recently went our separate ways. From time to time we even wear the same dark robes to prove it. And we have the same concerns about not putting our charges to sleep and getting them a little anxious about the final exam.

In church shopping for this book, I was occasionally curious about which denomination was best for me. And so in the service of full disclosure, here's the result of my taking the "Belief System Selector," a twenty-question sampling from more than two dozen world religions from SelectSmart.com. I'm not alone in my curiosity. The site gets about seven thousand hits a day and has even generated its own jokes. One patron claimed to have received a mixed test score of "100 percent Unitarian Universalist" and "100 percent Jehovah's Witness," which means that he knocks on doors for no apparent reason. On the basis of my "indwelling beliefs," here's where I belong and how much of me is affiliated:

HERE ARE MY RESULTS

1. Humanist (100)
2. Unitarian Universalist (92)
3. Atheist/Agnostic (81)
4. Theravada Buddhist (76)
5. Liberal Quaker (71)
6. NeoPagan (63)
7. Taoism (51)
8. Mainline to Liberal Protestant (47)
9. Orthodox Quaker (45)
10. New Age (44)
11. Mahayana Buddhist (39)
12. Baha'i (27)
13. Jainism (27)
14. Reform Judaism (27)
15. Sikhism (27)
16. Christian Science (18)
17. Hindu (18)
18. Latter Day Saints (18)
19. New Thought (18)
20. Scientology (18)
21. Seventh-day Adventist (15)
22. Mainline to Conservative Protestant (14)
23. Eastern Orthodox Christianity (9)
24. Islam (9)
25. Jehovah's Witness (9)
26. Orthodox Judaism (9)

I now think of myself as a cold Christian or, better yet, an "apatheist." I lift this coinage from a recent *Atlantic Monthly* article by Jonathan Rauch. It means "a disinclination to care all that much about one's own religion and an even stronger disinclination to care about other people's." This is not atheism, agnosticism, skepticism, secularism, and all the rest, because the apatheist believes that religion has an important place in every culture. And that place should be protected and made safe. We live in a Christian culture; we can't pretend to be unaffected by its profound influence. I'd be out of business without it. Apatheists also believe, however, that if a religion has to move out of its place, has to proselytize in order to be true to its calling, that it do so very quietly and politely. Knock first.

So, if you want to write a review of this book, here's your first sentence: "*Shopping for God* is just what you'd expect from an apatheist."

CHAPTER TWO

Another Great Awakening?

Somewhere in rural Pennsylvania in the mid-1950s, J. Melvin Stewart saw a rickety wooden sign with plastic letters, the kind of letters used for movie marquees, announcing an upcoming church function. Was it for a potluck dinner or bingo? Mr. Stewart is now in his mid-eighties, and he's not sure exactly where the sign was or even what the message was. But he does remember thinking that since it was hard to tell churches apart, a changeable sign out front might increase the gate. He was then in the home finance business. He was about to go into the church sign business.

Son of a minister for the Assemblies of God, Mel Stewart knew firsthand that poorly marked churches rarely had full parking lots. Steeples were a good sign if you were driving a horse and buggy, but they all look the same at forty miles an hour. This was a Saul on the road to Damascus moment. The J. M. Stewart Corporation of Sarasota, Florida, is now the nation's largest manufacturer of church signage.

Mel Stewart made his reputation with a marquee sign he called "The Witness." It was not like those little signs you saw entering a town saying that there's a Moose lodge, Episcopal church, and Kiwanis club up ahead, but a sign right out in front of the church, almost in the driver's face. It had moveable letters. Before Mel's sudden illumination, there had been a gentleman's agreement not to erect vulgar signs in front of churches. Religion was private. Signs were public.

Maybe such subtlety worked when there were no highways. But no longer. The steeple showed only that the building was a church, not which denomination or "flavor" of church. And that was Mel's real insight. The Witness would not just show the denomination, but, with the changeable letters, would spell out something to give the taste, the personality, the pizzazz of the place. In so doing, he would change forever what is called in church parlance "the last hundred feet"—the distance between the unchurched driving by and those pulling in.

Signs of Faith

The Witness has since developed into a visual cliché holding a verbal cliché. With moveable four- or six-inch letters, the same sign might spell out "Potluck Dinner" on one day or a nifty saying like "Dusty Bibles Lead to Dirty Lives" or "To Be Lifted Up, Go Down on Your Knees" on the next. Mel is the auteur indirectly responsible for:

"This Church Is Prayer-Conditioned"
"Remember the Rabbit Foot Didn't Work for the Rabbit"
"Under Same Management for 2,000 Years"
"No God, No Peace. Know God, Know Peace"
"CH _ _ CH. What's Missing? U R"
"God Answers Knee Mail—Log On"

Mel put some fluorescent lamps inside so that the sermonettes could be read at night. He even calculated that the higher the speed limit in front of your church, the bigger the font and the fewer the words on your sign. Today the J. M. Stewart Corp. offers seven models, from simple lawn marquees to casino-style, blinking, alphanumeric electronic displays that start at forty thousand dollars. Using his proprietary software, which asks the speed limit, the traffic flow,

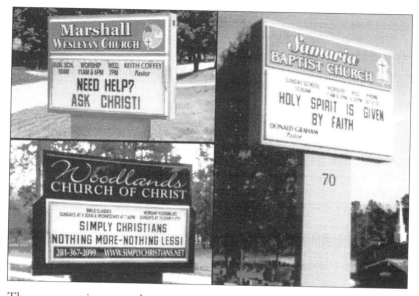

The marquee sign at work. (SOURCE: J. H. STEWART CORPORATION CAT-
ALOG, PP. 12–13.)

the size of your front yard, and the amount of other signage nearby,
you can order the sign that's right for you.

Such signs open up a fascinating subject: How do churches position themselves, how do they separate themselves from one another,
how do they break through the clutter of not just other religions but
other denominations? How, in short, do they get in your face to get
you in church?

And, at a slightly greater remove, what can we learn about marketing from studying intra- and extra-denominational competition—the winners and losers in the salvation business? Or, from a
slightly farther-out angle, if capitalism was informed by Christian
attitudes, as sociologists like Max Weber famously speculated, are
we now living in a time when the magnetic poles are being
reversed? Are Christian markets now being informed by capitalism? Can we see the invisible hand of Procter & Gamble in the competitive behavior of successful denominations, as we used to be able
to see the hand of God in the success of competitive businesses?

That's quite a stretch, I admit. Mel's three-second sermons on marquee signs are not on a par with the conversion of Constantine, St. Jerome's Latin Vulgate, the monastery at Cluny, Bach's and Handel's church music, John Wesley's taking sermons out of the church and into the field, or the Azusa Street Revival of Pentecostalism, but their effect is similar. They capture attention in order to make a sale. They are, in a word, *evangelical.* They take the message to the street. In the vulgate of marketing, they move product.

These signs, and this Burma-Shave way of doing business, are unique to American culture. True, you see most of them in the Bible Belt, where denominational competition is fierce. But there is hardly an American town that doesn't have a marquee or a marquee knockoff. You don't see them in Europe or in other cultures with dominant religions, like Roman Catholicism or Islam. As well, you rarely see them in front of synagogues.

Maybe these little signs capture not just what makes American religion American but what makes American culture American, and help show why this thoroughly commercialized culture is so powerful. When the French wished to disparage the English in the nineteenth century, they called them a nation of shopkeepers. When the rest of the world now wishes to disparage America, they call us a nation of salesmen. We don't think much about signs. After all, they are simply part of the water we swim in; we don't even know they're there.

Then again, sometimes we do. A few years ago, two churches in Stillwater, Minnesota, faced off, sign to sign. Rev. Steve Molin of Our Savior's Lutheran Church challenged Rev. Roland "Rollie" Mossberg of Bethany Evangelical Covenant Church to play a little church sign war. The first question posted on the sign at Our Savior's Lutheran Church: "Church Sign Trivia: List the 10 Commandments, in No Particular Order. Answer in One Mile." A mile southwest is the answer on Bethany's sign: "Trivia Answer: 3 6 5 9 10 4 2 7 8 1." Pastor Molin even calls himself the Church Sign Guy. His first message appeared four years ago when he went on vacation: "Now is a good time to visit. Our pastor is on vacation!"

Try explaining these signs to someone from anywhere else on the planet, and they'll usually be dumbfounded. Yet almost any North American gets it. We recognize that behind the fun is something serious. The signs capture attention in order to—again in the language of the market—make a sale. More specific, to make a sale of a fungible product (forgiveness and salvation) at a particular place (this church). The signs try to separate and—again in adspeak— *brand* the specific church. As we know from the battles we fight over meat patties, over beer brands, over Coke versus Pepsi, things can quickly get out of hand. Just consider these church signs:

"Thanks, Mom, for Not Aborting Me"
"What's the Price of Being Pro-Choice? Only 41,000,000 Babies"
"Ms. Is an Abbreviation for Miserable"
"Was It Adam and Eve or Adam and Steve?"

A mutation of these marquee signs appeared in the "billboards from God" campaign in the 1990s. Along the interstate they asked, "What Part of 'Thou Shalt Not . . .' Didn't You Understand?" and "Have You Read My No. 1 Best Seller? (There will be a test)." With funds from an anonymous donor, the campaign ran for three months in Florida. Then the Outdoor Advertising Association of America adopted these "GodSpeaks" sayings as its national public service campaign for 1999, putting them on ten thousand billboards in two hundred cities across America.

The campaign is back again, with a new set of one-liners and gentle questions all linked to a website. Here's some of what the motorist sees:

"The Real Supreme Court Meets up Here"
"One Nation under Me"
"Can I Even Know There Is a God?"
"Isn't Every Religion Really a Path to God?"
"Keep Using My Name in Vain, and I'll Make Rush Hour Longer"
"Don't Make Me Come Down There"

Either call the 800 number listed on the sign, or log on to the website given, and you find a familiar, conservative Christian response in "seeker-sensitive language."

What makes this in-your-face medium still more interesting is that now the United Methodist Church—the church that in the nineteenth century was the most innovative supplier of (again in marketing terms) "product," complete with itinerant preachers, preach-offs, sing-alongs, and camp meetings—has now been buying billboard space to display its denominational messages.

Although an often edgy interaction between buyer and seller and between seller and seller is second nature to us today, we have tended to think of churches as being exempt from the brutal hubbub of the marketplace. They most definitely are not. Churches are in the thick of things. And they have been there elbowing it out with one another for quite a while.

What is more interesting is why the perpetual ruckus in the faith business goes unnoticed. Lest you think I'm picking on religion, let me assure you that universities, museums, hospitals, philanthropies, and other putative nonprofits also compete for students, patrons, patients, and donors, sometimes roughly. But what separates religion is that this market usually operates in the dim candlelight of ineffable mystery.

So while belief in God is an act of personal faith, attending church is an act of choice made in public, and that choice is, and has been, up

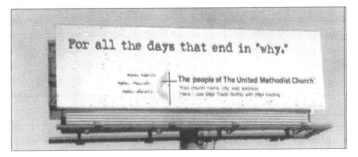

Billboarding for God, Methodist style. (SOURCE: IGNITING MINISTRY CAMPAIGN VIEWBOOK, VERSION 1.2.)

for grabs. Quite often the denomination that is the most successful is the one that understands the drawing power of whatever new media and new pitch have been developed. It finds a need and fills it quick. As we will see later, it is not by happenstance that today commercial advertising and denominational religion are joined at the hip.

The Altar Call

We usually think of religion as the unfolding of a sacred truth, and hence it is usually surrounded by "*Shhh,* please, don't be too picky." Just take the leap of faith and forget about the contradictions. But if you take the larger view, the historical view—if you will, the marketing view—you see that while American religious consumption stays relatively constant, the delivery is incredibly innovative. Plus, while you might think that people would become more or less interested in sacred truth when things in this world turn punky, such is not always the case. Often what excites the market is not increased demand but shifts in supply, innovations in packaging, new lingo, new sound system, new payment schedules, new pastorpreneurs. New signage.

When this happens in American culture, we get what has been called an awakening. This is a misnomer because it sites the stimulus in the consumer, not in the producer. Religion and religiosity are different. Religiosity usually happens when people have plenty of time and energy to respond to some new product development or delivery system. They start to clamor. An awakening is a burst in religiosity, not in religious faith.

In the 1730s and periodically until the Civil War, such clamors swept over different parts of the country. They were called revivals, but again the word choice is poor, because this implies a rebirth, a reawakening. It's not. It's just a spike in demand, almost always caused by innovations in supply. Very often these early revivals were the result of a new kind of charismatic preacher getting into or out of the pulpit with a new version of the product.

The second generation of pastorpreneur, appearing just before the Civil War, had the greatest success in goosing up the sensational. Observe the genius of Charles Grandison Finney, a Presbyterian preacher in upstate New York. Finney understood the dynamics of conversion, of inching toward the point of no return, and concurrently of the intense anxiety of being Left Behind. And he understood that before you make the leap, before you pay up to see what's behind the curtain, you need to sense that it's now or never.

P. T. Barnum had applied exactly this technique to the circus. *See it now; it leaves tomorrow.* He mastered the concept of a once-in-a-lifetime opportunity. After all, Barnum said, he was only doing what he had learned from church. Not for nothing did he call his circus audience his "congregation," and not for nothing did his critics complain of his self-evident blasphemy. As an editorial writer for *The Nation* perceptively noted, "He is the personification of a certain kind of humbug which, funny as it often appears, eats out the heart of religion." But, as Barnum would say, you take value where you can find it.

So what did Finney do? During his seemingly extemporaneous sermons, he installed a bench of hebephrenic believers at the front of the church, right at his feet. These people could be easily seen by the observers in the back. In fact, the up-front bench sitters acted very much like the supernumeraries on the stage in Elizabethan dramas. As William Shakespeare knew, if you can put audience surrogates on the stage and have them join in, the rest of the audience will go along for the ride.

Barnum always seeded his sideshows with enthusiastic shills. Notice that every once in a while, the auction houses Sotheby's and Christie's get nicked by the law for doing the same. It's what the mosh pit does at a rock concert, or why dance clubs have doormen trained to let certain people in while keeping others out. Lest you think this technique is used only by sleazy hucksters, the same process of generating buyer's panic is currently used by some of the admissions departments of Ivy League–type schools. They essentially give away their product to certain students during early admission periods in hopes of generating "I gotta go there too" anxiety with later consumers.

To effectively use buyer's panic, you have to have some appreciation of how consumption works in crowds. In a sense, the up-fronts were the "early adopters." Marketers can predict with eerie accuracy how consumers will behave once they observe others. Forget the product; it may or may not be important. Focus on who's buying. For a while there was a huge industry called "cool hunting," which looked for this front bench of buyers. They are, after all, the engine of consumer fads. Blame them for why at Christmas there is always some toy, like the Cabbage Patch doll, that is sold out.

And that's because once the early adopters make their move, the "early majority," or more careful consumers, inch forward, and after them the tsunami of the "late majority." Then it's over. Only the "laggards" are left, and we all know who they are and how they feel. They are the old, the weak, the Left Behind. An entire industry has been built on delivering the sensation of who gets left behind after the Rapture comes. That's because we may not know the feeling of epiphany, but we all know the feeling of "whoops, I'm alone."

Finney picked excitable women and a few volatile men who could be counted on to respond actively to his preaching. And he was a crackerjack preacher. His voice was booming, and his eyes were bright as hot coals. Finney would start sermonizing about the importance of conversion, saying how we were otherwise damned to hell, reiterating the danger we faced if we did not make the move. Soon. Now. Stirring hymns were sung in the background, and at strategic moments, seemingly impromptu prayers were said.

As the pressure from the pulpit increased, those front row penitents started to churn, well aware that behind them was the crowd of others observing their every move. They knew the drill. Sometimes his minions, under the guise of praying with the penned-up penitents, would egg them on until, like the proverbial dominoes, they soon tipped, one after another. As Finney poured out earnest pleas, supplications, and promises, the groans and tears would turn to shouts and wails. And then, best of all, the fainting. In the rapture business, nothing trumps fainting.

Up front Finney thundered on, seemingly oblivious to the wave cresting below and starting to flow back toward the casual observers. He couldn't be concerned. That was the work of God. "Whoever doesn't want to go to hell, come down front and accept Jesus," he softly announced. "Do you renounce the forces of evil? Then come down front and accept His free gift," he boomed. "Who wants to go to heaven? Then come down to the altar and get saved," he whispered. The format was the same: the questions; the surge and recoil; the promise of free gifts; the act now, the act-now-tommorrow-is-too-late ploy/gambit; the soft music; the prayer; then the surge from back in the pack.

For 1,700 years, the church had thrived without this call forward. Such a practice was never used by Jesus or His apostles. Polycarp, Tertullian, Ambrose, Jerome, John Chrysostom, Augustine, Thomas Aquinas, William Tyndale, John Knox, Martin Luther, Ulrich Zwingli, John Calvin, and Jonathan Edwards never invoked its use. But once the results were seen, it was soon picked up by Baptist and Methodist preachers and used everywhere. Men like D. L. Moody, Billy Sunday, and Billy Graham used these methods to bring thousands forward at the close of their services. The altar call is currently a staple of the Southern Baptist service. It's also called "dragging the net."

The altar call seemed to have disproportionate importance for women, not just for those on the bench, but those in the crowd. Women made up a majority of those Finney converted (perhaps as many as two-thirds), and they played an instrumental role in assisting the work of the revival. Often the first converted in their families (thus demonstrating their independence in spiritual matters), women believed that they had a special duty to carry the pressing message of repentance back to family members and others in the community. They organized prayer meetings in their homes to work up enthusiasm for the revival and engaged in house-to-house visits to encourage attendance at revival meetings. The prominence of women in revivals and in revival strategies struck some more conservative church people and clergy as questionable. And, as we will see, it still does.

It's hard to overestimate this marketing innovation. It soon merited a name: the "anxious bench." Finney was always trying new delivery, new techniques of coercion. His informal language (sometimes shocking), the scheduling of "protracted" or daily meetings, and the practice of praying for individuals by name galvanized the crowd. He encouraged simultaneous extemporaneous prayer, in a sense a precursor to speaking in tongues. And he perfected advance advertising to build audience expectation weeks before his arrival.

Like so many pastorpreneurs, Finney was not just able to project sincerity; he *was* sincere. He knew that part of his allure was that he was always on the move from town to town. Toward the end of his ministry, however, he had a chance to retrace his steps. He noted an amazing phenomenon. A few years after making the altar call, his converts did not act all that converted. Those who had sought the Redeemer did not appear to be very redeemed. There were some sincere converts, yes, but the vast majority of those who came down front were not changed at all. Most did not continue attending church. They wanted the sensation. They wanted to feel powerful feelings. They wanted—gasp—a kind of entertainment that he provided. They wanted the stories that carried powerful feelings, the sensations of rapture.

Are We Now Having an Awakening?

Just as the Holy Roman Empire was neither holy, Roman, nor an empire, so too the great awakenings were hardly great or awakenings. Instead, awakenings are an increase in religiosity because of new innovations in storytelling. Something happens—a camp meeting, a new venue, competitive prayer, a new musical instrument (organ first, now synthesizer), a new minister who does something different like going outside or holding a praise and worship dance, Pentecostal permission. Whatever it is, a new way of "doing religion" happens. Church becomes fun. Yes, *fun*. Attendance surges, and an increase in religiosity follows.

Similar transformations happen in politics, art, education, and other cultural fields as technology makes startling changes in delivery systems. Museums and universities now often compete not on the basis of inventory (number of books, works of art) or teaching staff but on what are called "competitive amenities." Think museum store, souvenirs, climbing wall, student union, football team. Although Melvin Stewart didn't know it, his little innovation in signage was at the leading edge of the most recent of these surges in the spiritual markets.

In many ways, the past few years have been a perfect storm of supply. Winds of new media, low pressure systems of new client-centered psychology, bursts of new technology like the internet, and especially the adaptation of entertainment devices like huge projection screens and amplified music inside church have made going to church something that it has not been for a while.

In fact, a case could be made that the most important influence on modern megachurch delivery is the rock concert. Successful churches have one thing in common: They are entertaining. Fun! And in an entertainment economy, the most successful product is the one with predictable sensation delivery. Religion has become, since the dour 1966 *Time* magazine cover asked, "Is God Dead?" nothing if not entertaining. Not only is God alive, He rocks.

In a sense, one source of our current enthusiasm for sensationalism can be sited a hundred years ago in a series of boisterous revival meetings held in a converted stable on Azusa Street in Los Angeles. In early 1906 a young black pastor named William Seymour preached for several weeks about how baptism in the Holy Spirit would allow the believer to heal, to see the future, and to speak in a spiritual language called *tongues*. As rock and roll would later transform swing music by making it overtly sexual, so too these enthusiasts were activating moribund Protestantism. You want the *evidence*? We got it. Get up and dance.

Like the other great pastorpreneurs, Seymour knew how to pack 'em in. The congregation met in the round, on the sawdust-covered dirt floor of the Apostolic Faith Mission—popularly known as the Azusa Street Mission. Like the modern megachurch, once wound up, the process never stopped. Thousands of people came to worship at three services a day, seven days a week, for almost three years. Seymour worked the crowd from the center of the room. The meetings were in the style of the black church, with hand clapping, foot stomping, and shouting. At the height of the Jim Crow era, the congregants included blacks, whites, Hispanics, and Asians, all from the Los Angeles melting pot—up to 1,300 people at a time.

The Africanization of American Christianity put the fizz back in the brew. Church became emancipation via sensation. And this excitement launched a global movement that overcame differences in class, gender, and race to congeal around the belief that the Holy Spirit still works miracles, yes, and these miracles can happen to you. Now. Today, there are about six hundred million Pentecostal and charismatic Christians whose roots are in this so-called Azusa Street revival. They make up the fastest-growing segment of Christianity, thriving especially in the southern hemisphere, and their beliefs have an impact on nearly every Christian denomination.

And this storm of religiosity has traveled across the religious denominations, activating always-eager Pentecostals, jumbling the staid Catholics with active splinter groups moving off every which way, and even stirring up Jews, who are seeking God in the mystical thickets of kabbalah. This increased enthusiasm accounts as well for a rebirth of pagan religions that look for God in the wonders of the natural world, in Zen and innumerable other strains of Buddhism, whose followers seek enlightenment through meditation and designer leotards. And in the efforts of American Muslims to achieve a more market-savvy Islam. Just look at Wicca and a host of ready-to-congregate groups who seem to sprout spontaneously after every rainstorm, "Hey, let's start a church."

While the old-line Protestant denominations have entered a period of desuetude, in their midst is one of the most explosive public manifestations of religiosity in America today: the megachurches. These churches, defined by the size of membership (two thousand plus) rather than by their doctrine, are popping up all over the country. Dr. John N. Vaughan, founder of the research outfit Church Growth Today, calculates that a new megachurch crosses the tipping point every third day. Their number has shot up from about 50 in 1980 to about 1,210 in 2005. They are replacing the old country churches that are going under at the rate of about one every eight days.

But now here's the kicker: while there is a lot more religiosity, the number of believers has not increased. The general demand is not budging. Those two groups, hot and lukewarm, that I mentioned in the first chapter are still in place. The supply is simply dividing the hot consumers into new niches, and these niches, true to their marketing mandates, are taking chances, making the news. Of 1,004 respondents to a *Newsweek/Beliefnet* poll in 2005, 45 percent said they attend worship services weekly, virtually identical to the figure (44 percent) in a Gallup poll cited by *Time* in 1966. Then as now, however, there is probably a fair amount of wishful thinking in those fig-

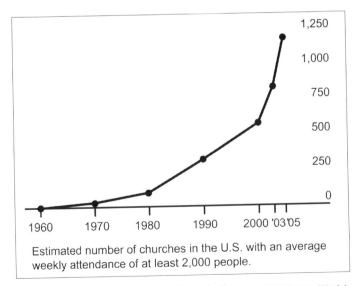

Estimated number of churches in the U.S. with an average weekly attendance of at least 2,000 people.

The big-box store comes to Church Street. (SOURCE: WALL STREET JOURNAL, APRIL 26, 2006, B1.)

ures; researchers who have done actual head counts in churches think the figure is probably more like 20 percent. There has been a particular falloff in attendance by African-Americans, for whom the church is no longer the main avenue of social advancement. Meanwhile their praise and worship music, and Pentecostal enthusiasm, have moved mainstream, essentially co-opted by the megas.

And what of this buried subset that barely makes the news? The fastest-growing category on surveys was not the hots and lukewarms but the stone colds. When "none" is a religious affiliation choice, more people are taking it. Note the best-selling success of Richard Dawkins and Sam Harris. We've seen the bumper stickers of believers. If the colds put their views on their bumpers instead of the "Don't Blame Me, I Voted for Gore" and "Practice Random Acts of Kindness," they'd look a bit like this:

"Religion is the great unmentionable evil — Gore Vidal"
"Religion is the most malevolent of all mind viruses
   —Arthur C. Clarke"
"Religion deserves no more respect than a pile of garbage
   —H. L. Mencken"
"At present there is not a single credible established religion in the
   world —George Bernard Shaw"
"Religions are founded on the fear of the many and the cleverness
   of the few —Stendhal"
"Religion consists in a set of things which the average man thinks
   he believes and wishes he was certain of —Mark Twain"
"Men never do evil so completely and cheerfully as when they do it
   from religious conviction—Pascal"

Still, if many colds are allowed to be "spiritual," they'll take it. The *Newsweek/Beliefnet* poll found that more Americans, especially those younger than sixty, described themselves as "spiritual" (79 percent) than "religious" (64 percent). And while almost two-thirds of Americans say they pray every day, nearly one-third meditate. So possibly what the colds don't like about organized religion is the *organized* part.

As with sensation delivery systems elsewhere—like music, dance, reading, movies, and television—many people want to *feel* spirituality. They want to experience epiphany, ecstasy, and rapture, and currently they want it in quick-release form. As religious historian Martin E. Marty of the University of Chicago has said of young believers today, "They don't want to hear that Joan of Arc had a vision. *They* want to have a vision."

If you pay attention to the surge of religiosity moving through American religious culture, you can see that it invariably spotlights the individual believer and delivers the goods lickety-split. No monastery time necessary. You don't have to carry a cross. The born-again experience—the sensation that successful churches are bringing to market with the same efficiency that luxury-goods suppliers are doing with purses and scarves—is one that gives the individual consumer/believer the most intimate and powerful experience (starting over) and does it with, as we will see, startling efficiency. Being born again is no trope; it's what this business is about.

A Short Political Aside

Should you ever wonder if we are experiencing an awakening of some sort, observe politics, which historically has been Geiger counter–sensitive to the shifting of religious plates. After World War II, the plates were stable. Old-line denominations were stuck in place. The lukewarms ruled. In 1960 the candidacy of John F. Kennedy, a Roman Catholic, shook things up by stirring ancient fears of Taking Directions from the pope. But nothing happened. Then came Jimmy Carter, an unabashed evangelical Christian, and Bill Clinton, an abashed evangelical Christian. Again, not much movement of the tectonic plates, but faith was at least being talked about in some way other than "I'm a Christian."

About the time Mel Stewart was developing his huge sign business, a middle-aged man in Midland, Texas—a man who had attended Andover, Yale, and Harvard, a man who was a scion of New England Episcopalianism—became a cowboy-boot-wearing oilman, a word-slurring good ol' boy, and a born-again Christian. He didn't hide it. He was caught up in it.

In a sense, George W. Bush is a personification of American religiosity. The events of September 11, 2001, may have been the trigger, but the charge was already loaded and ready to be fired. Dubya went from the warm side of American believers to the hot side. At the same time, the Episcopal Church, once known as "the Republican Party at prayer," woke up to find that not only had one of its own gone AWOL, but that its house was collapsing. The elder George Bush stayed where he belonged (Bill Clinton kidded him for being one of the "frozen chosen"), but the second one pronounces Jesus his "favorite philosopher" and trumpets America's mission to battle world evil. He got elected not because he stole votes from Democrats but because he found votes they didn't even know were there.

Junior's religiosity is no fluke. It came during a broad Christian revival that had been exploding for a while and which, if past is prologue, will eventually quiet down. But while it's aflame, he and many other Protestants who became hot sincerely use the Bible to help them cope and, beyond that, even read the Scriptures to understand and interpret unfolding events.

Bush has made no secret of the fact he thinks we are in a Great Awakening. According to the *Washington Post* (September 13, 2006), he spoke to a group of conservative journalists, saying, "A lot of people in America see this time as a confrontation between good and evil, including me . . . There was a stark change between the culture of the fifties and the sixties—boom—and I think there's change happening here. It seems to me that there's a Third Awakening." The White House wisely did not release a transcript of Bush's remarks, but the *National Review* posted highlights on its website.

Call it what you will, from Bush's campaign attacks on gay marriage, to the Supreme Court deliberations on the display of the Ten Commandments, to the decision to use the Terri Schiavo tragedy to gain political advantage, to the invocation of intelligent design and the never-ending question of a right to abortion, the one thing that is clear is that something is moving through the sensation markets. To believers it's almost rapturous to think that The Time has come.

This is prophetic Christianity, that typically American version of the old McDonald's Slogan, "You, You're the One." The believer not just overcomes the ambiguity of one God but many religions (of which only *mine* is the one true religion), and then steadfastly holds to supposed biblical predictions of the apocalypse. Blessedly innocent of history as well as the folkloric role of Chicken Little, prophetic Christians believe that every event leads to "Now it's really going to happen!" Over on the extreme Christian right, brought forward into serious consideration by Bush crusaders, are the Taliban-like literalists or reconstructionists, who believe in a reversal of women's rights, who describe the separation of church and state as a "myth," and who call openly for a theocratic government shaped by Christian doctrine. Some of these are the Promise Keepers, whom we'll look at later.

When religion gets this close to politics, however, the fire burns out. The lukewarms and the colds have all but captured the Democratic Party. The Republicans have the hots. Consider this: Americans who never go to church pull the lever for Democrats by a 2-to-1 ratio; those who attend regularly now vote Republican by a 2-to-1 majority. Currently religious temperature is the most accurate predictor of party affiliation and voting intention. Historically, that means a calm period ahead. The cold shower of real life puts out most flames.

Religion Is the News, Not Necessarily the Good News

But first we have to go through it. It has to become not just the *good news* but simply *the news*. And it has. Religion is big news. About a decade ago, in a keynote address to the Religion Newswriters Association, Bill Moyers noted, "For broadcast executives, news of the soul is no news at all." At about the same time, Stewart Hoover, a professor in the School of Journalism and Mass Communication at the University of Colorado, found that newspaper readers rated religion as an important topic for papers to cover (above sports, below education), but rated religion coverage as the one with which they were least satisfied. The "church page" or "the God beat" has largely been the domain of cub reporters. The *New York Times,* according to Gay Talese's *The Kingdom and the Power,* used to assign clerks and copy boys who aspired to be reporters to cover sermons, with editors on alert "for any signs of irreverence that the church coverage might reveal."

No more. Religion stories are all over. Like the goo in *The Blob,* this stuff is bubbling up everywhere. In fact, one could argue that

The president may have trouble with the word *crusade*, but not the History Channel.

most of the major domestic stories are now about religious issues. Think gay rights, abortion, Islam, intelligent design, and school prayer. Just do a LexisNexis search on *crusade*, and you will see how close to the surface the concept of holy war is becoming. Until he was told to hush, in 2001 George W. even used the word "crusade" to describe what he had in mind for the Middle East. The History Channel invokes the word's grisly history as a way to gather an audience.

The overarching story, and one that this book is about, is the shift since the 1950s in "doing church" and telling other people "the good news." What most people overlook is that a church is chosen, *purchased*, if you will, in an act that mimics consumption elsewhere. Although you can be spiritual by yourself, you consume the religious-experienced religion through a group, a church, and hence product switching is possible. The current awakening is both the cause and result of a massive amount of switching.

The efficient delivery of religion and frequent consumer switching have caused the decline of the mainline religious denominations and the increased growth of more conservative denominations and sects. The mainline suppliers, principally the Methodist, Lutheran, Presbyterian, and Episcopalian churches, which attracted over 60 percent of Protestants in the 1950s and were a majority among Protestants as recently as 1972, are currently closing down many of their outlets. By the 1990s only about 40 percent of U.S. Protestants were affiliated with these mainline churches. In addition, an entirely new kind of super-efficient church has exploded out there by the interstate, right next to the box stores, in large part the result of mass marketing.

How did the market transform so quickly? George Barna is a new kind of entrepreneur, the church consultant. He advises churches how to grow big and fast. In his 1988 book *Marketing the Church,* he diagnosed the problem: "My contention, based on careful study of data and the activities of American churches, is that the major problem plaguing the church is its failure to embrace a marketing orientation in what has become a market-driven environment."

Old-line religions got stuck with that old-time religion: forgiveness now, salvation later. They couldn't shift what was already in the supply lines. While their focus was on the world coming up, the real battle was in the here and now. The mainline denominations were providing a quiet place to go on Sunday with your consumption community surrounding you. But they were not delivering the sensation. They were not generating excitement. They were not providing forgiveness now, salvation now.

Meanwhile the more conservative denominations—including the Southern Baptist Convention, the Assemblies of God, the Pentecostal and Pentecostal Holiness churches—were growing like Topsy. They delivered on their brand promise. They were not your father's church. They were exciting. They have grown both in absolute numbers and as a share of the Protestant population, so the redistribution of Protestants is as much a story about how these denominations are growing as it is about how mainline denominations are declining.

Mark well: this shift, this awakening, if you will, is happening inside some but not all the Protestant churches. Even though the fraction of American adults who identify themselves as Protestant has decreased from 63 percent in the early 1970s to 54 percent in the late 1990s, the total number of Protestants has increased over time due to population growth. Believers didn't flood in from outside. Consumers were switching stores, from downtown, if you will, to out there in the mall by the interstate. George W. Bush is a harbinger of this change, moving from a high-church Anglican to a low-church evangelical Methodist. In a sense, he moved across town to do his shopping.

Understanding this shift in church shopping explains why the Southern Baptists are doing so well. They do an extraordinary job of niche marketing. In 2005 the 16.4-million-member Convention "planted" some 1,800 new churches by coupling church with specific locale. Just as Wal-Mart runs its inventory controls from each store, not from denominational HQ in Bentonville, Arkansas, so the Baptist Convention links its product to each individual church. So there are cowboy churches for people working on ranches, country music churches, even several motorcycle churches for bikers.

While Baptists may look as if their gaze is heavenward, they never take an eye off the gate. It's a key to their success. "How could anything bad be growin' so good?" The centrality of growth as a product informs other groups, such as the Mormons and the millennarian churches like the Seventh-day Adventists and Jehovah's Witnesses. They too are spinning the turnstiles with little or no centralized marketing. They are each often increasing membership by about 3 percent to 5 percent annually. And they are doing it the hard way, one convert at a time.

The process is incredibly time consuming, but they experience the efficiencies of cult marketing: few converts fall away. Freeloaders, the bane of any voluntary group dynamic, are kept to a minimum. If you've ever had a chance to encounter one of these groups as they are involved in their door-to-door marketing, you may well conclude that these authoritarian groups punish questioning, reward gullibility, and maintain distinct boundaries between Us and Them. But what they really do is generate powerful emotions and long-lasting commitment.

In a perverse sense, these are the luxury suppliers of religious goods. The expense ratios are kept high: the level of sacrifice, not just through tithing but through social commitment, is intense and long lasting. For these groups the sense of separation, even martyrdom, is clearly worth the price. After all, the price of salvation is separation.

When I think of how they sell, I'm reminded of this great ad from Cadillac. The ad, written by Theodore MacManus and titled "The Penalty of Leadership," ran only once, in 1915. It didn't have to run again. It was lifted from the pages of *The Saturday Evening Post* and applied to any product that was not selling itself so much as it was selling the sensation of separation it could provide. Sometimes we buy things to be "one of the Joneses," but occasionally we want to stand out, to really Lord it over others by showing we are different. And we're proud of the difference. Just read the body copy:

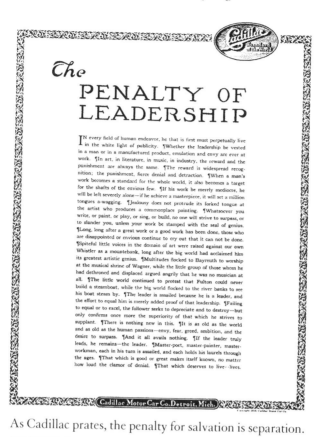

The
PENALTY OF LEADERSHIP

IN every field of human endeavor, he that is first must perpetually live in the white light of publicity. ¶Whether the leadership be vested in a man or in a manufactured product, emulation and envy are ever at work. ¶In art, in literature, in music, in industry, the reward and the punishment are always the same. ¶The reward is widespread recognition; the punishment, fierce denial and detraction. ¶When a man's work becomes a standard for the whole world, it also becomes a target for the shafts of the envious few. ¶If his work be merely mediocre, he will be left severely alone—if he achieve a masterpiece, it will set a million tongues a-wagging. ¶Jealousy does not protrude its forked tongue at the artist who produces a commonplace painting. ¶Whatsoever you write, or paint, or play, or sing, or build, no one will strive to surpass, or to slander you, unless your work be stamped with the seal of genius. ¶Long, long after a great work or a good work has been done, those who are disappointed or envious continue to cry out that it can not be done. ¶Spiteful little voices in the domain of art were raised against our own Whistler as a mountebank, long after the big world had acclaimed him its greatest artistic genius. ¶Multitudes flocked to Bayreuth to worship at the musical shrine of Wagner, while the little group of those whom he had dethroned and displaced argued angrily that he was no musician at all. ¶The little world continued to protest that Fulton could never build a steamboat, while the big world flocked to the river banks to see his boat steam by. ¶The leader is assailed because he is a leader, and the effort to equal him is merely added proof of that leadership. ¶Failing to equal or to excel, the follower seeks to depreciate and to destroy—but only confirms once more the superiority of that which he strives to supplant. ¶There is nothing new in this. ¶It is as old as the world and as old as the human passions—envy, fear, greed, ambition, and the desire to surpass. ¶And it all avails nothing. ¶If the leader truly leads, he remains—the leader. ¶Master-poet, master-painter, master-workman, each in his turn is assailed, and each holds his laurels through the ages. ¶That which is good or great makes itself known, no matter how loud the clamor of denial. ¶That which deserves to live—lives.

Cadillac Motor Car Co. Detroit, Mich.

As Cadillac prates, the penalty for salvation is separation.
(SOURCE: THE SATURDAY EVENING POST, JANUARY 2, 1915.)

In every field of human endeavor, he that is first must perpetually live in the white light of publicity. Whether the leadership be vested in a man or in a manufactured product, emulation and envy are ever at work. In art, in literature, in music, in industry, the reward and the punishment are always the same. The reward is widespread recognition; the punishment, fierce denial and detraction . . . Jealousy does not protrude its forked tongue at the artist who produces a commonplace painting . . . The leader is assailed because he is a leader, and the effort to equal him is merely added proof of that leadership. Failing to equal or to excel, the follower seeks to depreciate and to destroy—but only confirms once more the superiority of that which he strives to supplant. There is nothing new in this. It is as old as the world and as old as human passions—envy, fear, greed, ambition, and the desire to surpass. And it all avails nothing . . . That which is good or great makes itself known, no matter how loud the clamor of denial. That which deserves to live—lives.

MacManus knew nothing about cars, let alone about Cadillac. What he knew about was the deep yearning to see oneself as martyr to a cause. This ad made the Cadillac brand and for a half century protected its owners from the dreary truth.

In this mix of fungible products at different price points is a new kind of church that is far less expensive and far more inclusive. Instead of separating you from the Joneses, it puts you cheek to jowl with thousands of them and they separate the whole lot of you. It uses a different kind of marketing. Instead of intense one-on-one sales, it relies on generalized word of mouth. The megachurch, that application of big-box store to just-in-time salvation, is colonizing not just defunct malls but entire sports arenas such as the Compaq Center in Houston. The megachurch represents the cross-marketing of authoritarian religion with the human potential movement. It often has a comforting name with the word *community* in its title. And, just like the mall, the rest of its name usually refers to whatever natural site it bulldozed. So: In the Pines Community Church tells you what happened.

As is often the case in a consumerist society, the megachurch has succeeded in direct proportion to its ability to deliver sensation. I've attended many of these churches, and the one thing I'm aware of feeling as I walk back to my car in the spotless parking lot is "Hey, that was fun." The megachurch is the camp revival of the nineteenth century, except this version is 24-7-365. In fact, as we will see, the mega is the application of Woodstock (yes, *that* Woodstock) to religion.

The megachurch is the most sophisticated user of new delivery techniques. Drop-down JumboTron screens, accurate-enough amplification to hear the minister's breathing from the back of the auditorium (the new name for *sanctuary*), podcasts of specific sermons (called Godcasts), burst emailings on the subject du jour, services on your cell phone, the use of the internet and satellite technology for videoconferencing and linking to like-minded groups, sophisticated mood lighting and video to heighten sensations, electronic fund transfer, the replacement of "pew Bibles" and hymnals with easy-reading screen projection and soon to be on handheld mobile devices, the elaborate transformation of Sunday school into interest-based and age-sorted groups—you name it, if it delivers sensation and cost efficiencies, the mega will be using it.

We'll visit a few of these churches later on. They are not scary at all, and even though they bristle when called "McChurch" or "Christianity Lite," they know what they are doing. With low barriers to entry and with no established hierarchy other than a charismatic pastorpreneur, they can be pleasurable—at least at the weekend services. They are incredibly cost effective, since they are not just open for two hours on Sunday but essentially all the time. They have no denominational overhead to support, no home office in some faraway town, so they really are *your* neighborhood church. In fact, for some members, they become the *entire* neighborhood.

The door-to-door denominations, on one hand, and megachurches, on the other, are making life for mainline denominations hell. So the mainline groups are now doing a little defensive marketing of their own. I'll spend some time in chapters 5 and 6 looking at their self-promotion. But you may already know that the United Church of Christ (a descendant of the Congregational Church, itself a descendant of the Puritans) is currently running a campaign called "Still Speaking." Methodists, a century ago the fastest growing and most innovative supplier of sensation, thanks to camp meetings and itinerant preachers, have a very expensive campaign they call "Igniting Ministry." Episcopalians, blue bloods who once owned the status product but have now lost their market base, are running an anemic "Come and Grow." The Presbyterians, a generation ago one of the more innovative in church organization, are trying to increase traffic with "Stop In & Find Out." The various Lutheran councils, or *synods* as they are called, who started it all with the sixteenth-century break with what we now know as the Roman Catholic Church but who still have trouble among themselves, have never been able to have a one-church unified campaign. And the Unitarians, one of the few mainline denominations increasing in membership, often from disaffected members of other denominations, also have no central marketing but have cleverly built a brand persona by celebrating what is anathema to the lower churches: "marriage equality" and "open to all." Before we look at how churches take their product to market, let's see how markets work. Let's go shopping!

CHAPTER THREE

Let's Go Shopping: Brought to You by God®

I believe that an important reason why religion has gone from private to public, from in your heart to in your face, from lukewarm to hot, can be explained by brand switching. To understand this activity, we need to set the subject of organized religion aside and, as is often the case in modern life when things get a bit murky, go shopping.

For the moment at least, we need to strip off the bumper stickers that say "My God Isn't Dead, Sorry about Yours," and "God Promises a Safe Landing, Not a Calm Passage," and replace them with: "When the Going Gets Tough, the Tough Go Shopping"; "Shop 'til You Drop"; "He Who Dies with the Most Toys, Wins"; "People Who Say Money Can't Buy Happiness, Don't Know Where to Shop"; and "Work to Live, Live to Love, Love to Shop." In other words, let's try using the world of Mammon to explain the world of God.

Christian Consumers Are Consumers First

A key to understanding why and how American Christianity has become so dynamic is to appreciate the importance of material consumption as an expression of belief. Before we are spiritualists, we

In a world in which everything is marketed, shopping is no joke. (SOURCE, *NEW YORK TIMES MAGAZINE* SPECIAL ISSUE FOR RETAIL, FEBRUARY 16, 1997, P. 20.)

are materialists. Barbara Kruger's 1987 photographic screenprint "I shop therefore I am" is clearly parodic, but like all parody, first it tells the truth. The thing, the accessory, the hard good, is the unambiguous external sign of modern internal grace. "I shop, therefore I'm saved" is the modern extension of American religions. The sacred and the profane have always needed each other. No major religion compares with Christianity for its inventory of totemic stuff. Not for nothing is it at the heart of capitalism. According to a study by the market research publisher Packaged Facts, domestic sales of religious products are likely to grow to $9.5 billion by 2010.

It's been this way from the get-go. The first supplier of religious knickknacks to the Western worrier was, of course, the Roman Church. Two products are worthy of mention: the indulgence and the relic. They are still being sold, albeit in different forms. The indulgence was a promissory note essentially promising not safe passage into heaven but a jump ahead of your colleagues on judgment day. Some of the first printed texts, even before the Gutenberg Bible, were these indulgences. The relic was a bone, a fragment, a sliver of the cross—anything!—that had to do with the life and death of Christ, his disciples, and the saints. Why were relics so valuable that pilgrims would travel miles to observe and sometimes buy a smidgen for themselves? Because at the Rapture, proximity to this object was going to leapfrog the holder to the head of the line.

If you remember your Chaucer, you recall that by the time of the Pardoner's appearance in *The Canterbury Tales* (1386–1400), the jig was pretty well up, at least for the literate. Most of the travelers knew that the shyster was just selling pigs' knuckles, and they weren't buying. But recall that these pilgrims were on their way to Canterbury Cathedral to observe the relics of St. Thomas Becket, so they were not completely sure it was a con job. And if you remember your church history, you'll recall that it was the wild bubble in the indulgence and relic market a little more than a century later that so upset the literal-minded monk Martin Luther that he saw fit to draw attention to their abuse, and in so doing create the scramble market that we recognize today.

After the Reformation, holier-than-thou, self-righteous Protestants sneered that it had been the Church of Rome that had been making a market in what they called "holy hardware" or "Jesus junk." True enough. For a while, the Protestant churches, so pure and free of commercial taint, held the high road. Plus, for a while, they made a market in melting down Catholic icons and selling off church property. But eventually the Protestants were manufacturing their own holy hardware, what with Jesus thermometers, "magic lantern" slides, and the first Christian board game, Mansions of Glory. American churchgoers were especially eager to stock up on stuff. Lest we forget, this country was founded by both Christianists and capitalists. While states like Massachusetts were organized by the Massachusetts Bay Company to save souls, states like Virginia were organized by the Virginia Company of London to make money.

Pretty soon the Protestants were even generating their own relics. For instance, George Whitefield, the great Methodist evangelist, was dug up by believers who chopped off his thumb, which they shaved into amulets. And sold. In 1775 two Continental Army officers (one of them Benedict Arnold) reportedly stole the clerical collar and wristbands from his corpse and carried them into battle. By 1829 his arm had made a twenty-year sojourn to Britain to be prayed over before returning to his Newburyport, Massachusetts, burial vault. Much of Whitefield's ephemera and many of his possessions now reside in the library at New Jersey's Drew University, where they are still revered by good Methodists.

Where American Protestants excelled was with Bible printing and decoration—wonderfully ornate presentation items left conspicuously in the parlor for all comers to appreciate. According to religious historian Colleen McDannell, there was a glut of Bible editions between 1830 and 1860; no fewer than one thousand variations of God's word in print. On one hand, there was the going-to-church Bible, but on the other was a new profit center: the suitcase-sized behemoth that stayed at home. This Bible had the same purpose as today's plasma-screen TV in the modern entertainment room. In fact, the family Bible often sat on a majestic stand surrounded by all kinds of look-how-religious-we-are bling.

Still, until recently, Protestants could always claim that, OK, they had lots of Bibles, but that was only because the Word was so important. Times have changed. American low-church Protestants, who once railed against the shallow materialism of their no-longer-kissing cousins from Rome, are now shopping at the indulgence and relic markets. They are the ones who are now selling the pig's knuckles. Where once they enjoyed invoking the story of Christ throwing the money changers out of the temple, today the megachurches clearly welcome the merchants into their temples. The souvenir store is front and center, right next to the sanctuary, selling all kinds of logoed stuff. If you are a doubting Thomas, check out any of their websites.

As in so much of modern life, before all else, the belief statement is the fashion statement. We wear the designer's name, little pony, alligator, or initials over our hearts to announce our affiliation (as well as our willingness—and ability—to pay full retail). So consider such synergies as the iPod being transformed into a cross hung around the neck with a lanyard. Or what of a brand like Not of This World, which makes its way onto accessories like belt buckles. Go into a chain of stores such as LifeWay Christian Stores or Family Christian Stores, the nation's largest for-profit Christian retail chains, and you'll see aisles of undifferentiated objects inscribed, embossed, embedded with Christian iconography. In C28, a popular Christian store chain primarily on the West Coast, you see T-shirts bearing what looks to be a heavy-metal skull with biblical verses like this from 1 Corinthians 15:33: "Do not be misled: bad company corrupts good character." Should you ever go to a Christian rock concert, you'll see a veritable cornucopia of such message-driven merchandise.

Better yet, attend the Christian Booksellers Association meeting, and you'll see this same transformation of born-again religion into endless memorial objects. Don't let the *Booksellers* in the name fool you. It's a modern vanity fair. Most of the five hundred retailers and vendors are not selling books but a vast array of "Christ-honoring product," like children videos (the wildly popular *VeggieTales* series plus the latest installment of *Bibleman,* an animated action hero); jewelry (Fisher of Men rings and endless variations of the cross); sportswear (from Extreme Christian Clothing and Fear God); comics (not just biblical stories but versions of DC Comics' *Infinite Quest* series, in which our superheroes seek help from a higher power); computer games (from companies like Left Behind Games, Digital Praise, and GraceWorks Interactive); parlor games (Bibleopoly and Scriptionary, plus a game modeled on Risk, which involves world military domination, called Missionary Conquest); countless T-shirts with bumper sticker mottoes, auto sun visors that say "Jesus Is Lord" on one side and "Need Help! Please Call Police" on the reverse; neckties in patterns of "angel paisley" or "burning bush;" "spiritually inspired messages" for your answering machine; chewing gum (Testamints, the breath-freshening candy with a cross impressed in the center and a verse of scripture on the wrapper); and all manner of what used to be associated with those icon-worshiping Catholics with their dashboard Jesus and designer rosary beads hanging from the rearview mirror.

Such goods often seem to hang on with a smirk of irony, unable to decide what side they're on. Is this purposeful? I don't know. What sense do you make of a talking Bible called the GodPod, diet books such as *What Would Jesus Eat?*, or a wristwatch with a solitary *11* on the face, so if anybody asks the time, a brochure advises replying: "You see, it really doesn't matter what time it is; we're in the eleventh hour. Would you like to know Jesus and prepare for His coming?" Or what about a Christian boomerang ("Love always returns"), and a balm called Fragrance of Jesus? Is this wink-wink or what? Perhaps one needs to be reminded that a quarter of the readers of *The Da Vinci Code* believed it to be telling the truth about the Catholic church.

While it's easy to decode the fact that teenage girls of the newly empowered religious right have emptied Christian store shelves of WWJD bracelets ("What Would Jesus Do?"), what to make of a product called Wait Wear—underwear with slogans like "No Vows No Sex," "I'm Saving It!" and "Virginity Lane: Exit When Married"? Who's the intended reader? By the time they're parsed, virginity may be no more. When the Style section of the *New York Times* ran a piece on "A Ring That Says No, Not Yet" about the growing use of chastity rings, even the Gray Lady seemed more amused than affronted. But what about the ring wearer?

And what of the Evangelical Environmental Network linking the teachings of Jesus with the fuel economy of cars, warning the big automakers to quit making SUVs? Trying to provoke support from religious car buyers, the EEN website asks the question, What would Jesus drive? Another question might be *why* would Jesus drive? If you really want to see the bumper sticker confusion at work, consider the "Jesus Is My Homeboy" T-shirts that Ashton Kutcher, Pamela Anderson, Ben Affleck, and Jessica Simpson are all reported to wear. And who sells them? Among others, Urban Outfitters.

Perhaps retail has become one of the few ways that we can talk about religion without squabbling. We use it to make statements, what used to be called value judgements. Take the material that is the stuff of our times—denim. No area of consumable is more powerful or more interesting than this cotton fabric. Denim is essentially a rugged weave of colored threads, usually blue and white, which became the stuff of durable work clothes in late nineteenth century and of fashion statements a century later. The product itself is interchangeable; the bolt going to Levi's is pretty much the same as the one heading off to Gloria Vanderbilt.

Sure, cut, design, color, hand stitching, hand washing, and wear and tear signs can all make jeans more interesting (and expensive), but at the end of the day it's just another pair of jeans. As we have learned with products like this (numerous and interchangeable), the narrative (brand) becomes important. What's in a jean's name? As opposed to a rose, pretty much everything. When a product achieves fungibility, marketing starts.

True Religion Apparel manufactures, markets, distributes, and sells True Religion Brand Jeans in the United States, Canada, the United Kingdom, Europe, Mexico, and Japan. They have become one of an elect company of "it" jeans. You can buy them at places like Neiman Marcus, Saks Fifth Avenue, Henri Bendel, Bloomingdale's, Nordstrom, and Barneys. You cannot buy them at Wal-Mart. They sell for about two hundred dollars. True Religion's big break came in connecting with celebrities such as Jessica Simpson and Cameron Diaz, who appeared in magazines wearing the jeans.

Since denim is so eloquent as a sender of messages, consider also the appearance of "bad jeans," which attempt to get into your face with a little sneer. Cheap Monday jeans have a satanic logo—a cross turned upside down on the forehead of a skull—presumably to make Christians angry. As one might expect, they are especially popular in countries in which the evangelical is kept at bay, Sweden in particular.

Shoppers' *Choice* Is Crucial

Indeed, with the exception of furniture and major appliances, it is possible to outfit your entire self and home in Christian products—bird feeders to body lotions, luggage to lamps. It has been said that the medieval peasant lived surrounded by such iconography, from the door frames incorporating the cross, to his eating utensils laid out in the shape of the cross, to the cross on the church. We're coming close. Clearly, religiously informed objects are now a part of the modern scene, asserting their place in a multicultural world. Just as we use manufactured stuff to say, "I am a Mexican American," or "I am gay," so too do we say, "I am an evangelical Christian." The key, however, is that the statement is not about belief as much as about an entire lifestyle. The new Christian decked out like a bumper covered with stickers considers his faith not something to exercise in private on Sundays but something to do in public, in front of you. It's not just something to believe in; it's something to wear.

As a matter of fact, the mall store is not all that far from the megachurch. The big megachurches look eerily alike, a slightly different version of Safeway. A number of observers have pointed to the often provocative similarities between the medieval cathedral and the modern department store: both are concerned with salvation via consumption, getting the Word out (proselytizing/ advertising), and ranks of affiliation (devotion/brand loyalty). Furthermore, both have sacred texts (Bible/catalog), functionaries (clergy/clerks), signs of spiritual election (salvation/goods), holidays (religious/sales), heroic lighting (stained glass/spotlights), music (hymns/Muzak), and financial transactions (tithe/purchase and collection plate/cash register).

With the appearance of the megachurch, the similarities are no longer mere analogs but reality. In many megas you find gift stores where you can buy logoed merchandise just as you can in the mall. Not by happenstance are both athletic jerseys and church T-shirts called spiritwear. In the modern world we often know where we are by what we are buying. While it may seem paradoxical that big churches are also in the trinket business, it's not just a source of profit but of community.

So let's go down the road to your mall store to see how the act of shopping not only leads to the ultimate act of buying but also expresses empowerment. All successful retail has one thing in common. The customer wants to feel in control, and to do this there needs to be choice. Shoppers don't tell you this. The store does. A decade ago the average grocery store carried about 9,000 items; the average stock is now 24,000, and the big ones double that number. Even more interesting is that since 1991, the number of brands in the store has tripled. In other words, not only have stock keeping units (SKUs, as they are called) exploded, the names of essentially interchangeable items have expanded even more. In 2004 the U.S. Patent and Trademark Office issued an incredible 140,000 trademarks, about 100,000 more than twenty years before. Go into Wal-Mart sometime and simply observe the amazing redundancy of choice. The place is packed, yes, but with many versions of almost the same product. Delete *almost*.

Before the automobile, the self-service store, and the little shopping cart, you had to ask a clerk for help. You put your groceries up on the counter for all to see. There were no brands. You bought right from the barrel. The grocer knew your name. You knew his. Your parents shopped there. Choice? There was none. As Henry Ford famously said about this kind of shopping, you could have your Model T in any color, so long as it was black.

Now go grocery shopping. No one knows you, because almost no one representing the store is there. The shelves are often restocked by the vendors to make sure that their goods are being properly displayed. Go down any aisle. What do you notice? Not just the packaging but the rather incredible repetition. Name it: toothpaste, yogurt, cola drinks, soaps, soups, ice cream—what you find is about eight or so different varieties and then about ten or so subsets of each.

Revlon makes 158 shades of lipstick. Want a more unisex product? Spend some time at toothpaste. What you see is Colgate, Crest, Tom's of Maine, Aquafresh, Aim, Close-Up, etc. Then look closely at just one brand, and you'll see versions for whitening, cavity protection, tartar protection, sensitive teeth, different flavors like baking soda, as well as different sizes, consistency, and shapes. Plus, much of this gets duplicated for the kiddies. All told, Crest comes in thirty-six different versions.

Who's the hottest supplier in the supermarket business today?

Whole Foods Market. Check out its fruits and vegetables: "724 produce varieties available today—93 organic selections." Over in the cheese section, 14 types of feta alone. Go to Starbucks. Look at the menu. What's nonfat decaf iced vanilla latte all about? Forget food. Home Depot has more than 1,500 drawer pulls. Amazon.com gives every town a bookstore with 2 million titles, while Netflix promises 35,000 different movies on DVD. The supplying of choice, needless choice, is everywhere, liberating to some, but to others a new source of stress.

During the last couple of decades, the American economy has undergone a variety revolution. Instead of simply offering mass-market goods, businesses of all sorts increasingly compete to give consumers more personalized products, more varied experiences, and more choice.

Now this explosion of choice has become second nature to some of us, mostly the young. It unbalances older types, like my colleague Barry Schwartz. His book *The Paradox of Choice: Why More Is Less* mourns the loss of a simpler world. In fact, Professor Schwartz does a riff on what it's like to go into the Gap to buy jeans. What kind? asks the fresh-faced Gappie: boot cut, fatty bottom, button fly, low rise, baggy, utility, stonewashed, sandblasted, whiskered, faded, black, carpenter? The poor professor is fazed. He doesn't want to change denominations.

Unfazed, however, is the regular consumer. The Gap's real customers are young people. They know how to handle this kind of choice. They've grown up on it. They have no cognitive frustration with choice, even when it doesn't exist. They've grown up with the old AT&T offering "the right choice"; Wendy's, "there is no better choice"; Pepsi, "the choice of a new generation"; Coke, "the real choice"; and Taster's Choice Coffee is "the choice for taste."

Even advertisers don't understand the phenomenon of unnecessary choice in places where there are no distinctions. While older types become cragfast, unable to decide, younger people pass right by. Just another multitask to them. Remember that this overflow of proffered choice most often happens when end products are almost indistinguishable, when there are few ingredient differences, when (now in the religious sense) there is little doctrinal separation.

If we were logical shoppers, as we claim, we would go down to the local library, read *Consumer Reports* and find out the marginally best version of toothpaste, soap, blue jean, and buy it. We would know that everyone was also logical because, over time, when we returned to the store, there would be fewer and fewer varieties and subvarieties as we gradually all bought the best. Just the opposite seems to happen.

The grocery store, again, if it were logical, would have shrunk to the size of a 7-Eleven. And so too would other venues that sell essentially interchangeable products. Instead of some forty kinds of SUV, there would be one or two. Instead of all those labels of bottled water, only a few. Instead of an aisle of jellies and jams, just a shelf. And just to make things more perplexing, instead of brands (Oreo) and subbrands (Oreo Double Stuf) and brand extensions (Oreo Jell-O Pudding Snacks), there would be mainly generics, store brands. And yet this is not what has happened.

What has any of this got to do with modern religion? If you are perplexed and impatient, this might be a good time to log on to www.SelectSmart.com/Religion and then click your way through the Belief System Selector. It will give you a sense of the explosion of religious choice experienced by young believers today.

The Effects of Plenitude

Back in the 1970s, Theodore Levitt, an American economist and professor at Harvard Business School, observed this paradox: similarity produces distinction.

> There is hardly a company that would not go down in ruin if it refused to provide fluff, because nobody will buy pure functionality. Without distortion, embellishment, and elaboration, life would be drab, dull, anguished, and at its existential worst.

This similarity happens whenever you get a phenomenon that cultural anthropologist Grant McCracken calls *plenitude* in a product line. Shoppers will, over time, move to about eight different choices and then to about eight more choices of subsets. The naming or branding process becomes progressively more important as the ingredient separation diminishes. Distortion, embellishment, and elaboration are taking hold.

But Sheena Iyengar and Mark Lepper, psychologists at Columbia and Stanford Universities, respectively, have shown that as the number of flavors of jam or varieties of chocolate available to shoppers is increased, the likelihood that the shoppers will leave the store without buying either jam or chocolate goes up. The professors found that shoppers are ten times more likely to buy jam when six varieties are on display as when twenty-four are on the shelf. They tried all kinds of variations. Customers could try as many flavors as they wanted. After tasting the jam, they got a coupon for one dollar off a jar of any flavor. Half the time the sample table offered six flavors, and half the time it offered twenty-four. Thirty percent of the customers who tasted jams from the small selection later bought a jar, compared to only 3 percent of those who sampled from two dozen different flavors.

Here's the take-away: if you can give the right number of choices (say a handful), and if you can separate them by brand appeal (emotion), you will sell more jam, chocolate, coffee, cola, than if you give shoppers no choice or too much choice. In other words, consumers will lock on to a specific brand and deeply affiliate not by a taste memory but by the fact that the choice has been made. *Their* choice. They're in control.

For instance, as the number of mutual funds in a 401(k) plan offered to employees increases, the likelihood that they will choose a fund—any fund—goes down. For every ten funds added to the array of options, the rate of participation drops 2 percent. And for those who do invest, adding fund options over about eight increases the chances that employees will invest in ultraconservative money-market funds. But keep the choice pool small and brand the choices with terms like *growth, value, emerging markets, small cap,* and you'll sell more. Better yet, investors will hold on to the fund even though they see the fund performing poorly.

Later I'll hazard an explanation for the limits to choice based on our ability to remember and enjoy stories, but for now let's just stick with the process of choosing between and among fungibles. What we seem to like is the process of some choice, and that choice is based not on what is in the product but what surrounds it. Could it be that if we buy the sizzle and not the steak, it's because there's something about the sizzle we like?

Branding 101: It's All about the Story

My favorite explanation of what happens to valuing choice in a world of plenitude is this conversation from the BBC sitcom *Absolutely Fabulous*. Edwina receives a gift of earrings from her daughter. "Are they Lacroix?" Edwina asks eagerly. "Do you like them?" asks her daughter. "I do if they're Lacroix," replies Edwina.

That's because the only way to distinguish an interchangeable product is to tell a story about it, and the stories themselves become the repositories of value. But why are stories so important? For a very simple reason: as opposed to most fungible objects, humans respond emotionally to stories. Americans are criticized for being too materialistic. Often this criticism comes from the pulpit. Yet, ironically, we are not materialistic *enough*. If we knew how to value the world of stuff, we would not need stories to serve as the markers of value. Things would just mean. Instead we have to install meaning, tell a story. That sounds self-evident, but it's crucial in understanding the modern commercial world. And, as we'll see, the modern religious world as well.

We seem hardwired to emote when someone tells us a powerful story. The process starts early, with simple parent-to-child stories. Different stories generate different emotions, and it's culture specific. So a sad story makes us cry, a funny one makes us laugh, a pornographic one arouses, and so forth. The general term under which this amazing response system travels is *genre*. No other animal experiences it, and all human cultures develop it. Or else they die out.

The telling of a story about a product to generate an emotion is called branding, and the story is told in many ways, such as through advertising, packaging, endorsements, PR, word of mouth, logos, and you know the rest. Great commercial brands make you feel some emotion, although the feeling is often so quicksilver fast that it never reaches consciousness. Coke, Nokia, Duracell, Nike, FedEx, Intel, and McDonald's separate themselves from the almost perfect substitutes by fostering the story, the brand, because brand-meisters know that you can "own" specific feelings, whereas you can't own unique ingredients. Often the sensation is in itself meaningless and totally independent of the product's characteristics. Think Coke's "The Real Thing" going up against Pepsi's equally meaningless "Next Generation." But the sensation carried in these murky colas is clear: integrity versus being with the in-group.

As a rule, the more commodified an industry, the more important the branding process; and the more emotional the brand story, the more successful the product. *In your face* becomes not a term of disparagement but of success. That's because *on your face* is where the emotion is displayed.

One of the hazards of branding is that narratives run out of steam or, more accurate, run out of audience. From time to time they have to get refreshed, or the consumer will essentially say, as does the listener to the bedtime story, "Been there, felt that." Brand loyalty is really adspeak for story effect. That's why companies are continually changing what seem to be great campaigns even when they seem to be working. Just when you think they are really compelling, they are actually wearing out.

As companies have spent enormous amounts of time and energy introducing new brands and defending established ones, Americans have become less affected, which translates into less attention, less genuine emotion. Not by happenstance have we developed a nifty disease to express this condition: attention deficit hyperactivity disorder, or ADHD. We give the disease to our kids, but to some degree, it's also ours as consumers.

"Brand shifting" is common among young people. A study by the retail-industry tracking firm NPD Group found that nearly half of those who described themselves as highly loyal to a brand were no longer loyal a year later. Even seemingly strong names rarely translate into much power at the cash register. Another remarkable study found that just 4 percent of consumers would be willing to stick with a brand if its competitors offered better value for the same price. Young consumers are continually looking for a better deal, opening the door for companies to introduce a raft of new products not just in hopes of exploiting your brand switching but of bollixing the competition. Just observe the cola aisle.

But here's a key point: Once a brand choice is made, usually in late adolescence, it sticks for a while. That's why most advertising (and the culture that it carries) is directed toward teenagers. It's been estimated that it costs about $200 of marketing to get a fifty-year-old to change his brand of beer, but only about $2 to get an eighteen-year-old to do the same. And the kid isn't even legal. In fact, if you look at beer advertising, you'll see that the target audience is well under the legal age, just as it is with cigarettes. Joe Camel was a kid's cartoon for a reason. Hooked early, the user will stay true—not to the product but to the brand.

Two generations ago, consumer-goods markets, rather like their current religious counterparts, were very stable. Stories held firm, to some degree, because the number of suppliers was small, and consumers didn't have much disposable income or time. If you had a set of trophy brands, you could be pretty sure that most of them would still be around two years, five years, ten years from now. Consumers were loyal, if only because there was a paucity of linked choices. So with cars, for instance, you would start driving a Chevy, move to an Olds, up to a Buick or Pontiac, and then—epiphany!—a Cadillac. The process took a lifetime. Similarly, in the religious markets you might start Baptist, move across town to the Presbyterian church, then end up an Episcopalian (or even a Unitarian!). The process might take a few generations. Now it's a hop and a skip.

Branding Ideal: The Cult

I teach at a large, impersonal university filled with anxious young people, the demographic most prized by advertisers for the reasons discussed. Each day as I cross the campus, there is often a little knot of very intense students clustered around someone speaking. Over the years, I've walked through the Moonies, Scientologists, TM-ers, Hari Krishnas, Maranathas, and countless evangelical Christians, itinerant and local. I know many of them. From time to time, I ask one of them to speak to my advertising class. Brother Jed Smock is my favorite. He sees himself as a modern-day John Wesley, and I have learned a lot from him about selling. He is not the stuff of the Heaven's Gate religious cult, Jim Jones, David Koresh, or Charles Manson, but he generates something that is provocatively similar to what happens in other nonreligious marketplaces.

Jed is a master of small-group foment and ferment. What's going on in those little cabals as I walk through them is close to what was going on among the first Mazda Miata owners, iPod users, early Starbucks drinkers, Manolo Blahnik wearers, Beanie Baby collectors. Stories are being told. Intimacy exchanged. Community built. The cult story is the promise of total affiliation. *My way or the highway.* This is the kind of affiliation that Apple Computer owners have, that Harley-Davidson has created, that Snapple, Saturn, and VW once had. The cult brand is so dynamic that it pushes all else aside. Clearly at some level, it's dangerous (after all, it can exact the highest price: martyrdom), but before that level it's the goal of every marketer.

Understanding how brands get and lose their cultic concentration is to understand why two generations ago the Methodist Church was going gangbusters, generating intense affiliation, yet today—what's a Methodist? Why do true believers sometimes puncture themselves, walk on their knees until they bleed, fast until they are skeletal, or join a monastery and go mum? And then, why do they suddenly switch allegiance? Or, from another angle, how and why did certain bones of particular saints and paraphernalia of the Christ become relics to our great-great-grandparents. They went on pilgrimages and crusades to celebrate these stories. They paid sacrificial prices to get this product.

When the brand allegiance is in place, it can sometimes be fierce. Note that religion is almost always the source of martyrdom. If you are going to wrap some plastic explosive around your belly and blow yourself up, chances are you are going to do it in the name of faith. You are dying to have the product.

But stories can wear out or be told at cross-purposes. Belief peters out. Denominations rise, shine, evaporate, and fall. In 1985 Coca-Cola infamously introduced an identity-blurring new brand, New Coke. It quickly found out the cultic nature of its constituency. A massive consumer backlash ensued, and the company quickly reinstated its familiar Coke Classic. You'd think that Coca-Cola would have learned from that betrayal of faith the importance of having a unique product personality, a stable doctrine. But today the company sells sixteen versions of Coke, including such exotic variations as Coca-Cola Zero, Diet Coke with Splenda, and Coca-Cola C2. What's a Coke? (What's a Presbyterian?)

Mercedes-Benz is making the same mistake. If you wander into a dealership, you're faced with the following lineup: A-Class, B-Class, C-Class, E-Class, S-Class, CLK, CLS, CL, SLK, SL, M-Class and G-Class. The prices are all over the place, as is the narrative. The result is that in Europe, Mercedes-Benz is not even listed as the top brand. The Audi A8, BMW, Maserati, and Jaguar have taken over this position. Same thing is happening here to our faith in the brand. Can advertising repair the damage?

A few years ago Young & Rubicam the old-line advertising agency, produced a study of brands in which it famously stated that "brands are the new religion." How else to explain why thousands of people get married in Disney theme parks and buried in Harley-

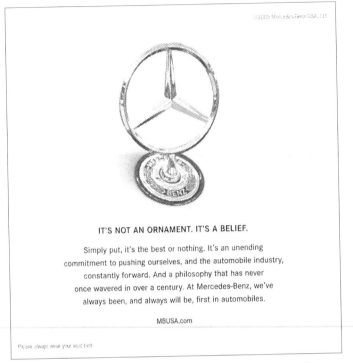

IT'S NOT AN ORNAMENT. IT'S A BELIEF.

Simply put, it's the best or nothing. It's an unending
commitment to pushing ourselves, and the automobile industry,
constantly forward. And a philosophy that has never
once wavered in over a century. At Mercedes-Benz, we've
always been, and always will be, first in automobiles.

MBUSA.com

Please always wear your seat belt.

The nameplate as icon: Mercedes knows that at some point
steel and plastic becomes religious.

Davidson brand coffins? While it's easy to see the fetishizing of
goods down at the supermarket, it's a bit hazier with the fetishizing
of belief over at the church. What is idolatry really depends on
which side of the church door you are standing. My objects are relics;
yours are rubbish.

Verily, I Sell unto You: Where Commercial Branding Came From

Forget branding for a moment. Forget hard goods. Just think *over-supply of interchangeable product*. Imagine that you sell a product
with these characteristics: (1) does everything, (2) costs nothing, (3) is

available 24-7, (4) comes with a lifetime warranty, and (5) is protected from competition by the state. How would you sell it? This exercise may help you understand why the American religious marketplace is so fascinating to study as an economy of buyers and sellers, a Babel of storytellers. It will also help you appreciate the claim that American marketing arose directly from American Christianity. Ministers of salvation became ministers of goods. What's happening now, as I write this, is that branding is making the return journey back to religion. Today competitive denominations use exactly the techniques that they had originally innovated and which were then perfected during what is naively called late capitalism.

It is no happenstance that the first formal advertising men, or "attention engineers," who helped bring about the rise of consumer culture, were steeped in the Christian tradition. They understood both the nature of yearning and how to franchise it. They knew the language of sincerity. They knew the power of promise, large promise. They knew how to make the sale and close the deal.

During the late nineteenth and early twentieth centuries, advertising was a white upper-middle-class Christian endeavor, in part because most of the educated population was Protestant, and, in part, because the procedure for selling manufactured answers to life's present problems was so similar to what religion had developed to sell future redemption. "You deserve a break tomorrow" became "You deserve a break today."

Look at the early apostles of advertising. Among the most important ministers of commerce with deep evangelical roots were: Artemas Ward, son of an Episcopal minister, whose slogans for Sapolio soap were almost as well-known as the songs of Solomon; John Wanamaker, a staunch Presbyterian who considered the ministry and whose marketing genius helped create both the modern department store and holidays like Mother's Day that give us reasons to shop there; Claude C. Hopkins, who came from a long line of impoverished preachers, preached himself at seventeen, and translated his talent into copywriting for beer, carpet sweepers, lard, and canned meats; James Webb Young, who sold Bibles door to door as a true believer until he went to work at J. Walter Thompson, where he did much the same job; Helen Lansdowne, the daughter of a Presbyterian minister, who studied three years at Princeton Theological Seminary before applying her talents to selling all manner of products to women; Theodore MacManus (copywriter of "The Penalty of Leadership" mentioned in chapter 2), one of the few devout Catholics in early advertising, who held honorary degrees from three Catholic colleges and was the master of the "soft sell" until he quit, disgusted with advertising, especially its huckstering of cigarettes as health foods; Rosser Reeves, son of a Methodist minister, who mastered the "hard sell" and left as his legacy the Anacin ads with all those hammers pounding their anvils; Marion Harper Jr., president of his Methodist Sunday school class, who went on to manage McCann-Erickson; and F. W. Ayer, a devout Baptist and Sunday school superintendent, who gave his own ad agency his father's name, N. W. Ayer & Son, because it sounded more established, and then coined the motto "Keeping everlastingly at it" to make sure the point was made. These are only a few of the priesthood of advertising, but the list shows that almost to a man (and occasional woman), the early advertisers came by their theological zeal honestly.

Bruce Barton, Salesman for Christ

Of all the evangelical confidence men, none was more influential in translating magical thinking into sectarian matters than Bruce Barton. And none was more typical. Son of a Congregational minister, young Barton considered the ministry, had a nervous breakdown, took up magazine writing, and then edged over into commercial selling. Once a success at copywriting, he joined with others to form the still-going-strong B (for Barton) BD&O advertising agency. Barton did the selling for the likes of General Motors, Lever Brothers, DuPont, and General Electric. He was central in coining not just the phrase but the concept of "Better Living through . . .". In so doing he recharged the central American belief in the frontier, in redemption, in second chance, in being born-again.

In his forties, Barton felt it was time to pay back his debt and perhaps relieve a guilty conscience for having spent so much time helping the friends of Mammon. He did this in a characteristically American Protestant way. He wrote a book of instruction for others less fortunate on the way to success. In the context of literary history, Barton's book *The Man Nobody Knows* (1925) fits into a robust genre of "How would Jesus act if He were alive today?" Best-selling books like Charles M. Sheldon's *In His Steps* (1896), in which readers were encouraged to imagine what life would be like if they were to respond to day-to-day problems by consulting the Lord, were as popular as how-to-be-your-own-best-friend books are today. Barton's Jesus was an advertising executive busy at "his father's business," selling redemption by the newly named but ancient devices of advertising.

In *The Man Nobody Knows,* Jesus and his little band of twelve entrepreneurs are shown carrying the Word to the modern world. He is no "lamb of God" but a full-fledged salesman out in the marketplace. We see a dapper Jesus at a cocktail party or a ballgame with the rest of us, a man among men who knows well what His people need and who struggles to explain how to get it. The omniscient narrator, the Voice of Advertising, often glosses the text with up-to-date information on selling techniques, but essentially the chapters represent a Christological musing on American business.

Here's the calculus, according to Barton: Jesus was a businessman; advertising is a business. Jesus spoke in parables; advertising speaks in parables. Christianity is a product; advertising sells products. Jesus performed miracles; advertising works magic. The similarities are too powerful to overlook. As Barton once said to a meeting of advertising agencies, "If advertising speaks to a thousand in order to influence one, so does the church." However much Barton's Babbittry in the cause of faith may seem Philistine, it cannot be denied that he made the connection between the two merchandising systems. If ever a man understood the old bromide "Religion afflicts the comforted and comforts the afflicted," it was Bruce Barton.

As religion has co-opted modern marketing, modern marketing has returned the favor.

Should you ever doubt the intimate connection between sacred and profane selling, you need only consult the modern magazine. For here you will see the legacy of Brother Barton. Christian cultures with few objects tend to load up their heaven with deluxe objects, while, as admen now know, cultures with a surfeit of objects tend to sacramentalize them in the here and now.

In chapters 5 and 6, I analyze some of the new Barton-esque campaigns coming from the branding efforts of individual denominations (especially the Methodists) as they battle for market position. In many ways they are mimicking the old-style corporations delivering product through a franchise of local retail outlets. To some readers it will seem sacrilegious to think of Christianity as one of a handful of religion suppliers in the world faith markets, individual Christian denominations as discrete manufacturers of essentially fungible lines, and that sweet little church on the corner as the outlet often hanging on for dear life lest that big Wal-Mart megachurch on the outskirts of town drain its pews. But, in the spirit of Barton, not to think this way may be a sacrilege of a different kind. The Chapter 11 kind.

If the templates for commercial and religious business are similar, it may be because consumers of both yearn for a certain kind of experience, expect a certain kind of brand story, and desire a certain kind of community. While thinking about believers as customers seems almost too vulgar, thinking about consumers as believers is precisely what modern marketing is all about. Maybe Bruce Barton was not far from the truth. While it was Jesus Christ who made the religion, it was St. Paul who built the marketplace church.

Denominational Brands, Born Again and Again

The first rule of Marketing 101 is this: for a product to be viable over time, there has to be an indwelling thirst, a yearning, a desire, a demand. Marketing does not create desire, however comforting it is to believe this. We are not victims in the hands of satanic salesmen. If we were, why would 80 percent of new products fail, including those with the best advertising? The shelves of capitalism are littered with the likes of Edsels, Corfam shoes, New Coke, eight-track stereo, Betamax. So too the shelves of religion. Think Shaker, Rappite, Amana, Oneida, Brook Farm. Marketing exploits desire, yes, but it does not invent it.

Much is made by those who hold the commercial world in disdain—many of whom speak from the pulpit—that the desire for Heineken or Lexus or DeBeers or Nike is installed by crafty admen into stupid consumers. This is the hypodermic theory of consumption. According to this theory, the dolts in the mall are there because they have been injected with yearning and now fritter away their earnings buying stuff they don't need. These yearnings of Mammon displace the natural reaching out for God. Presumably, we would all be eating tofu, piddling around in our Birkenstocks, and reading the Bible if left alone.

Conversely, many in the secular world—often preaching in the groves of academe—are convinced that the desire for organized religion is equally ephemeral to the human condition and made compelling only by those priests injecting the hypodermic needle of anxiety into the same dolts. In this view, the priest is injecting the fever of sin while at the same time he just happens to have the palliative forgiveness. Presumably, to this group, we would all be eating lettuce, walking around barefoot, and reading Percy Bysshe Shelley if left alone.

In all transactions there is a buyer and a seller, and both actively cooperate in providing the choice and then making it. Sometimes it seems that the seller is getting the upper hand. And sometimes he is. The most famous example is the tale of Listerine, in which what was really sold was halitosis, not mouthwash. In ad jargon, you don't sell the product, you sell the disease.

Ponder this: before Listerine there is no mention in popular literature of bad breath. Yes, people had diseases in the mouth, rotting teeth, and open sores. To us they would have stunk. To them they didn't. We have learned how to smell bad breath. And be repelled by it. The dreaded effects of halitosis ("Always a Bridesmaid, Never a Bride" was the famous campaign) have become part of what we call "common knowledge."

Motivational psychologists call the process *constructing discontent.* We are persuaded not so much to buy a product as to remove some dissonance and reestablish a perceived equilibrium. It just so happens that the product stands foursquare in the path of recovery from the contrived affliction. To be sure, this is nothing but a protection racket, as the company selling you the relief is also the one creating the deficiency.

In fact, if you go into your bathroom, you will see that almost every product there has been introduced into common use by generating constructive discontent. Body odor came from Lifebuoy soap, athlete's foot came from Absorbine Jr. liniment, the "five o'clock shadow" from Gillette razors, tooth film from Pepsodent toothpaste, and split ends from Alberto VO5 shampoo. Teeth, hair, mouth, beard, skin, underarms—you name it—if you can feel anxious about it, it is dealt with in the bathroom. This is the only room in the house that always has a door and almost always has a lock.

Could the same be true of religion? The church is the one building that used to pride itself on having no lock. But in many ways it operates on the same principles. You enter this space to be relieved of all the grime that, to a degree, is also applied in this space. In all cases, however, the participants must be willing, even anxious, to change, to sense some new stories, hear some narrative, have some explanation of why things happen. You are not duped into believing in sin any more than you are duped into believing in halitosis.

This view of negotiated meaning is increasingly being acknowledged on both sides of the altar. Ministers who are paying attention to the turnstiles know who is coming in the front and who is leaving by the side door. They also know how close this process is to the commercial world. Clearly what is called "mutual gains" is occurring, and it is happening rapidly because there is such a fluid market—choice, plenitude, fungibles, brand switching. Today there is an active population seeking religion in the same way they look for

household goods; they are shopping, switching pews until—
bingo!—they find the one they affiliate with. At least for a while.

The central connection between consumption and religion is
demonstrative; it requires shopping. You don't buy and hide; you
buy and show off. Climbing rates of church switching—4 percent of
adults in 1955 moved from the church of their parents, to more than
30 percent in 1980, to about 50 percent today—clearly have to do
with mobility, a liquid class structure, and increasing intermarriage.
But they also have to do with plenty of choice, an eagerness to take it,
and a desire to display the result.

So What Are the Brands of Faith?

Forget toothpaste. Forget religion. You know the phenomenon of
plenitude is taking over, with branding and brand extension occurring, the minute you see a consumption category named like this—
Protestant Christianity—with subsets like this:

Baptist	Mormon	Unitarian
Methodist	Presbyterian	Catholic
Lutheran	Episcopal	Congregational

which then break into subcategories like these:

Baptist
American Baptist Association
American Baptist Churches in the USA
National Baptist Convention of America
Southern Baptist Convention

Methodist
African Methodist Episcopal Church
African Methodist Episcopal Zion Church
United Methodist Church

Lutheran

American Lutheran Church

Evangelical Lutheran Church in America

Lutheran Church—Missouri Synod

Wisconsin Evangelical Lutheran Synod

Mormon

Church of Jesus Christ of Latter-day Saints

Community of Christ (formerly known as the Reorganized Church
of Jesus Christ of Latter-day Saints)

United Order Effort Restoration Church of Jesus Christ of
Latter-day Saints

When you see this kind of explosion in supply, you know the consumer is king.

Does a shopping mentality affect religious choice, or does religious choice affect a shopping mentality? Ask yourself, Is there a difference between, say, the old Episcopal Church logo, "The Episcopal Church Welcomes You," and the newer one: "The Episcopal Church: We're Here for You." It's clear that, especially in the last generation of baby boomers, consumers are increasingly buying spiritual experiences and buying into spiritual communities rather than accepting their father's religious Oldsmobile. And it's also clear that the successful churches are the ones alert to and even encouraging of these new conversations. Let's look at two examples of this process: what is called the "metrospiritual" and the do-it-yourself "designer religion."

METROSPIRITUAL

Metrospiritual mixes up luxury and religion. It's the spiritualizing of consumption. Think Whole Foods. Here is the emblematically metrospiritual company repeatedly telling shoppers, "We *believe* in a virtuous circle entwining the food chain, human beings, and Mother Earth: each is reliant upon the others through a beautiful and delicate symbiosis. Being green is our doctrine." Or consider another store, Anthropologie, where every object comes with a windbag story in which *calm, enrich, renew, inspire, connect,* and *heal* are incantations. "Renewing hand cream made in a monastery deep in the Czech Republic" is typical. Or what of The Body Shop, which advertises itself as a place that would never advertise because that violates its doctrine; and Aveda, which makes cosmetics, for goodness' sake, "connecting beauty, environment, and well-being" or, as it says on its website, "striving to set an example for environmental leadership and responsibility." In this same category is the rise of eco-travel to spiritual places like Peru's Machu Picchu and the Himalayas rather than to Las Vegas or Rio, hybrid cars that make you feel virtuous without having to take the more sensible mass transit, or even adopting a child from a Third World country à la actress Angelina Jolie rather than from the wrong side of your own tracks.

What makes metrospiritualism powerful is the crisscrossing of material stuff with religious sensation, the display of shopping with sanctimony, the self-conscious invocation of redemption with the holding of things. Of course, you are paying more for the experience; that's just the point. But this experience is not deluxe because of high price but because of high principles. Starbucks is high price, but fair-trade coffee is high commitment. In a sense, you are demonstrating your redemption via consumption; you are indeed born-again. It's not accidental that metrospiritualism in consumer goods and stand-alone megachuches in the religious markets happen concurrently.

DESIGNER RELIGION

Look carefully, and you can see the same pick-and-choose pattern in what is disparaged as do-it-yourself, or designer, religion. Once again the emphasis is on sensation, not denominational affiliation, and hence the control is in the hands of the consumer, not the supplier. That's why you often hear something like this: "I'm an Episcopalian, but I'm really into yoga, and I just read *The Tibetan Book of the*

Dead." Or: "I'm Roman Catholic, but I believe that priests should be allowed to marry, and I use birth control—but I still go to mass." Or: "I was raised Baptist, but my husband is Jewish, and we don't attend church or synagogue, but we just saw *The Passion* and were deeply moved." If you ever wondered why Buddhism has much more success in the form of books and Zen audiotapes than it does in attracting followers to join an institution, here's the reason. It's a major part of mix-and-match religion, something to spice up the mix.

In this à la carte, off-the-shelf religion, the mix of beliefs and practices involves blending the familiar narratives of mainline religion with Buddhism, astrology, yoga, reincarnation, and faith healing, with perhaps the seasoning of the day like tai chi (an Eastern meditation and exercise discipline characterized by slow, relaxed, circular motions), channeling (a New Age practice in which individuals claim to speak words and advice from the deceased), kabbalah (a form of Jewish mysticism that contemplates the origins of the cosmos and the existence of good in the world), and Sufism (a mystical strain of Islam that involves rhythmic chanting of sacred verses, poetry, ecstatic music, and dancing). In a world in which shopping has become a creative act, you make your own God gumbo.

As with clothing, belief consumers will mix and match a costume of beliefs almost like accessorizing. It's perfectly acceptable to wear your Gucci loafers with your Kmart T-shirt and your Ralph Lauren eyeglasses. A *USA Today*/CNN/Gallup survey found that 45 percent of those polled said they pay more attention to their "own views or the views of others" than to "God or religious teachings" in deciding how to conduct life. In response to another question, 44 percent said that Christianity is not the only true path to God. And, again, the major suppliers—the fashion police, so to speak—have confronted this not by denouncing it but by accommodation. In the last generation, many congregations have introduced charismatic forms of worship, stirring music, and ecstatic dance into the service.

Customization is an aspect of shopping. And it increasingly happens where plenitude occurs. You may bemoan the "customer is king" thinking and believe it is undermining American education, religion, media, and health care, but this thinking also reflects the fact that culture itself has become the result of creative choices made by the consumer. In the jargon of the human potential movement, the client/consumer/believer is becoming empowered. To many cultural critics, treating groups of students, patrons, patients, and penitents as "customers" or "clients" is having a serious negative impact on America's schools, churches, hospitals, media, and government. But to the consumer, it's a sign of shifting power and more immediate gratification. And it's at the heart of why Christianity is moving from in your heart to in your face.

The idea of being a customer also has tremendous intuitive appeal to most Americans because it implies greater attention and accountability from suppliers. They have to hustle. Who doesn't want to hear "May I help you?" It feels good for a reason. Neuroscientists say that the brain is pleasurably stimulated with the neurochemical dopamine when we have mildly novel experiences of pleasure. Little wonder that since the 1960s, we have dropped the word *citizen* and substituted *customer* or *consumer*. At the same time, we've substituted *seeker* for *believer*.

To paraphrase the Ford Motor Company slogan, quality is not job #1, customer satisfaction is. That's why after you buy the car, the company pesters you with phone calls asking whether you're happy with the product, and each time you take the car in for service, it interrupts you again. The company isn't trying to sell and service a car (the car is quite like all the others), it's trying to sell and service a relationship. Or the illusion of one. As you are being put on automatic hold, you hear, "Your call is very important to us." It's annoying because it's so obviously insincere, but you can see why they do it. The call is important, not the customer.

The implications for this kind of relationship-marketing are profound. Citizens have rights and responsibilities, but consumers have only rights, with virtually no responsibilities. Gimme. Feed me. Save me. To be a shopper/seeker is to be privileged, exempt from duties. After all, the shopper/seeker has a mission. Nowhere is this clearer than in the rise of a new kind of church that ministers not only to spiritual issues but to the feel-good entitlement of brand-shifting shoppers. It's a ministry of what are called "felt needs." It's a ministry of experiences, and a direct function of supply surplus.

Here, if you want to see an example, is an email sent by Pastor Bill Hybels to the listserv of Willow Creek Community Church, explaining why they should attend Palm Sunday service. I'm on the email lists of a number of megachurches, and this sort of communication is typical.

Dear Enews Friends,

I hope this email finds you well. I know that many of you are reading this from your computer at work so I'll be brief . . . This weekend I will be teaching the final installment of the "Uphill" series we have been in for the last four weeks. The subject matter is "The Ultimate Sacrifice." For some reason I have a stronger than usual level of anticipation about this upcoming service. It might be because I know all of you are back from spring break, which means the whole Willow family will be reunited. It might be because of a unique video presentation that our creative team has spent tons of time preparing for you. It might be because this is Palm Sunday and the beginning of Holy Week. I am not sure, but I am fired up and ready to go. I hope that you and your family and friends will be joining us. Here in South Barrington we hope you will join us whether you have 30 minutes or 3 hours to invest. You will enter the main lobby through a breath-taking display of inspiring art. There's a surround sound experience that will help all of us imagine what Jesus heard during the time leading up to his death. Have you ever wondered how much a first century cross weighed? We will help you figure that out when you come. For those of you who would like a full length reminder of Jesus' final hours, we will again be showing *The Passion of the Christ*. Additionally, there will be a 35-minute FX Good Friday experience for families and six different unplugged worship gatherings in the lakeside auditorium. Again, please check out the website for times, but don't pass up our Good Friday events. I am confident that they will spur you on in your walk with God.

Easter weekend we will gather with thousands of our invited guests from all over Chicagoland to celebrate the power of the resurrection. The planning and prayer that has gone into these services would humble you. I think God is going to work in an unprecedented way throughout the entire Willow family this Easter. As always, we e-ticket these services so that everybody can be assured of a reserved seat.

That's it for now, other than to ask for fervent prayer for the Chicago Cubs. It is opening day at Wrigley Field and without divine intervention, it could be another long year.

Blessings,
Bill

Many old-line denominations have been concerned about this religious shift from gatekeeper to carnival barker. God's presence may be chosen from among a myriad of offerings on a spiritual buffet, and whichever choice you make is right for you. This shopper-friendly approach to religion, to being spiritual, is a threat to the church proper that cannot be overlooked. Our Lady of Sales replaces Our Lady of Perpetual Sacrifice.

When you check the Church Growth Movement, a consortium of fast-growing evangelicals, you come across the language of Marketing 101: client acquisition, experiential marketing, intentional purchasing, postdecision dissonance, seeker services, and the like. These are the churches that hire full-time media staff, programming consultants, stage directors, drama coaches, special-effects experts, and choreographers to put on the show Pastor Hybels promises above. While it has been the lower Protestant denominations that have harvested the crop of undecided consumers, it has been Catholic theologians who have provided most of the serious commentary on this movement.

As one might imagine, the church most sensitive to this ever-hydrating explosion of choice is the church that once had the market monopoly, the Roman Catholic Church. As opposed to Protestants, this church has been able to contain much of the fragmentation engendered by the Protestant niche marketing. To some degree this is the result of a long heritage of competitive orders like the Franciscans, Jesuits, and Benedictines, which have been able to make brands and subbrands that stay inside the corporation.

While Catholic theologians have been sensitive to the dynamics of the marketplace, it has been the pope who has spoken out most eloquently on its danger. In August of 2005, speaking to a World Youth Day festival, Pope Benedict XVI warned against what he called "D-I-Y" religion. Stay away from the marketplace, he warned. "If it is pushed too far, religion becomes almost a consumer product. People choose what they like, and some are even able to make a profit from it. But religion constructed on a do-it-yourself basis cannot ultimately help us."

Ironically, the pope managed to identify what is perhaps the single most important feature of contemporary religiosity. You shop for it. You put it together; you don't buy it fully assembled. But it is wrong to think of the D-I-Y aspect of our culture as self-indulgent, wrong-headed, or opportunistic. This is to miss the anthropological point, and to underestimate how formidable commercial marketing has become for even faithful hearts and minds. Religion is hardly alone in being influenced by the shift in agency. The same thing has happened in higher education and in the world of the arts, for example.

Still, the Catholic voice is raised against the customization of religious belief while the Protestant voice is, in the main, silent. This is because of the Protestant habit of individualism in religious matters (viz, the Reformation) but also because it is precisely this act of shopping for God, of choosing religiosity, that now characterizes much of the Western Protestant landscape. It's not doctrine that is obligatory. It's all about choice. About doing it yourself.

Materialism versus Religion: Let's Give It a Rest

This might be an appropriate time to call a truce in the needless war between consumerism and religion. They have learned from each other how to sell, and neither one of them will go away. They need each other, and we need them both. Perhaps the battle is not between them as much as because of them. We may line up to listen to the narratives of both Mammon and Christ and be aware of a contradiction, but not of mutual exclusion. As your kid will tell you, a good fairy tale for a winter's night is not the same as one for a summer's day.

When we go shopping, be it for fast-moving consumer goods or slow-moving redemption goods, it is because we are seeking a narrative that makes us feel powerful and perhaps even makes the pursuit worthwhile. Religion will not be pushed to the periphery of life, nor will consumerism be shunted aside. What seems to change is the amount of friction between them. We're fighting about how much religion in the public square is appropriate, about whether religion belongs in the classroom, about the place faith has in our politics, law, and even art. And this has been going on for a long time.

It's time to stop fighting about religion and recognize that we are hardwired to seek its palliative effect and purpose. And it's time to admit that materialism and spiritualism—consumerism and religion—are not in opposition but simply part of the complex meaning-making equipment of being human. Just as religious types are admitting the allure of the material, so can materialists admit the allure of the spiritual. As the English writer Samuel Johnson said, "Nothing can please many, and please long, but just representations of general nature." Faith is part of human nature.

And so is stuff. We were materialistic from the get-go. We like to hold stuff, trade stuff, steal stuff, bury stuff, and fight about stuff. We like to make things, and then we like to make things make meaning. Sometimes we find stuff like gold and diamonds and then add the value later. When we get tired of them, we sometimes question their value. But until then we like to *sacramentalize* stuff.

If you'll notice, people who rail about the value of things tend to be mature; conversely, people who really like things tend to be adolescent. This distinction exists in cultures that have lots of things and those that don't. Cultures with lots of stuff tend to invest that stuff with transcendent meaning. Think Evian water and the Prada baguette purse.

Much of that stuff with sacramental meaning is called luxury. Cultures without much stuff tend to place their deluxe stuff in a next world. When anthropologists ask Americans to inventory heaven, they mention few things; in fact, they are often stumped. But ask Christians in other countries—say, in Africa or South America—and they can name the streets of gold, number the bolts of silk, and Cadillacs for all.

Think back on the history of Western culture. In medieval times there was a shared knowledge of heaven, of what we'd find there. Gradually with the rise of the mass production of things, that knowledge moved over into the manufactured world, and heaven started to mean simply the world after death. Consider the endless images of heaven in the Renaissance and their almost total absence today.

And we are spiritual just as clearly as we are materialistic. As Oscar Wilde said, with only a slight wink, "The true mystery of the world is the visible, not the invisible." Forget specific gods and their complex metaphysics for a moment. Just acknowledge that spiritual life has been around for a long time, almost as long as materialism. Consider that despite the vast number of religions, nearly everyone in the world believes in the same things: the existence of a soul, an afterlife, miracles, and the divine creation of the universe. And we all want the same product: the sensations of forgiveness and salvation.

So religion is not the skunk at the garden party; religion is what keeps the skunk out. The skunk is chaos and the intense anxiety it engenders. And, rather like the choices of jam, in one sense it really makes no difference what the religion is so long as it addresses the lack of order and provides a spiritual narrative for the seeker. A recent Gallup survey found that 95 percent of Americans believe in God, but of those, fully one-third believe in a nonpersonal God, something akin to "spirit," "ultimate spirit," "God Presence," or some other such organizing notion. The Barna Research Group concurs. It estimates that 1 out of 5 Americans are what it calls "New Age practitioners," a category that really seems to mean self-administered religion. As well, Beliefnet, which cosponsored a survey with *Newsweek,* claims a figure of 64 percent respondents who said they were "religious" but almost 80 percent who described themselves as "spiritual." This suggests that while the touchy-feely is now dominant, it is often in the service of some overarching system. All these studies conclude that we are learning how to link the belief in a personal God with a passion for the world of stuff.

In the world of customization, Americans increasingly imagine the divine as panentheistic, that He is both in the material world and beyond it. God is not distant and removed, but intimately connected to me and my place in the world. He is here more as a storyteller than as a watchmaker. In this sense, much of megachurch religion is capturing the vitality of the human potential movement, providing context more than truth. The distinction between spiritual and religious is becoming a blur. They are not in opposition but acknowledgments that a nonmaterial world of intentionality exists and that it somehow resolves the Escher-like confusion of our personal existence. In this context note that the Serenity Prayer, which became important in Alcoholics Anonymous circles, has also become a kind of banner text for many Americans in the twenty-first century: "God grant me the serenity to accept the things I cannot change; courage to change the things I can; and wisdom to know the difference." Note the subtle invocation of materialism, of the here and now, of the consumerist world.

CHAPTER FOUR

Hatch, Match, Dispatch, or Baptized, Married, Buried: The Work of Denominations

In the spring of 2005 I decided to go church shopping. At first I started by attending a different church every Sunday in a little community about twenty miles from where I live. The community is Melrose, Florida, and I chose going there because the town I live in, Gainesville, is home to the University of Florida and hence ecclesiastically tainted by academics. Years ago I had attended the local Unitarian church. It was like a university departmental meeting. As Huck Finn said about life with Aunt Sally, "I'd been there before." I wanted to go to church with people who didn't think about going to church, who just did it.

Melrose is rife with churches. Back in the 1930s and 1940s, before the railroad opened up the southern part of the state, Melrose and its sister town, Keystone Heights, had been the terminus for Yankees seeking warmth. Thanks to these snowbirds, many of the churches are old and architecturally interesting. In and around town there are Trinity Episcopal, Eliam Baptist, United Methodist, Ochwilla Baptist, Orange Heights Baptist, and then this mouthful: Little Melrose Church of Jesus Christ, Old Regular Faith and Order, Northern New Salem Association, which, understandably, meets only sporadically.

But better yet, north on Route 21 between downtown Melrose and Keystone Heights, is a little strip of about five miles that had just what I wanted: churches clustered side by side like fast-food joints, gas stations, or automobile dealerships. These churches are newish, variously sized, and denominationally redundant. There is Church of Christ, Melrose; Lake Ann Baptist Church; Open Arms Community Church; Believers Worship Center: Church of God; Faith Presbyterian Church; Keystone Christ Church; Christ Evangelical Lutheran Church; Keystone United Methodist Church; Keystone Presbyterian Church; Friendship Bible Church; and one budding mini-megachurch, Trinity Baptist Church.

As we've already discovered, an open marketplace results in division, not unification. Although there is always much talk of ecumenicalism, the natural process is division. As a general rule, Protestant churches split by nature and unify in desperation. When a church joins another, or when a denomination links up with another, weakness—not strength—is usually the reason. And why does splitting happen? The most common reason is petty squabbling over what seems like such minor differences. The most common explanation, however, is doctrine.

As much as I wanted to church shop the entire market, I had to cut down on the number of aisles, or I'd experience what every shopper knows: dreaded sensory overload. I'd end up like Professor Barry Schwartz, silent upon a peak of Gap jeans in the Darien mall. So I decided not to attend the Catholic church (which wasn't really contending for brand switchers anyway, at least not obviously), no synagogues (which was easy because there were none; plus, observant Jews have shown little interest in proselytizing outside the established consumer base—although that is changing), no Unitarian churches (they were all in Gainesville), and (here's where I really backslid) no African-American churches.

I know, I know. I willfully neglected one of the most important sources of innovation in modern Protestantism, and I did it solely for selfish reasons. It was often embarrassing enough to appear in khaki pants, cotton shirt, and horned-rim glasses, trying to hide a pen and notebook, fumbling with the hymnal, and then being set upon by well-meaning parishioners asking me to please fill in the visitor card. I just didn't think I could inflict myself on black churches without causing them (and myself) even greater consternation. As you will see, in Orlando, Florida, I happened on FaithWorld, a black megachurch, and it was by far my most interesting church experience. In thinking about this, however, I came to understand and contribute to what Martin Luther King Jr. meant when he said that "eleven o'clock on Sunday morning is the most segregated hour in America."

Let's face it. I am a lily-white northern Vermonter. I have a bit of a Yankee twang, I think, and the demeanor of a college professor, I know. No matter where I went, I'm sure I upset things a bit. It's not just the Heisenberg Uncertainty Principle at work, but the simple fact that a new face in a country place is a shock. The bigger the church, the better for me. Most of these were country churches with about a hundred attendees. I fit in best in those churches that did not ask you to do anything such as come forward or lead a prayer or even say hello. I did worse in places where I was invited to attend the Wednesday men's-only study group. The megachurch is populated with people just like me. In fact, as I began to realize, these country churches are part of the reason for the megas.

An example of my fouling the water occurred at the United Methodist church in Melrose. When I arrived, the kindly minister, Don Dalton, asked me in front of the congregation of about thirty why I was attending, and I told him I was passing through town, staying with friends, and wanted the comfort of my fellow Methodists. Halfway through the sermon Pastor Dalton decided he'd refresh the membership with a little rebaptism. Out of the blue, he asked everyone to come forward—and then added the caveat, everyone *already baptized*, that is. I had to stay put. I was terrified. I'm not sure what I feared, perhaps that the holy water would burn, but, from the looks I received, I certainly wish I had gone forward.

Church Shopping

What I was seeing around me in these north Florida churches was a sliver of one of the most extraordinary scramble markets in the world. It's a minimicrocosm of one of the many macromarkets in ethical monotheism. Once again, I'm not talking about God; that's a belief. I'm talking about a delivery system or, better yet, a family of systems divided into franchises called denominations, each of which supplies a slightly different narrative. I was looking at the detergent aisle filled with different versions of essentially the same soap.

The history of Christianity since the Protestant Reformation is, in a sense, the history of marketing itself, the development of self-conscious branding as a competitive device in an oversupplied market. In fact, selling God, the activity known as proselytizing, is a uniquely Christian/capitalist concept. And it depends on competitive suppliers. Religions exchange sensations for some investment by the believer. That's the brand promise. A story told, a feeling felt, and for this sensation the believer sacrifices something. That's the quid pro quo without which no religion can get up and going. Sometimes the believer just contributes attention, but if that's the case, the religion will soon flop. (As we will see, the megachurch has figured out how to exploit freeloaders, but they are the exception.) Usually nothing kills faith faster than freeloaders. Why should I pay if you get the benefit? If I am sacrificing to be saved, infidels had better be punished.

You Can't Know Value without Paying

We usually think of church payment in terms of tithing. The collection plate is a kind of aide-mémoire of more serious pledging as well as a way to inform the uninitiated that payment is part of the process. We usually think the tithe is for church overhead or missionary work or building a playground for the kiddies. But tithing is far more important. It shows that the narrative has worth.

In every country church I attended, I heard about the importance of tithing, sometimes even double tithing, something I had never heard of before. In every megachurch this was stepped up a notch— tithing and growth were preached as doctrine. "Giving 'til it hurts" was part of a recitative reading. Much pulpit energy was expended on whether tithing should come off gross or net income, and much focus on the timing of such payment. It was always referred to as "giving to God," and the implication was that this was an invest- ment demanded in the Bible.

What makes the payment schedule so interesting is that the more I researched tithing, the more nonbiblical it appeared to be. As far as I could see, no one in the pews seemed to mind. In the Old Testament, tithing was a way for the Israelites to support their priestly tribe, the Levites, who did no work outside of their sacred duties. In fact, *tithe* appears in the entire Old Testament only twenty-seven times, mostly in passing. It is discussed in any detail only in five places, and these references are, at least to this English professor, conflicting.

The New Testament says nothing in favor of tithing. Neither Jesus nor Paul commanded believers to give 10 percent to their local church or, for that matter, to go to church at all. Jesus mocked the scribes and Pharisees who tithed (Matthew 23:23), and denounced a self-righteous Pharisee who boasted about tithing (Luke 18:9–14). The writer of Hebrews observed that the old tithe was collected by the Levites, yes, but times are different now: "For the priesthood being changed, there is made of necessity a change also of the law" (Hebrews 7:5,12). So New Testament giving was generally freer, less legalistic than the Old Testament; although in one case, perhaps the exception that proves the nonrule, church members were struck dead for failing to give 100 percent (!) to their church (Acts 5:1–11).

So if tithing is not mandated or really even suggested, why do both buyer and seller today maintain the fiction that it is specifically mandated by God? The answer is clear. In shopping cultures, where value is attributed by price points, the tithe announces value. Like free advice, if you give the service away, it becomes worth what you have paid for it. Conversely, high price implies high value. This pricing pattern is called the Veblen effect after the curmudgeonly

American economist who coined the concept in *The Theory of the Leisure Class.* Perceived value directly increases with price.

The tithe is the Veblen effect made manifest. Tithing shows that the narrative has worth. Payment is sacrifice, and sacrifice is price, a sign of value. As well, it's a barrier to freeloaders. Nothing dilutes brand value more than the fact that someone sitting next to you is getting the same service for a cut rate. The minute you see those little polo-pony shirts from Ralph Lauren on sale at Sam's Club, you know that the brand is stressed. Calvin Klein almost went into Chapter 11 when he started selling his line at JCPenney.

Again, Observe the Cult

When the freeloaders and brand detractors are removed and the sacrifice level is high, a religious cult may emerge. A cult will often increase the level of sacrifice by transforming the tithe into a different currency. They often ask members to estrange themselves from others by wearing special clothing, shaving or not shaving hair in various places, behaving in observably eccentric ways, and generally carrying on as if the belief system were not only the sole way to get access to the next world, but the only way to fit into this one.

We live surrounded by cults, and they continually intersect with mainline denominations, often energizing them. Some of the best known (or most notorious) cults came out of the sixties, groups like the Unification Church, Krishna Consciousness, or the Children of God. They have shrunk in size, to be sure, but not before they influenced other suppliers in the religious economy. Other non-Christian orientations, from Wicca to trance channeling, are experiencing an upsurge. In many of the new religions, the traditions of the West and the East are being fused (for example, Scientology, Shambhala, Rastafarianism), while in others new elements, like the belief in UFOs, are being added to the mix (Heaven's Gate, the Raelians, Burning Man).

Cults get a bad name when the tithing levels go ballistic. In my lifetime just a handful of the thousands of new religions in our midst have become so centripetal that they tithe themselves into a maelstrom. The mass suicides of members of the People's Temple in 1978, and the Order of the Solar Temple in 1994, 1995, and again in 1997 are a tribute to the goosing-up of the Veblen effect. We explain them away by focusing on apocalyptic systems of belief, charismatic styles of leadership, and increasing social isolation, but what these cults are really doing is what other religions also ask for but in more moderation: gradually upping sacrifice in exchange for sensation.

This process of upping the tithe is profoundly appealing, especially for many young people. Cult members tend to be smart and hardworking, with markedly better-than-average educations, and overwhelmingly middle- to upper-class backgrounds. I see them everyday. They are in my classes. Often they are my better students. They join specific groups because members of their family, friends, dormmates, or associates at work have joined. True, they affiliate because they have spiritual and philosophical questions for which these groups provide clear and often quite sophisticated answers; and, true, they yearn for camaraderie, affection, and a sense of purpose in life that outstrips the meager offerings of our "buy one, get one free" choices. But what the members really want are the sensations the cult story delivers. In a way, in a most perverse way, they are the ultimate luxury shoppers, paying confiscatory prices for something not particularly well made.

Long before Route 21, Christianity Was a Cult

When a cult hits pay dirt, it becomes a full-fledged religion. Recall that Christianity began as a fierce sectarian movement within Judaism. With the missionary efforts of St. Paul, it became a cult movement in the larger Greco-Roman world. A hundred years after the death of Jesus, there were only seven thousand to eight thousand Christians in the world. Christianity has never been so vibrant as when it was combative, edging over into the pagan beliefs of the Romans. One wonders if the same vitalization process is now occurring as Islam is edging up against it. But also realize this: when you have a plenitude of fungible suppliers, cults are inevitable as a marketing position.

Consider the Mormon Church. This currently docile church (with some exceptions that are now making news for polygamy) began with a few hundred followers in upstate New York in the 1830s. It's very hard to take Joseph Smith and the tablets seriously, and that's precisely how the freeloaders were unloaded. The tithe was that you uprooted yourself. Then, properly isolated and anxious, the sect exploded. With an estimated rate of growth of about 43 percent per decade in the early twentieth century, there are now about thirteen million Mormons throughout the world. Domestic growth has now slowed.

As with other systems, the tithe is higher the farther the system moves away from the center. The so-called Wasatch effect is the phenomenon that explains why Mormons in Salt Lake City are less sacrificial than those in the hinterlands. This condition is also seen in marketing, where it is sometimes called the "Atlanta effect," explaining why drinkers of Coke tend to be dedicated in direct proportion to miles out of Georgia. Separation makes the heart grow fonder. Or, maybe like sausage, it's not good to see how it's made.

Grasping how cults succeed seems easy, but it's not. The road to paradise is littered with also-rans. The failure ratio is probably close to that of new commercial products—about 90 percent fail in the first year. *The World Christian Encyclopedia: A Comparative Survey of Churches and Religions in the Modern World,* published every other year by Oxford University Press, counts them up. It takes two volumes and runs to eight hundred pages. Why? Because there are almost ten thousand distinct religions in the world. Each day about two more are added. The exceptionally lucky ones become cults, and maybe only a fraction of 1 percent of those ever last longer than ten years.

Epiphany Sounds Good but What Does It Look Like?

So what does a cult give the believer that makes joining worthy of sacrifice? What does the leader promise that moves the undecided over the tipping point? Along with community and forgiveness, the ostensible product of most religious cults is safe passage to the next world. For lack of a better word, the brand promise is "elevated consciousness." What you feel next is the epiphany.

In Christianity, that "believer's sublime" is even laid out in a central story. The first epiphany occurred after the birth of Christ, when three wise men felt elevated after they saw the infant Jesus. They were "wise men" for a reason. They were skeptics. But viewing the divinity of God in the body of a mortal filled them with a peace that passeth all understanding, in the biblical phrase. They were transformed by a vision; in a sense, reborn.

In the religious context, this sensation goes by a number of names: enlightenment, rebirth, Paulist conversion, sublimity, out-of-body experience, transcendence, among others. The sensation usually happens in a group of like-minded individuals at a particular time following certain rituals, many of them keyed in to music. Sometimes it is achieved alone, helped along by fasting and contemplation.

If you were to ask the churchgoer if he or she is conscious of seeking this sensation, it's doubtful you'd be answered, "Yes, I'm here for the sensation." In fact, chances are you'd be spurned. Sooner ask the Harlequin Romance reader if she is trying to feel romantic yearning, the horror filmgoer if he is trying to get the shivers, or the viewer of *Hamlet* if he desires to feel pity and terror. Only the consumer of pornography will tell you why he looks at it, which is why "I read *Playboy* only for the articles" is such an easy-to-understand joke.

In its most vulgarized and solipsistic state, epiphany is what currently is marketed as a *God wink*. Here the believer is encouraged to take some coincidence, like winning the lottery or recovering from sickness, as evidence of a higher power at work. So Squire Rushnell, in *When God Winks at You: How God Speaks Directly to You Through the Power of Coincidence*, tells of a woman who goes to church and just happens to sit next to the birth mother she was seeking. The mother was attending services for the first time! "Every time you receive what some call a coincidence or an answered prayer, it's a direct and personal message of reassurance from God to you," he contends. Narcissism itself becomes proof of divine selection.

In 2005 an unprecedented study was released by the National Opinion Research Center at the University of Chicago. The National Spiritual Transportation Study attempted to limn spiritual transformation as a human experience susceptible to statistical study. Over the last twenty years, many studies have looked at near-death experiences, but epiphanies have been neglected. Until recently. One obvious reason is because this kind of experience is currently being retailed as part of the general Protestant experience. If Joan of Arc can have visions, why not me? If the wisemen were reborn, well, here I am. If the Pentecost of holy visitation could descend on 3,000, then why not 3,001?

To do the study, researchers conducted one-on-one interviews with more than 1,300 randomly selected people across the nation over a five-month period. What they found was that the majority of people (60 percent) who had undergone epiphanies did so before age thirty, and such experiences tended to have long-lasting effects. Nearly 65 percent of those who said they had undergone such spiritual transformations (or about 38 percent of all Americans) used the term *born-again* to describe their experience. The study's other findings include:

- About half of those who had spiritual transformations said these events were preceded by religious activity, such as attending a retreat or worship service, or by a personal problem, such as illness or the death of a loved one.

- Blacks (64 percent) are more likely to have a spiritually transforming experience than whites (50 percent).

- Spiritual transformations are more common among Protestants (62 percent) than Catholics (30 percent).

- Such experiences are least likely in New England (24 percent), most likely in the South (60 percent), and average in the Midwest (42 percent).

Since religion, in brandspeak, "owns" the out-of-body experience, it protects its territory from competition. While a few churches use drugs like peyote as part of the process, in the Christian churches this is unusual. Chanting and fasting, however, have a long history, especially in the Catholic orders, of producing out-of-body feelings.

Consequently the church usually lobbies the state to control consciousness-raising drugs. That is, until the explosion of psychotropic drugs (Prozac, Zoloft, Paxil, Wellbutrin, and a host of other antidepressants) in the 1980s and 1990s. With about 15 percent of the American population now using these drugs, it's hard to argue against them. But once several studies showed that people with religious faith reported themselves as happier than those without such faith, the church relaxed. Of course, the people with the highest happiness scores tend to be martyrs about to kill for their belief.

In the nineteenth century, Romantic spiritualism as practiced and recorded by the likes of Wordsworth, Whitman, Shelley, Keats, Coleridge, Thoreau, and Emerson gave transcendentalism the proper epiphanic meaning. The sacred text was nature, and the poets drank it in to experience the "sense sublime." As works like "Tintern Abbey," the "Intimations Ode," "Endymion," "Hymn to Intellectual Beauty," and the "Over-Soul" essay show, the democratization of epiphany was one of the more revolutionary aspects of the early nineteenth century. Look at paintings from what is now called American Luminism (Fitz Hugh Lane, John Frederick Kensett, Martin Johnson Heade, Frederic Edwin Church), and you can literally see over the horizon into the beyond.

Not for nothing was the Second Great Awakening in the U.S. contemporaneous with the rise of Romanticism. Both movements sought the same level of elevated consciousness. The Romantic poets and painters were fond of experimenting with drugs, especially the opiate laudanum, as a method of generating expanded sensations. As Aldous Huxley pointed out in the once-startling, now-tame *The*

Doors of Perception, the pharmacological version is almost a perfect mimic of the religious. Ingesting LSD or peyote may give you a sensation of out of body. It's called a *trip* for a reason. You're spaced out.

This generation's LSD is a drug called Ecstasy, and its promise is in its name. What this drug holds out is a high eerily close to its ritualized cousins in religious settings. Entering culture as part of "rave" entertainment, Ecstasy produces sensations of immediate detachment, lightness, loss of drives such as hunger and sleep, and especially a sense of renewed confidence and optimism. That this sense of renewal should be tied to music and communal excitement is no happenstance.

Little wonder that a generation that has known this experience on the street and at the rock concert should want to patronize churches that promise its deliverance in the pews.

What Does It Look Like?

Historically we have had to trust prose descriptions of the effect of rapture from eyewitness reports, usually of camp meetings in the nineteenth century or the big-city revivals of the early twentieth. The reporter is usually a scoffer. So the reports center on how evangelical preachers worked the already primed crowd into a passion, and, just as predictably, the authorial tone is a little smug and self-satisfied. After all, the observer is not experiencing the event but observing from afar. In the "move of the holy spirit," we are told, some members barked like dogs, showed signs of apparent drunkenness, rolled around on the ground, and generally cavorted like those possessed. Or like drunk children. Most reporters understandably neglect the behavior of the others who were not in the look-at-me performance mode and doubtless assumed the slightly spaced-out posture of the "Hallelujah, I'm saved!" that the camera has opened up the experience for observation.

One of the best places to see this effect is in a recent (2005) book of black-and-white photographs by Steven Katzman called *The Face of Forgiveness: Salvation and Redemption.* Katzman spent a number of

The look of epiphany: Brownsville Assembly of God, Pensacola, Florida, 1999, and Toronto Airport Christian Fellowship, Canada, 2000. (SOURCE: STEVEN KATZMAN, *THE FACE OF FORGIVENESS: SALVATION AND REDEMPTION.*)

years at evangelical meetings around the world simply photographing believers in a state of ecstasy. He tried to capture that moment in which the holy spirit moved through the congregation. Up go the arms, back go the heads, and down go the eyelids. Like many human emotions, it's contagious and moves through a crowd once the initial tipping point has been crossed.

Another place to see the effect of rapture is in a documentary film made in 1967 by Peter Adair called *Holy Ghost People*. This little gem was rightly hailed by anthropologist Margaret Mead as one of the best ethnographic films ever made. It is affecting because it is so nonjudgmental. These people are sincere. Here is a ragtag group of West Virginian Christians who are clearly after the emotional wallop of rapture, even if it means physical trauma. They handle poisonous snakes. That's the tithe. Better yet, they taunt these poisonous snakes, not like teenage boys but like would-be martyrs. The feeling must be like what the suicide bomber feels as he is tucking in the explosives around his midriff. Or, as one of the handlers says after what is essentially dancing with a snake in his face, "You don't wanna do it, but you feel so happy when it's done."

This sect has taken the promise of St. Mark to heart: "And these signs shall follow them that believe; in my name they shall cast out devils; they shall speak with new tongues; they shall take up serpents, and if they drink any deadly thing, it shall not hurt them; they shall lay hands on the sick, and they shall recover" (16:17,18). They literally feel protection from danger by confronting poison. They are after what one of the young men calls "the evidence." In many respects this confrontation seems the opposite of the dull dutiful Sunday church, but it is not. These believers find in the lure of ineffable danger something close to what the penitent finds in the expectation of Judgment Day. Of course it's dangerous. That's the point.

Clearly they have learned how to choreograph the event. They've done it before. Music and dancing stir them up. For a while it almost seems as if the snake rattling his tail is accompanying the music like the tambourine. What separates these Pentecostals from the rest of us is that this group has taken the frisson of belief to an immediate climax. Show me the evidence!

Adair's camera dispassionately records this "quickening power," which takes over even the most blasé members. They *want* the ecstasy state. Inside the church they can give full play to their emotions, shrieking, flailing, crumpling to the floor, talking in tongues, drinking poison, and handling snakes—as a competitive test of their faith, yes, but also as a way to get out of themselves and their dreary lives. With no ostensible leader, they work up each other by praying loudly, gyrating, falling to the floor, until the snake boxes are brought out.

In a later chapter I'll talk about the importance of men in church, but here I'd just like to note that the older men pick up the snakes in an almost taunting way, throwing them to the younger men, as a test of courage. I was struck by the fact that the men are wearing white shirts and ties, Sunday clothes, and that they kiss each other on the lips as the church service begins. If you ever want to see the role of men in religious sects, here's the place.

Admittedly, the service consumer of an ordinary Sunday along Route 21 is nowhere near their level of cartoon vibration, but the emotional goal is eerily similar. On a number of occasions I saw it operate in megachurches, especially Orlando's FaithWorld. You could watch the enthusiasm for epiphany slowly percolate through the crowd as people filed into the service. They wanted to *feel the Lord.* They often had their arms held halfway in front of their bodies as if to state their willingness to raise them higher. You could tell well before the music started what was going to happen. And they could tell too. While easily observed in African-American churches, the sensation also ripples through all vibrant churches, albeit at a more moderate frequency. If history is any guide, the more repressed a church gets about delivering it, the crustier and more hidebound it becomes. Cults revel in it, however, and that is part of their appeal.

The Suppliers Named

Although there are hundreds of Protestant denominations (some Catholic apologists claim there have been more than twenty thousand, but that's more to buttress their claim of anarchy outside the *one true faith* than a tribute to fair counting), there are really just a handful of serious suppliers now doing business in America. When they started they had one thing in common. They were cultlike, they promised they were cleansing the dross and offering the pure experience. They were getting rid of the intermediaries between penitent and God. Over time they became self-conscious denominations, more concerned about consolidating gains than extending risk.

What is extraordinary to the apatheist is that each of them still considers itself more true than the others even though they all recognize that the others are making exactly the same claims. Since there is no Church of America, no centralized supplier against whom they can all compete, they compete against one another, in every venue, all the time. In so doing, they provide a continually roiled market, which not only increases the aggregate demand but continually rewards the risk takers. Well, some of them, up to a point.

Since the market is huge and getting bigger, let's first get a sense of the general edges. Here are some (not all) of the big-box suppliers:

American Baptist Churches, USA
Christian and Missionary Alliance
Christian Church (Disciples of Christ)
Christian Methodist Episcopal Church
Church of God
Church of the Nazarene
Coalition of Spirit-filled Churches
Cumberland Presbyterian Church
Cumberland Presbyterian Church in America
Episcopal Church
Evangelical Covenant Church
Evangelical Lutheran Church in America
Evangelical Lutheran Synod
International Church of the Foursquare Gospel
Lutheran Church—Missouri Synod
Moravian Church in America
National Association of Congregational Christian Churches
Presbyterian Church (USA)
Reformed Episcopal Church
Southern Baptist Convention
United Church of Christ

United Methodist Church
Wisconsin Evangelical Lutheran Synod

As a kind of shorthand I'm going to use the general terms, sliding together groups that have often fought bitterly to become separate.

Anabaptist and Baptist
Anglican / Episcopalian
Calvinist / Reformed and Presbyterian
Lutheran
Methodist / Wesleyan and the Holiness movement
Pentecostal and Charismatic
Quakerism
Restoration movement

You should also be aware of a still more compressed shorthand. When talking about the *mainline* Protestant denominations, like the seven sisters of women's colleges or the Ivy League, the denominations referred to include:

American Baptist Churches in the USA
Christian Church (Disciples of Christ)
Episcopal Church
Evangelical Lutheran Church in America
Presbyterian Church (USA)
United Church of Christ
United Methodist Church

When you look at the specific ingredient differences between and among these denominations, you will be, I think, amazed at how razor-thin the content separation really is. As they say in the academic world, the fights can be so nasty because the stakes are so small. Often humor is a more trustworthy guide. Here's a joke from the 1930s:

Walking across a bridge, I saw a man on the edge, about to jump. I ran over and said, "Stop. Don't do it."

"Why not?" he asked.

"Well, there's so much to live for!"

"Like what?"

"Are you religious?"

He said, "Yes."

I said, "Me too. Are you Christian or Buddhist?"

"Christian."

"Me too. Are you Catholic or Protestant?"

"Protestant."

"Me too. Are you Episcopalian or Baptist?"

"Baptist."

"Me too. Are you Baptist Church of God or Church of the Lord?"

"Baptist Church of God."

"Me too. Are you original Baptist Church of God, or Reformed Baptist Church of God?"

"Reformed Baptist Church of God."

"Me too! Are you Reformed Baptist Church of God, Reformation of 1879, or Reformed Baptist Church of God, Reformation of 1915?"

He said, "Reformation of 1915."

I said, "Die, heretic scum," and pushed him off.

And now to be a bit more reductive, and possibly unfair, here's my brief explanation of the ingredient separations in your neighborhood churches.

- The United Church of Christ is what used to be called Congregational, which was the Puritans, who were English Calvinists. The Puritans started as a fierce cult, produced great preachers (Cotton Mather, Jonathan Edwards), and, for a while, hankered to become a monopoly religion. They almost succeeded. As the old saying goes, the Puritans left tolerant Holland in order to find the freedom to be intolerant in the New World. They are now just the opposite; the result of endless dilutive mergers. They separate themselves by making independence a selling point and acceptance almost a fetish. In adspeak, their unique selling proposition is that they own political correctness.

In faith markets, when a supplier goes from purity to unification, it's usually a sign of brand exhaustion.

• Also on the left, so to speak, is the Unitarian Church, sometimes called the church without the steeple. Or the church without heaven. It grew out of Congregationalism and sometimes travels by its whole name: the Unitarian Universalist Church, or UU for short. Unitarianism and Universalism developed separately. Universalist congregations began in the 1770s. They were robust and intense, in many ways like the Quakers. Other Protestant congregations, many established earlier, began to take the Unitarian name in the 1820s. Over the decades the two groups converged in their liberal emphasis and style, and in 1961 they merged to become the Unitarian Universalist Association. Headquartered in Boston, they believe in a loving God who will save almost anyone. Often they like calling themselves non-Christian, even heretics, if only to distinguish themselves from those who think that acceptance of any creedal belief is necessary for salvation. Their ranks are growing, often with the disaffected from other, more straight-laced denominations and Jews, but they have demographic disaster ahead. You can't be sustained by older brand switchers. You need young consumers.

• The Quaker Church has more historical importance than current impact. It also started as a cultish desire to strip away all corruption, to go to the sacred text, and to get to the "inner light" held by each individual. Their proper name is the Religious Society of Friends, but Quakers were called that for a reason. They were, like the Shakers, denigrated in name for their cultic behavior. And they showed it. No longer. They are not as keen on parsing the Bible, nor are they entirely sure who Jesus really was, nor do they quake. To join the church you have to be convinced that you are following your own genius. In a sense, this is the ultimate Reformation church: get rid of everything but the faith. And then keep it to yourself. That is, until something Important happens and then the Quaker can practice the Economy of the Closed Mind: think Susan B. Anthony, conscientious objectors, *High Noon.*

- The Episcopal Church in this country is what Anglophiles have for the Anglican Church. Henry VIII created it opportunistically when he wanted to get a divorce and marry yet again. A nifty irony is that the denomination is now in free fall because of marriage—this time gay marriage. And gay ordination is a problem too. Another paradox: it's the African branch of the Anglican Church that is organizing the hard-liners. The Episcopal Church is about as close as we have ever gotten to a national church, what with the National Cathedral in Washington, DC, and membership of almost every president of the country and master of industry in the early twentieth century. It's not too ludicrous a statement to assert that this church was mortally wounded not by gay marriage but by the SATs. Blue blood lost out to meritocracy. You now get into Harvard by doing extraordinary things, not by being in the *Social Register*. In the little college town where I live, there are eight different versions of Episcopal Church, some not talking to one another about any number of things, most especially the Book of Common Prayer and the ordination of gays. And that condition is typical. Episcopalians used to nickname their churches and cherish irony. They could afford to. No longer.

- The Lutheran Church is the granddaddy of all the Protestants and in many ways the most stern. They often remind you about it. After all, they were formed to set the Catholic Church right. Faith, grace, and the Scriptures are what gets you into the next world, not toadying up to the priest. "A Mighty Fortress Is Our God." If you are Lutheran, you can never hide. Garrison Keillor has made a good living making fun of how much trouble Lutherans have having fun. This religion seems to work best in cold climates, but whenever the Lutheran Church becomes the national church, as in parts of northern Europe and Scandinavia, it falls apart. Lutheranism thrives on being contrary.

- The Presbyterian Church is also concerned about spiritual rigor. If Catholic indulgences don't help, then what about divine grace? Providence resolves depravity. But how to organize a church around this idea? Community is formed in groups called *presbyteries,* hence the name. An important religion in Scotland, where it got strength in opposition to Anglicanism, it seems to lose concentration without a countervailing force. As Mark Twain said of his own mild-mannered denomination, "no frenzy, no fanaticism, no skirmishing." Presbyterians are distinctive in two major ways: they adhere to a pattern of religious thought known as Reformed theology and a form of community that stresses the active, representational leadership of both ministers and church members. They are currently hemorrhaging membership in large part because of the trouble of brand definition.

• The Methodist Church descends from John Wesley, who in the eighteenth century felt "strangely warmed" by reading Luther. That warmth turned to real heat when his cult broke from the Church of England to assert the importance of individual choice. Wesley "took it to the street." The service was exciting and made revivals into one of the most compelling new ways to "do church." In a strange way, televangelism is a descendant of this kind of delivery system. The camp meeting, which was the Chautauqua educational events at the high end and summer camp at the lower, moved through American nineteenth-century culture like a hot breeze. Alas, no longer.

• The Baptist Church starts as a no-brand church stressing the importance of self-denial and self-control. Read the Bible. Decide for yourself. Initially it wants to clean up things by stressing asceticism, which is why it focuses on individual choice. You decide if you want to be baptized, which can be pretty exciting. The Amish and the Mennonites broke off into free-standing brands, and you can see by their cultic fee schedule (the clothes, the refusal to "modernize") how intense the root religion can be.

There are all kinds of Baptist subbrands like the Primitive, Missionary, Free Will, General, Regular, and Independent. But the most expressive denomination is currently the Southern Baptist Convention (SBC). In theory this church is seriously egalitarian, but in practice it can be autocratic and intolerant, even anti-intellectual. This denomination thrives on trouble. And that friction is part of the reason why the SBC is the biggest U.S. Protestant group, with a reported membership of 16.27 million in 2005. The other reason for success is that it delivers the goods: go here to be born again, experience epiphany.

Want to be a Baptist minister? Get some followers together, and you're in business. Forget seminary. The services are exciting because the ministers are continually innovating and taking chances. The SBC doesn't advertise. It doesn't have to. Member churches have great word of mouth and a compelling product. They deliver. They have never forgotten the value of the altar call not just for gaining converts but for reminding the saved which side they are on.

• Aligned with the Baptists, in the sense of keeping sensation central, are the Pentecostal Churches, an omnium-gatherum term for churches that travel in loose groupings like Assemblies of God or the Christian Churches. They make religion into music. In a sense, they take Methodism seriously and ask for entire sanctification; hence pentecostalism or the process of filling up with the Holy Ghost. Believers gloss this promise as a modern-day fulfillment of Acts 2:4, the biblical passage in which the Holy Spirit descends on the disciples after Christ's crucifixion, resurrection, and ascension. But from a marketing point of view, these churches are delivering on the promise of other denominations—strong feelings of salvation right now—cutting out all the extraneous doctrine.

Religious Economies Theory

How do these denominations compete? How do they bring product to market? How do they price it? Assuming that the decision to buy into one of these systems of belief is voluntary, then the successful supplier must be delivering something in demand. And, as we have seen, the attraction is most probably not doctrinal; it is sensational.

The history of American Protestantism is that some provider figures out how to deliver the sense of epiphany in such a compelling way that brand switchers make their move. They start moving consumers down what is called in commercial marketing the *buy-hole* or perhaps in religion marketing might be called the "belief hole." Over the years

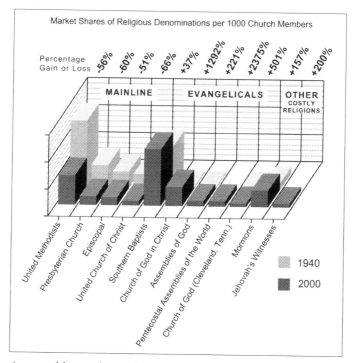

A scramble market: who wins shares, who loses. (SOURCE: ROGER FINKE AND RODNEY STARK, *THE CHURCHING OF AMERICA, 1776–2001,* P. 246.)

the faith hole for various denominations has expanded and contracted.

I don't think it's entirely coincidental that these denominational distinctions became especially important in America during the 1930s, about the same time that other such distinctions between almost equals were being made among hard goods. Take cars, for instance. The great contribution of Alfred P. Sloan at General Motors is that he took Henry Ford's idea of mass-producing a product but then gave it brand separation. Often the cars had the same chassis— body by Fisher—but different nameplates: Chevrolet, Pontiac, Oldsmobile, and Buick. So too perhaps American Protestantism.

In academic circles the economic approach to the study of faith markets travels under the unfortunate rubric of "religious economies." It's a bad word choice for a culturally compelling subject. Religions are usually not competitive; denominations inside them are. I prefer "denominational shopping theory" because it gives the context of alternative choice among parity suppliers, consumer empowerment, the ability of end users to make judgments about what's being offered, and the need for suppliers to continually shift their brand narratives.

Call it what you will, the religious marketplace has been around for a while. The observation that denominations move in markets starts with Adam Smith's observation that self-interest motivates clergy just as it does secular producers. Here he is on the subject of how suppliers have to hustle in a free market:

> The teachers of |religion| . . . in the same manner as other teachers, may either depend altogether for their subsistence upon the voluntary contributions of their hearers; or they may derive it from some other fund to which the law of their country may entitle them . . . Their exertion, their zeal and industry, are likely to be much greater in the former situation than the latter. In this respect the teachers of new religions have always had a considerable advantage in attacking those ancient and established systems of which the clergy, reposing themselves upon their benefices, had neglected to keep up the fervour of the faith and devotion in the great body of the people . . .

Smith's insights were essentially stiff-armed for two hundred years because the general subject of churches getting down and dirty was considered not just vulgar to study, but sacrilegious even to utter. While it might be permissible to think that schools compete for students or that museums compete for patrons or even that hospitals compete for the sick, certainly there were no markets being made for penitents. Transcendence is not beef patties, for goodness' sake. Such a view is unspeakable to all but a few historians.

Ministers, however, knew better. You had to hustle, or your congregation would be poached. Charles M. Sheldon, who would go on to write the incredibly popular *In His Steps,* the basis for the "What Would Jesus Do?" bracelets, spent some of his early preaching career near where I spend my summers. In his reminiscences of life at the Waterbury Congregational Church in Vermont, he was aware that the Methodists next door were pulling part of his crowd. He tried to figure out why. He found out. He hired their organist, and his attendance soared. He acknowledges this coup in his memoirs, realizing that his fellow pastors would understand.

It took the rest of us a little longer to appreciate the obvious: churches compete. Since the 1970s, and especially in the past few years, economists and sociologists have returned to Smith's insights to foreground a central truth of religion. Religion is a choice pretending to be a calling. Viewing religious behavior as just another purchase decision (rather than an exception to it) and seeing doctrine manufacturers behaving like widget makers (rather than as ordained Voices of God), researchers have been analyzing religious affiliation/choice at the individual, group, and market levels.

In retrospect, the turning point in the economic study of churches was the awarding of the Nobel Prize in 1992 to University of Chicago economist Gary S. Becker. Professor Becker started turning on the lights of economics in such dark rooms as crime, drugs, and even family interactions. It is in Becker's work that a whole school of economists like Steven Levitt, author of *Freakonomics,* find their inspiration. You get a sense of how combustible this economic approach to human concerns is in the fact that Levitt subtitles his book *A Rogue Economist Explores the Hidden Side of Everything.* Why *rogue,* and why have such matters as social affiliations been *hidden* from economic study?

While we prefer to think that faith and widgets exist in different orbits, sooner or later the markets for belief were going to be illuminated. Economists have now started to inch closer to such theological questions as the price of God. How is He shopped for, purchased, and paid for? Who are the luxury suppliers? What happens to discounters? How are surplus inventories handled? And what happens to suppliers who start extending the product into other areas like schooling, housing developments, or politics? Is there any way to predict the futures markets in religion? If so, who's long and who's short?

Let's put it this way: why *not* attempt to understand what happens in an open market by studying such matters as market share, customer satisfaction, cost-benefit analysis, return on investment. In this sense, a denomination is a collection of churches that is made up of intelligent and sensitive believers doing business as a broadcast network. Who's tuning in? Why not construct a paradigm (or borrow a paradigm from business) that allows an explanation of religion in terms of cost and reward?

Of all the scholars who have been confronting these queries, none has been more influential than Rodney Stark, now at Baylor University, and Roger Finke, at Penn State. They have written voluminously about the history of the "churching" of America, applying marketplace interpretations to the rise, shining, evaporation, and fall of various denominations. Their work started when, as graduate professor (Starke) and grad student (Finke) at the University of Washington, they came across a trove of unstudied data: a United States Census Bureau survey of religious behavior in 1906. This kind of data is no longer collected. As a sign of our nonjudgmental, hands-off times, we are hesitant to invade the privacy of religious affiliation. But our grandparents weren't. They considered religion like country of origin: you couldn't control it, so why not mention it?

The Churching of America

If any one book typifies the religious economies approach it is Finke and Stark's *The Churching of America, 1776–2005: Winners and Losers in Our Religious Economy.* From the title alone, you can see the thesis. In a few words: since colonial days, the United States has gone from a nation in which most people took no part in organized religion to a nation in which nearly two-thirds of American adults do. Here are the numbers that beg explication: 17 percent of the population were "religious adherents" in 1776, 37 percent in 1860, 53 percent in 1916, 59 percent in 1952, and 62 percent in 1980 and 2000. Go figure.

But it's the subtitle that carries the stinger: "Winners and losers"!

You can almost see the good divines and old-time pew holders, rolling their eyes. Yes, you can't judge the quality of a book by the best-seller list, nor can you tell if a movie is one you'll enjoy by looking at the weekly grosses. And a high Nielsen rating doesn't mean a TV show is entertaining for you. In fact, these may be contrary indicators for many. But you'll certainly learn a lot more about what people are really consuming by following the popcorn-of-their-choice trails than by listening to the critics, apologists, or those with the vested interests.

In a sense, Finke and Stark follow the popcorn. And in so doing, they question, if not demolish, much conventional wisdom about so-called American exceptionalism and offer in its place a powerful model of what happens when the markets are open and all comers are welcome to scramble for customers.

Here's just a bit of what they uncover. Although it's comforting to think that America's founding fathers and mothers were a pious lot concerned with building a church-going "Christian nation," such is poppycock. Church membership was low, premarital sex was rampant, and ministers were often randy. In addition, there is no evidence that the so-called great awakenings were caused by demand. What caused them was a new kind of marketing, of enthusiastic preaching, a new delivery system organized by competitive preachers who left their staid church perches and took chances in the field. The leading denominations of 1776, Congregationalists, Presbyterians, and Episcopalians, lost market share because they ceased to supply a sensational product.

The authors point out that denominations that grow, such as the conservative Southern Baptist, Mormon, Jehovah's Witnesses, and Assemblies of God, have often succeeded precisely because they demand the most time, money, and sacrifice from their members. Such suppliers do not see themselves as one of many. They see themselves as sole suppliers. Yet, converts do not get spiritual because they are stupid, scared, or superstitious. Consumers are not tricked or duped. They make rational choices about religion and actually are rewarded for their time and money. Americans want their religion to be sufficiently spicy, vivid, and compelling so that it can offer them rewards of great magnitude. Yes, it's magical thinking, an especially potent variety of competitive behavior. Is there any other kind?

Criticism

As one might imagine, such a violent rocking of the religious boat has provoked much sea sickness. Some have questioned the individual sets of data used by the authors, some the specific conclusions as they relate to specific denominations, and some the necessarily reductionist nature of fitting a putative nonprofit into the template of a money-making enterprise.

But the most vehement concern was expressed in the *vade mecum* of ecumenical thinking, the magazine *The Christian Century,* by a preeminent historian of American religion and an ordained Lutheran minister. Martin Marty, the retired Fairfax M. Cone professor of religion at the University of Chicago (an irony to note in passing is that Fairfax Cone was one of the great advertising men of the twentieth century, a man who helped build the premier agency Foote, Cone & Belding in Chicago) first accuses Finke and Stark of a "consistently sneering" tone, and then unloads:

> Finke and Stark's world contains no God or religion or spirituality, no issue of truth or beauty or goodness, no faith or hope or love, no justice or mercy; only winning and losing in the churching game matters.
>
> The authors enjoy using a kind of "in your face" approach to "religious economies." Most students of American religion use some economic insights and market metaphors, but Finke and Stark reduce everything to the language of "regulation," "cost and benefit," "maximizing," "collective production," "good bargains," "opportunity costs," "consuming," and so on.
>
> They dismiss, demean, or disdain almost all other sociologists of religion—the main exception being two or three who have collaborated with them—and, while picking up on a couple of

creative revisionist monographs, they trash all authors of "general religious histories." *Trash* is not too strong a word: they accuse this company (to which I belong) of "sloppy scholarship," of "glaring, systematic biases," and of simply being and remaining "ignorant."

Finke and Stark misrepresent, distort, quote out of context, and overlook revisions made by all the general historians whose life work they think they can repudiate thanks to their recently discovered laws of history.

In respect to (a) collegiality and recognition of others' scholarship, (b) scholarly nuance, and (c) good counsel to church leaders, the score for Finke and Stark can be reduced to Winning, 0; Losing, 3.

A Defense from a Different Field

As you might imagine, this view of religion inflected with economics is anathema to many more believers than critics. Like Professor Marty, you yourself may be having trouble with it. But since it's so important to the rest of this book, let's try a similar explanation of an analogous delivery system.

I am a schoolteacher. I teach literature. In many ways I am like a minister. My job comes directly from the church. All the names in my world have been lifted from the ecclesiastical one: My boss is the *dean;* his boss is the *provost;* and his, the *chancellor.* These are all names borrowed from church business; in fact, these are the names of those who handle church monies and enforce church policies. From time to time I still wear the flowing robes of the clergy to prove the provenance of my job. My students call me *doctor* not because I am one but because before there were medical doctors there were doctors of divinity, those priests who practiced the same exegesis of text that I perform. School buildings and church buildings often look the same. In fact, the school where I teach is done in what is called academic gothic. If you really want to see it done to the nines, look at the campuses of Yale, Duke, or the many American schools that attempted to copy the look of Oxford and Cambridge, which, in turn, were parts of the church.

From time to time I even use the same sales pitch as do my churchly counterparts. If you will spend time with me and my subjects, I say, you'll have a better life. I have some sacred texts to explore, and my job is to introduce my parishioners to what I think they mean. I don't like to admit how shaky my interpretation is; in fact, I often reject out of hand the idea that I could be mistaken. But in the back of my mind, I know better.

No matter, I promise them that if they do well and attend to their studies, they will be better for it. I indoctrinate them, literally. The works I teach are from something called the canon, and schoolteachers pretend that the canon is stable and timeless. But it's very much like the Christian canon—a lot of it is up for grabs.

In the 1920s I. A. Richards, a famous literary critic at Oxford University, played a whimsical but profound trick on his graduate students. He gave them a sheaf of miscellaneous poems—some written by "great masters," some written by also-rans, some even written by himself—and asked the grad students to evaluate them as "works of art." If great art is self-evident, he thought, then surely these future teachers will be able to distinguish creative genius from popular dross. They couldn't do it. They were just as likely to mistake the treacle of a Hallmark card for the masterful confection of an Elizabethan sonnet. My sacred texts may not really be all that sacred, because in order for them to become sacred, they need me. That's my job as priest.

Some Christians are unnerved by the fact that nowhere does God itemize the sixty-six books that make up the Bible. Many believers have at best only a vague notion of how the church arrived at what is called the Canon of Scripture. Even after becoming more aware, some believers are uncomfortable with the process by which the New Testament canon was determined. For many, it was what appears to be a haphazard process that took far too long and seems a bit—what?—political.

Ditto my world. The stuff in the high-lit canon is called art, or in my case, literature. From matriculation to graduation, we mimic the catechism of church life. You must take it on faith that this is the Word. Churches and schools foster communities built around what sociologists like to call a "commonality of desire." Woe to the student who asks why. And we charge our students a little tithe for the experience; often the higher the amount, the higher the perceived value. And we give them a diploma when they are confirmed.

We even have our relics. Many academic libraries have storehouses of rare books under lock and key. The better the school, the bigger the cache. Since the advent of the photocopier, these rare books have essentially no scholarly value. We never admit that. We never suggest that we unload these relics to collectors for top dollar, but we all know that if you were to put a turnstile up in front of the rare book room, it would soon rust. Having them is part of how we generate our value. Using them is not.

Students and teacher want a powerful experience. On my students' side, they want (or at least some of them may want) sensational experiences, epiphanies, breakthroughs. On my side, I want to provide them with this, and I'll shift things around to see that they get it.

I also want to have full classes. I want good job evaluations. I compete with my colleagues. And my colleagues and I compete with other suppliers of this experience at other schools. In other words, I have my individual congregation inside a denomination, and this denomination struggles with others to get the highest number of incoming students and transfers. We want our students to have a rewarding experience because at some level we know that their later contributions will help support us. When necessary, I inflate the grades a bit.

Like believers, students increasingly shop for this experience. Often they don't go to the school of their parents. For a number of reasons, there's a lot of brand switching. Once at a school, there is a period at the beginning of the semester that used to be called "drop/add," now called "shopping around." In the first few days there is standing room only as students come by and taste the flavor.

They know how to do this. For them it's an extension of channel surfing. I try to frighten them during the first week with how tough my grading is, so that I won't get too many freeloaders looking for a gut course. Freeloaders can ruin a course, just as they can a congregation.

In the general sense, I always keep one eye on the crowd once it's thinned down to the true believers. What do *they* want? Do they want easy poems or hard ones? Long or short? Male or female authors? Novels? Do they want hard tests? Sometimes they do. Or do they want quick and easy? And how about grades? I am a hard grader. By that I mean I give more than As and Bs. I find that my good students really like that. They like knowing that someone is getting a D. It makes their B worth something. I use guilt and fear. The final exam is coming, I remind them. It counts for a huge percent of their grade. My colleagues and I joke that if you don't give them a tough final, they won't come for the last half of the semester.

This same scrambling process is going on between departments. That's how we are funded. A class with too few students gets dropped even if the subject is important. Adios Chaucer, not because the professorate doesn't think he's still important. We know he is. But the classes won't fill. Say good-bye to Milton and Spenser. Nothing is more mortifying than to be called into the chair's office a few days before classes start and be told that your class didn't make it. Too many empty pews.

Just as Adam Smith predicted that open markets in religion would cause clerics to hustle, so too do open markets in higher education cause faculty to jitter. A sign of the process: when we are talking enrollment, we call students "FTEs," or Full Time Equivalents. More telling: in parts of the university, they are called clients. Still more telling: most semesters my department teaches more courses in television and movies than in literature.

As the composition of the classroom changes, as more women or African-Americans or, in my case, Cubans, enroll, I have to start shifting my subject matter lest I be left behind by a congregation moving elsewhere for stories. How come African-American literature appeared about twenty years ago? Where did feminist literature suddenly come from? How come my department is hiring people in Caribbean studies? A generation ago such subjects didn't exist. These works were not in the canon.

What happened was that we suppliers of the catechism, of art appreciation, realized that we were tapping new markets and so we shifted out some of the Dead White Males to let in the Literature of Others. We didn't do this because we were ecumenical; we did this because we were looking for business. Our business, remember, is growing enrollment, yes, but not just by the raw numbers. No, what sets us apart is growing the numbers of the most selective students. Every year we are judged by *our* Vatican, *U.S. News & World Report*'s annual "America's Best Colleges" issue. The most important internal figure is how many students we refuse. Whom we refuse to accept is, in a sense, more important than who gets in.

Now, would we ever admit this? Never. Ask, as I have, various ministers how much they tailor their sermons and church experience to increase not just the gate but the quality of those who come through the gate, and you'll be met with rolled eyes. "What! Me pander to only parts of the congregation? We're open and affirming. Just like Jesus." For many in the education and religion businesses, just the mention of market pressures is anathema. Try coining a concept like religious economies and call it "academic economies," and see where it gets you. Arched eyebrows. But when it's a roomful of just us, we certainly do admit it to one another.

No Joking Matter

Although the competitive-market model may be applied grudgingly to higher education or art museums, it still seems somehow inappropriate when stuck onto the forgiveness-and-salvation business. Professor Marty is right. Religious-economies theory contains "no issue of truth or beauty or goodness, no faith or hope or love, no justice or mercy; only winning and losing in the churching game matters."

Still, it does open up one of the more interesting approaches to denominationalism. Churches operate in markets. And, if churchmen find it unappealing, they may be forgiven, just as economists should be indulged if they have trouble finding any elevated purpose in the dreary world of supply and demand.

That said, however, such a cost-and-benefit approach does lead to some interesting speculation about churches in the future. As I write this, *The Economist,* that cheeky and often provocative mouthpiece of British business reporting, has published a conjecture on its website. In a piece titled "A Marriage Made in Heaven," they report on a rumor making its way around England. Remember how the behemoth AT&T—monopoly supplier until the 1970s—was broken up into a handful of squabbling denominations? These regional suppliers nickel-and-dimed each other to death. Now bit by bit the "baby bells" have reconfigured and remerged themselves back into the monolithic single supplier—AT&T. It took time and wasted a lot of money but it was worth it.

Why not consider a massive remerger of a vast Rome-based corporation and a smaller rival with headquarters in southern England? Let's face it, says *The Economist,* there really was no good business reason for the acrimonious separation of the Anglicans in the sixteenth century. Such rejoining has obvious rewards, but obstacles remain.

> As with any merger, knitting together rival management teams could prove tricky. Each disagrees on the nature of the Eucharist and the ordination of women. Recognizing the pope as the boss of a merged corporation might also prove a sticking point. The Anglican brand also looks troubled. It lacks a clear business model and suffers from open divisions among top managers who have far more devolved authority. Many managers are engaged in a bitter dispute over the hiring of homosexual staff in its American subsidiary. In contrast the Catholic church has a clear line of command between its chief executive, its 4,700 senior executives and 400,000 line managers around the world.

Yet potential synergies abound. Combining workforces could allow for significant cost savings, though job cuts might prove unpopular. Buoyant property markets mean that a merged church could profit handsomely by selling surplus assets, many of them in prime city-centre sites. As the two organizations would not benefit equally—the merger would in effect be a Catholic takeover of its smaller rival—Anglicans may prefer a looser bond, perhaps hiving-off some assets into a joint-venture or even, looking to the heavens, embracing something akin to the code-sharing agreements between big airlines. Whatever form the merger eventually takes, if any, at least the two groups have shown they are serious about getting the mass-communication business in shape for the 21st century.

If there is one thing we have seen from the history of denominations it is that, for all the vulgarity of it, business logic has always elbowed dogma aside when denominational growth has started to ebb. *The Economist* may joke, but the prospect that the Anglican Church (perhaps taking with it the right-wing of the American Episcopal Church) might one day return to the Roman Catholic fold might indeed be a strategy to confront the rise of the pentecostals, evangelicals, and megachurches. The day after *The Economist* observation appeared it was picked up *in toto* by the *Wall Street Journal*. Perhaps business people realized that it was, at some level, no joke. If there is one thing we have learned about the competitive nature of human institutions (be they in the service of higher education, art appreciation, or the salvation of souls), it is that there is no joking around when they really get down to business. Shhh, please, now things are finally getting serious.

CHAPTER FIVE

Holy Franchise: Marketing Religion in a Scramble Economy

Mainstream denominations are in deep trouble. Membership in the United Church of Christ has dropped every year since 1965, from 2.1 million then to 1.3 million today; Methodists, known for heartfelt discipleship and care for the needy, have seen their missionary ranks thin from 2,000 before 1950 to just 93 in 2004; the Presbyterian Church has been losing about 40,000 members a year and, if this continues, will have zero members in 2053; and don't even ask about the Episcopalians, who can't decide if they're even a denomination any longer. The mainlines used to own the market; now they account for just 16 percent of the U.S. population.

What happened? There are any number of explanations. First is the obvious. The majors forgot how to sell. Or just don't care. If you want proof, look at the fastest growing denominations, and you'll see what they have in common. They are selling, selling, selling, 24-7. Missionary zeal is at the heart of their attraction, not just because showing the Way to others is a source of jubilation, but because it means that you yourself must have found your way. The value of the *next* sale (the convert) proves the value of the *previous* sale (yours).

The person who is selling Amway is in many ways not as concerned about your purchase as his own. While it looks as if everything

133

is directed at the "next customer," it all relates back to the last customer. You. How to make your purchase worthwhile is to continue the selling pyramid forward. That's why what growing churches sell is . . . *growth*. "If this soap wasn't so good, would it be selling so well?"

In the spring of 2006 I attended a Jehovah's Witnesses convention. The affair, which lasted three days, explained how to sell the product, how to interact with the hesitant believer, and how to make the sale. And then how to feel good about yourself. While the entire convention was preparing you to go back out into the missionary fields and convert others, I realized that everyone there had essentially had the sale made to them. They had all bought in. But without the next purchaser, their "goods" were worthless. It was a pyramid scheme—the value of your purchase was in the actions of the next consumer.

But there are other more subtle reasons for the decline of mainline denominations. Obviously the great effacement of social distinctions caused by rampant commercialism removed the social hierarchy of who's going to what church. Church denomination was a social marker. In the first part of the twentieth century, you could often "buy" a family pew. It was yours. Your name sometimes was engraved on a little plaque. Plus, the farther up front your pew, the more prestigious your social status.

Just as by the end of the twentieth century, no one really cared about how many generations your family had lived in your town, what clubs you joined, or, to a considerable degree, the color of your skin, no one cared where you worshiped, let alone if you had your own pew. In fact, by the end of the twentieth century, no one cared if you even went to church.

In 1929 a young theologian, H. Richard Niebuhr, caused a storm by dissecting "The Social Sources of Denominationalism," a landmark study in American religion. He railed against the social use of religion as just another affiliation product—what is known in marketing as a "badge" good. Changing badges was a sign of upward mobility. For Niebuhr, denominational divisions based on social class represented nothing less than a "moral failure of Christianity."

Today if someone wants to know your social status, he looks at the car you drive, the label on your clothes, where you vacation, your choice of commercial brands. The brand name on your refrigerator has replaced your brand of church—a Sub-Zero in the corner trumps Our Lady of the Upper Crust down the street. The label has gone from inside the social garment, as it were, to the outside, viz., the polo pony, the alligator, the initials of some designer. "Does my Lexus fit with my watch band?" is more likely the reflection of the modern J. Alfred Prufrock than "Should I tell people I'm a Methodist?"

Another reason denominations lost their centripetal force was the rise of a different kind of mobility. The average person now changes houses ten times and jobs eight times in his life. The culprit? The car. You are no longer stuck in your father's church. Plus, the car means that you can church-shop to your heart's content and never be noticed by those who might censure you.

Magnifying this mobility in getting to church was the profound shift in family mobility. If you moved your residence five times, you may have switched your spouse at least once. Half of marriages dissolve. Religion is a family experience, not just for the present membership but for the future. The best predictor of future affiliation is childhood indoctrination by the parents. The believer doesn't fall too far from the family tree. However, the family tree for many kids is a forest.

With divorce, the child's religious indoctrination usually goes with the custodial parent. This not only weakens the link but makes the next linkage more tenuous. When they grow up, children of divorce are 62 percent more likely than children of nondivorced parents to no longer identify with the faith of their parents. And they are far more likely to quit the endeavor altogether, considering religious choice not just superfluous but part of a traumatic memory.

These migration patterns are exaggerated by a demographic phenomenon first pointed out by University of California at Berkeley sociologist Michael Hout in the *American Journal of Sociology.* For the last fifty years, women from conservative denominations have had one more birth, on average, than other Protestant women. Couples from those mainline churches are averaging fewer than two births each; in short, they are not reproducing themselves. According to Hout, the demographic explanation accounts for 70 percent of denominational change, while the remaining 30 percent stems from the growing efficiency of conservative denominations in holding on to their own. Thus to find the root of the historic shift in American Protestantism, look not to the pulpits but to the nurseries.

Here's another reason why denominations lost their groove. Ministers have traditionally moved around, usually following inner light, not paycheck. In the nineteenth century the Methodist church gained its explosive growth by sending out its emissaries to every nook and cranny—one-on-one selling. This intimacy was supplemented with itinerant preachers who popped in for evangelical camp meetings. Baptists did the same with low-entry qualifications for pastoring, which meant that almost any congregation could find a homegrown leader. But as denominations settled down, control was applied from above so that there was uniformity with the product. Ministers were appointed. The home office decided where and when things happened. Over time local eccentricities were polished away, pastors came from the same cloth, and the experience became predictable, rather like a meat patty and a Coke.

A few generations ago, before the mainline denominations became businesslike, your church had a long-term pastor who saw to it that his flock stayed close to home. He baptized you, married you, buried you. Over time, however, this lifetime bonding has gone the way of other jobs for life. Move up or move out.

A study conducted in 2005 by Ellison Research among a representative sample of 872 Protestant ministers explored the job situations of ministers in the United States. The average American minister has held a paid job in ministry for 19 years and has spent an average of 15.6 of those years as a senior pastor of one or more churches. The average minister has been the senior pastor of his or her current church for 7.7 years. Average time spent in the same job for middle management in a commercial business: 7.6 years.

What used to be a sinecure has become just another step up the corporate ladder. The statistics show that it's much more common for a pastor to take a job at a different church due to a promotion than it is for a pastor to move to a new church because of *a calling*. Many clergy are themselves concerned that pastors do not spend enough years at one church. Only 31 percent feel that the average pastor stays the right amount of time. One-third believe the average tenure is a little too short, and 26 percent feel it is much too short. If you are trying to build brand loyalty at the neighborhood store, you can't keep shifting the manager.

Pastors are acting more and more like their compatriots in the business world. They move because they are promoted, demoted, or fired. They want better pay, better working conditions, a change of scenery, or, increasingly common, a spouse gets a job elsewhere, and they tag along. Relatively few pastors have left a job because they wanted to pastor a smaller church (4 percent) or because their church closed down or ceased to exist (2 percent). They move usually for the same reason the rest of us move: advancement.

Among Methodists, the most common reason for a job change is being transferred (80 percent). Church switching is more common among Methodist pastors than among other denominational groups, as is wanting to move to a larger church. Methodist ministers are much less likely than average to have left a job to start a new church, to have felt God's call to go to another church, or to have been fired. They themselves know the problem. Almost three-quarters of them are concerned that they don't put down deep enough roots. Such an irony: pastoral mobility, an advantage in the nineteenth century when it generated excitement, has become a hindrance in modern times, when the church is often valued as a still point, and the parishioners are the mobile ones.

What all these social transformations—lack of social class distinction generated by church affiliation, rise of a divorce culture, mobility of parishioner and pastorate—have done is to aggravate an inherent problem of voluntary associations. It's just too easy to leave. In church parlance this is called "slipping out the side door," which carries the nice touch of thereby not having to meet the pastor for the bonding handshake. People most often leave a cooperative group when the friction possibilities are high inside and the stigma penalty is low outside.

In studies done on apostasy in England, nearly three-quarters of the people left churches over a disagreement on what seems to be minor issues, from the way the organ is played to the seating arrangements. It's the little things like the choir robes, prayer book, hymnal, or flower arrangement that cause silly arguments.

So too on this side of the Atlantic, shrinkage is often a cumulative effect of small matters, not substantive disagreements. In *Why Churches Die* (with the rather daunting subtitle *Diagnosing Lethal Poisons in the Body of Christ*), two Baptist preachers practice what they call "spiritual forensics." They find that the motivations for leaving are rather like those for exiting book clubs, health clubs, fraternal groups, trade unions, and neighborhood associations: someone gets pissed off at someone else.

In 1958 only 1 in 25 Americans had left the denomination of their upbringing. By the end of the century, more than 1 in 3 had left or switched. Today nearly half of all people raised as Presbyterians, Methodists, and Episcopalians have left the faith—or at least the denominations—of their forefathers.

When you find this kind of loosening of ties to brands in the commercial world, you very often find a rise in generic producers, house brands. So when the market for, say, bottled water starts to collapse, as it has recently, there is not necessarily a turn back to tap water or an increase in colas but a movement to off-brand water, essentially no-name water—still bottled, but at a lower price. Consumers maintain the need for the product, but lose the bond to brand.

The Generic Product: Spiritualism

No problem is more pressing for old-line Protestantism than this "trading down." Since content differences are minimal, one of the most important connections to develop is brand loyalty. Nothing is more dangerous than seeing someone switch; nothing more detrimental than arriving on Sunday to sense that fewer people are there; nothing worse than knowing that the megachurch out by the interstate is growing. And what accounts for the mega's growth? Church literature from one megachurch, Valley Cathedral of Phoenix, proudly proclaims that it began with persons from thirty-four different denominations.

Could this flux downward in the faith markets partly explain the eruption of spiritualism, the pure generic of denominational religion, religion without the brand? According to a recent survey from the MacArthur Foundation, 7 out of 10 Americans say they are religious and consider spirituality to be an important part of their lives. But about half attend church services less than once a month, or never. They are the Great Unchurched Believers—80 million adult Americans who claim membership in no denomination, church, or other religious institution.

In so many respects, the New Age movement seems feather headed, whether it be belief in astrology, channeling, crystals, fire walking, I Ching, Maharishi this-or-that, massage, meditation, numerology, power spots, pyramids, third eye, tofu, vibes, yoga, or free-range chickens. Such Shirley MacLaine stuff seems so crunchy granola, so perfect for those people who don't want to be bothered by real complexity and prefer the faux variety. But spiritualism is to religion what alternative health is to modern medicine or home schooling is to education: in a sense it's the reassertion of individual control and a rebellion against the control of self-appointed experts.

The mantra "I'm into spirituality, not religion" often means, I want the feelings without the overhead. While much of spirituality is pure nonsense—marketing, packaging, psychobabble—it is practical and personal, more about stress reduction than salvation, more therapeutic than theological. It's about feeling good, not necessarily about being good. It's as much about the body as the soul. It's health masquerading as belief, the Church of Dr. Phil, the Chapel of Oprah.

I mention this because the repackaging of spiritualism is at the

heart of many megachurches. For what you see in these huge muta-
tions of "I'm OK, you're OK" and traditional denominational religion
("they're not OK") is what in marketing is called the "experiential
sell." In a sense, the megas are the triumph of the generic.

That's why, as you walk the aisle of the spiritual supermarket, you
can see the repackaging in progress. First Baptist Church becomes
the Family Christian Center, while the Lutherans across town are
reborn as Grace Community Church. And it's the secret of the success of a new kind of pastor like Joel Osteen. Spend a few hours
watching his weekly television show or read his *Your Best Life Now*,
and you can see the migration of spiritualism back into a church setting. As admen say, sell the feeling, throw in the product for free.
(Plus child care, a sports club, and a guaranteed parking place.)

Church Marketing Inc.: The Historical Basis

What can the mainlines do, how can they regain market share, how
can they convert some of that spiritualism back into demand for
their services, how can they staunch the flow of apostasy? One possible answer is . . . advertise. Use commercial speech to reassert the
availability and importance of the religious product. When markets
are expanding, no one really thinks about advertising. When markets are contracting, no one thinks about anything else. Oddly
enough, we've been here before.

Almost a century ago the entire religion market was contracting.
The great flurry of post–Civil War excitement had died down (fraternity restored), science (especially evolution) was starting to efface
the claims of divine creation, and a general sense of national purpose
(manifest destiny) was in the air. It was in this context that one of the
most innovative treatments of church marketing was produced.

The so-called Progressive movement in American culture of the
early twentieth century sought to revitalize the dreary status of
denominations with an appeal to social utility. In a sense, this was
spiritualism mixed not with the human potential movement, as it is

now, but with the industrial revolution. Shouldn't brothers on the assembly line also be brothers in Christ? Why should getting and spending be so bleak and uninspiring, pitting men against men, and company against company?

One of the most articulate spokesmen for the pollination of religion and the marketplace was a product of the Lower East Side of New York, a Bowery Boy, the Rev. Charles Stelzle, a devout Presbyterian. Of his many contributions to the Progressive movement (supporting urban ministry to the poor, organizing workingman's missions, welcoming immigrants), none was more important than his belief that if churches were to be at the vanguard of social change, they must make themselves attractive not just to the nonbelievers but to the unchurched as well. And to do this, churches had to enter the marketplace and toot the horn.

In 1908 Stelzle published his remarkable *Principles of Successful Church Advertising,* remarkable because he is absolutely unapologetic and cunning about how to go about getting converts. How should we know where to go to church if not by information, and why should church information not be distributed like information about soap or, perish the thought, booze? So the book is filled with tips on newspaper advertising, outdoor billboards, leaflets, logos, appropriate typefaces, and the like. He ends his introduction with this peroration:

> The Church should advertise because the method is successful in legitimate business enterprise. To narrate the story of modern business advertising would seem like a fairy tale. Suffice it to say that the successful principles which have been discovered in this experience will be dealt with in their proper place in this study. If the Christian men in the Church have found this method so successful in their commercial life, what unanswerable objection can be brought to bear against the use by the Church of the same methods?
>
> The Church must advertise, because it is slowly but surely losing ground in our great centers of population, which are inevitably to dominate the nation. Indeed, from all parts of the

world, there come stories of losses in membership, either comparative or actual. In the face of this, dare the Church sit back and leave untried a single method which may win men to Christ, provided that this method be legitimate?

One can never overlook the fact that the specific church that Charles Stelzle was attempting to position was the Presbyterian Church. In high Victorian times, it was the Presbyterians, in many ways the serious big brother to the Methodists, who were arguing for the strict and obedient social conscience. From founder John Knox, who battled the forces of the backsliding English in his native Scotland, to Thomas Cartwright, who did it to them on their own turf, Presbyterians took it to the streets. In ad jargon, its unique selling proposition was that Presbyterians took a stand. In fact, Stelzle was arguing for advertising very much like what is now coming from the United Church of Christ.

If public advertising was the tribute Presbyterians paid the soiled world of commerce, then the price of doing good was doing a little bad. Other denominations were neither so bold nor so confident. In fact, since the mainline ministry saw itself as above the market, anything with the whiff of commercialism was to be held at arm's length. This is the context, however, that produced Billy Sunday and later Billy Graham, raised as Presbyterians and close readers of Stelzle. Before you save souls, you fill pews.

While other denominations may have spoken to one another *about* the market of Mammon, these Presbyterians went *through* the market of Mammon. But they were the exception. To a considerable degree, this hesitancy has as much to do with the nature of advertising as the nature of religion. Although many wits have observed that religion and advertising have a commonality—namely, to comfort the afflicted and afflict the comfortable—the simple fact of the matter is that advertising is rarely used for an entire category. In other words, you advertise the brand not the object, or in religious context, the denomination not the belief.

Here's why. Make all the machine-made biscuits, shoes, cigarettes, automobiles, or computer chips you want, you can't sell effectively until you can call it a Ritz, a Nike, a Marlboro, a Chevrolet, or an Intel 386. If everybody's biscuits are in the same barrel, and if they look pretty much the same, it probably doesn't reward you to urge people to buy biscuits. Chances are they won't buy *your* biscuit.

So if you are in the forgiveness and salvation business, you rarely advertise the path of righteousness; instead you advertise the Presbyterian path. The only time you see what is called *category advertising* is when you have a monopoly supplier. Think diamonds, for instance. When DeBeers controlled most of the world's supply, it could run a campaign called "A Diamond Is Forever." But the minute you lose monopoly control, then you advertise the DeBeers diamond.

Category Advertising

If you want to see category advertising in religion, you have to go to the single-supplier cultures. Both the Catholic Church in Europe and the Anglican Church in England have made desultory attempts at category advertising.

The Catholic Church, which after all invented church advertising by using the package (church building) and plasma (church walls and ornamentation) to distinguish between and among the various mendicant order venues, is now publicly skeptical of marketing. In fact, it's occasionally downright hostile. Its public view, expressed in a policy document "Ethics in Advertising," criticizes commercial advertisers that make "deliberate appeals to such motives as envy, status seeking, and lust."

Back in the days before the FCC opened up the airwaves to individual churches, the Catholic Church ran mostly public service ads in the service of what is now called family values: love your neighbor and keep tabs on your kiddies. For years it also allowed a most charismatic and unfailingly kind spokesman, Bishop Fulton J. Sheen, whose television show *Life Is Worth Living* often outdrew Milton Berle, to spread not the Word but the ethos of a compassionate and caring organization. In a sense, the bishop was a precursor to the TV star Mother Angelica and what she calls the Global Catholic Network, as well as Sister Wendy, the British nun and art enthusiast on the BBC.

But the Vatican pulled back from category advertising, fearful that it would be confused with the hurly-burly of proselytizing denominations. After all, that had been the knock on the Church of Rome; namely, that it was too concerned with aggrandizing its own membership at the expense of Protestants. However, from time to time individual churches would go off on their own, as did the St. Lawrence Martyr Catholic Church in Redondo Beach, California, when it ran an ad under this headline: "Did the Catholic Church Screw Up Your Life? Sorry. Give Us Another Chance."

That said, the church has had a specific and burdensome problem: a priesthood under siege. Since 1965 the number of ordinations has plummeted. In the last decade, enrollment in graduate-level seminaries has dropped from 8,325 to 3,308. Thousands of parishes are without a resident priest, and the average age of Catholic clergy is climbing. Not only has the priesthood suffered the blight of association (real and imagined) with child molestation, but there are fewer and fewer young men willing to live a life of celibacy. Should the priest shortage continue, no doubt celibacy will become optional for diocesan priests. Such a move would increase seminarians, and the priest shortage could be over.

Until then: on one recruitment poster, a young Roman Catholic priest in full cassock stands before a black backdrop gripping a cross in one hand and a rosary in the other. A halo of light surrounds him, but his expression is far from angelic. He stares grimly at the ground, his eyes obscured by dark sunglasses. That's all. The poster is a takeoff on ads for the movie *The Matrix* and was developed by a youth minister in the Archdiocese of Indianapolis to send a message about enrolling in seminary. Priests, like the Keanu Reeves character in the film, fight for good in a tough world. But such ads are run only locally and in tightly controlled venues like parochial schools.

Not so hostile to advertising, however, is the English spur of the Roman Catholic Church. The Anglican Church, beset with low attendance and little in the way of interesting things to see or hear, has had to battle for market share. During the booming commercial markets in the late twentieth century, the government Prime Minister Margaret Thatcher changed the law to allow religious groups to advertise on television and radio. President Ronald Reagan had already opened up the FCC to allow religious programmers to buy broadcast time, in effect creating channels like the Christian Broadcasting Network. The Church of England took note. It issued a report, cheekily titled "Paying the Piper," which made the following points:

1. Advertising should be used as part of the churches' communication strategy.
2. The role of advertising as an appropriate means of communication in its own right was affirmed.
3. A strong recommendation was made that Christian advertising should be ecumenical.
4. The report encouraged the churches to engage in commercial advertising.

Should you look at the website www.churchads.org.uk, you'll read this: "We believe that advertising can be a creative, effective, appropriate, even amusing means of communication for the church. We recommend that advertising be considered as part of the communication mix." Although the third point (ecumenical ads) is nonsensical unless you are a true monopoly supplier, the genie was again out of the bottle.

So what have the Brits been seeing? Posters such as:

• An image of Jesus saying "Surprise!" to his disciples three days after they buried him.

• An image of the Virgin Mary in the manger with mussed-up hair, being visited by the three wise men. The copy reads: "Bad hair day?

You're a virgin, you've just given birth, and now three kings have shown up."

- Jesus as the Marxist revolutionary Che Guevara, peering down on motorists from billboards across the country.
- The Last Supper depicted as a corporate board meeting.
- A long-haired Jesus clad in a designer suit, and the representative of computer giant Microsoft portrayed as Judas.

You can imagine the response. Needless to say, the specter of the anti-Christ, Madison Avenue, was often invoked by the outraged Brits. The campaign made little difference. The Church of England's Sunday attendance continued to fall by an average of 4 percent per year. According to the people who put the campaign together, the ads were not supposed to address declining attendance, but to build the brand. If you spend any time studying ad agencies, you know that this is self-serving mumbo-jumbo.

The Church Ad Project

At the same time the British Anglicans were experimenting with commercial speech in the service of upping religious consumption, so too were the American Episcopalians. The Episcopal Ad Project, now called the Church Ad Project, was started in the 1990s by George Martin, an Episcopal minister and adman in Minneapolis. Like his fellow Anglicans, he realized that an entire generation was bypassing his church, and you couldn't bring them back by the hard sell. So his ads were visually clever and linguistically sophisticated. They captured the wink-wink tone of the old English church, that wry self-satisfied sense of belonging, but without offering something new and distinctive. In other words, in ad lingo, they entertained without selling. Or without insulting intelligence. Have a look.

In other ads, we see pictures of Santa Claus and Jesus with the

If you can't beat 'em, join 'em: selling church affiliation à la Madison Avenue. (SOURCE: CHURCH AD PROJECT CATALOG.)

question "Whose birthday is it, anyway?"; a picture of the Bible over the line "The Original Power Book"; a snowboarder flying upside down through this headline, "You're self-confident and self-reliant, but it never hurts to have a backup"; a picture of a chalice under this heading, "Over 10 Trillion Served"; the external shot of an Episcopal-looking church, "The leading place to invest in futures"; under a picture of crucified Christ, "Body piercing is nothing new to us"; a picture of the prayer book under "Weekly prophet sharing"; the Energizer Bunny against the headline "Has the true meaning of Easter gotten a little fuzzy?"

True to the American spirit of "find a need and make money from it," the Church Ad Project went commercial, incorporated itself, and now offers camera-ready ads for placement in newspapers and magazines that can be customized with a local church's "tag." Almost ten thousand churches have used its service for ready-made ads, cards, posters, T-shirts, and radio spots.

The Church Ad Project has not been without competition. One of the biggest suppliers of "ready product" is Impact Productions, a nonprofit ministry based in Tulsa, Oklahoma. All told, the company has produced forty-three commercials, which it rents to more than 1,300 churches nationwide for broadcast in their immediate areas. Impact charges an average of $833 for a church to use a single commercial for two years. The commercials are grouped by stage of life so that concerns like parenthood, divorce, moving in, and moving away are addressed. You name the group, and the company claims, it has just the commercial to attract them.

In many marketing respects, what we see here is the same as selling dairy products, soap, or gasoline. There is little if any product differentiation, so the ads themselves, like the products, are interchangeable. Rule 1 in Marketing 101: don't sell the product, sell the brand. But individual churches want to think of themselves as unique, and these ads, ironically, serve only to homogenize them. One of the reasons that the nondenominational megachurch has been so successful is that it can focus its marketing on a specific demographic and capture all the wasted expense of preaching both to the choir as well as to the dedicated uninterested.

Single Supplier Marketing: Marble Collegiate

So what can the individual mainline denominational church do to sell its particular brand? Often not much. The old standby has been to buy a small box ad in the newspaper to run on Saturday, as churches have been doing since the late nineteenth century, but all you can really do in such a setting is promote the upcoming sermon and list service times. The modern website now more than ever accommodates this function. And, thanks to Mel Stewart, you can change your church marquee sign more often and make the text snappier.

If you're adventurous, you can buy trailer time before the features are shown down at the local cineplex or buy relatively cheap time in the spot market of cable TV. Ironically, since broadcast deregulation in the mid-1980s, the networks don't have to run PSAs (public service announcements), so the prices have gone way up. For a while in the 1960s, a nonprofit could buy thirty seconds in the dead of night for around $15. Now, thanks in large part to the profusion of infomercials, those days are over. Even the Mormons, who have been buying airtime since 1987, have found it too expensive. They currently spend about $4 million per year on cable alone. And, of course, your ad will probably run late at night. That, however, may not be a problem if anxious seekers are your demographic. What's better than the eleventh-hour convert at literally the eleventh hour?

But if you are a big church with deep pockets, standard advertising may be worth a try. Here's an example. Marble Collegiate Church is one of the oldest places of worship in Manhattan. In fact, as the Collegiate Reformed Protestant Dutch Church of the City of New York, it is the oldest Protestant organization in North America, with continuous service since 1628. But that's not its claim to fame. Norman Vincent Peale is. Peale was the pastor of Marble Collegiate from 1932 until 1984 and one of the most influential religious figures of the twentieth century. The author of forty-six books, including the all-time inspirational bestseller *The Power of Positive Thinking,* he was the first of the pastorpreneurs. With Marble Church as a base, the appropriately named Peale launched far-reaching innovations during the 1930s, 1940s, and 1950s. Star of radio and TV, he was one of the first to preach the gospel of adaptation. In many ways Peale was a harbinger of a more aggressive kind of God merchant, the megachurch maestro.

For better *and* for worse. When you get church growth centering around a charismatic figure (and anyone who saw Peale's broadcasts knows how good he was), you can predict what will inevitably happen. He can't be replicated. He's irreplaceable. And with the pastorpreneur's death comes the gradual ebbing of what has gathered, namely, an audience more compelled by personal dynamism than by doctrinal substance. (Many megas are about to discover this.)

So what did Marble Collegiate do after Norman Vincent Peale's retirement? Since the church had found its growth spurt at the edge of the then-nascent Christian entertainment industry, it hired an ad agency to help it find new members—brand switchers—and at the same time keep its regulars in place. The story is best told by the adman it hired, John Follis of the Follis ad agency. Here he is telling his compatriots on Madison Avenue of his exploits in *Adweek* (January 8, 2001):

> Well, listen to this. Three years ago, I hooked up with a client you wouldn't expect to see on an agency roster: a church. Most houses of worship don't offer "back-to-church specials" or package deals to heaven.
>
> The Marble Collegiate Church, however, is not your typical church. Far from the judgmental dogma often associated with Christianity, Marble Church is a cool place with a variety of relevant groups and programs. The $8 buffet brunch ain't bad, either.
>
> To the uninitiated, it may seem strange to market a church like a box of Kellogg's Frosted Mini-Wheats. Well, obviously, you don't market a church like a box of Frosted Mini-Wheats.
>
> How then?
>
> By selling spiritually. More specifically, by selling God. Selling God—what a concept. (I thought I'd seen it all after working on infant anal thermometers.) Even with all the product attributes, God is still a tough sell. I've had people tell me they "just love the campaign," and when I ask if they've visited Marble, they reply, "Oh, no! I don't go to church."
>
> I can totally understand that attitude, since I felt the same way before Marble. It's also why it's critical that the church have a kick-ass website. For those turned off by church, www.marblechurch.org is a much more palatable option.
>
> And three years after the initial effort, I'm happy to report the campaign is working.
>
> Despite the tough sell and tiny budget, membership is up more than 30 percent, traffic to the website has tripled, and overall awareness is remarkably high. I use this case to suggest that whether it's a church, a temple, or a box of Pop-Tarts, it does make a difference when you believe in what you're selling.

And so what did Follis create for a campaign? In his terms, "a highly creative guerrilla marketing campaign." Ads appeared in Long Island publications like *Hamptons* magazine, *Dan's Papers* on Long Island, and the *Fire Island Tide,* as well as in city venues like *New York* magazine, *Time Out New York,* and *The Village Voice.* Marble Collegiate's message has been put on postcards in trendy bistros, on mobile billboards driven around Manhattan, and on boarded-up building sites. But the corker was an airplane banner that caught the eyes of sunbathers from Jones Beach to the Hamptons one Labor Day weekend. Instead of hawking suntan lotion or happy-hour drinks, the sign read: "Make a Friend in a Very High Place. marblechurch.org." You can see the campaign at www.follis inc.com/service1.htm.

The church attained adman's heaven with free publicity in the *New York Times, USA Today, Time,* New York *Daily News,* and *Adweek,* and then sanctification by appearing in a college textbook, *Principles of Marketing* (Prentice Hall, 2004) as a case of effective marketing on a limited budget. A follow-up study indicated that more people had heard about Marble from the ad campaign than from all its TV and radio broadcasts combined. What makes this fact particularly impressive is that these TV and radio church broadcasts ran weekly for forty years, while the in-your-face ad campaign from Follis averaged less than three out of twelve months for just four years.

Such seeming success was soon imitated because plagiarism is, after all, the highest form of advertising. So the Church of the Heavenly Rest a majestic Episcopal house of worship at Fifth Avenue and 90th Street in New York City began using similarly amusing ads, including two campaigns a year geared to subway poster display. A typical message: "Sex Doesn't Mean a Thing." In smaller type, it continues: "Neither does race, age, economic status, political affiliation. Or whether you believe in God. If you need help, you won't be turned down. You've got to start somewhere. Start now."

But here's the problem: although getting your name out and saying something witty will increase attention in the short run and perhaps even goose-up consumption for a few Sundays, in the long-term the future for old-time denomination-based churches isn't very rosy. As the old quip says, the only thing that great advertising does for a mediocre brand is let it go out of business quicker by spending more money.

The Revival of Revival Marketing: Franklin Graham

To have the clout to launch a campaign like Marble Collegiate, you need a large customer base and targeted media. That's why advertising in the Hamptons for a Manhattan church makes sense. But what if you're just a small-time, small-town operation with a small pocketbook and a big geographical area? Somehow you have to make your service unique and compelling.

Back in the eighteenth century, the Methodists found out how to do it. In 1738, quite by accident, George Whitefield, a colleague of Charles and John Wesley, stepped into the pulpit in Bermondsey, England. Whitefield was, to say the least, an enthusiastic performer. He was the Elvis Presley of his time, preaching the Word and gyrating the rapture. A huge audience gathered outside to see the show. Although it was against the law to preach in the open air (except for executions, where the sermon was more of a last rite), Whitefield took his congregation to the countryside, thereby starting a kind of preaching called, appropriately enough, "open air."

Open-air churching exploded in the United States. Between 1738 and 1770 Whitefield made seven visits where he showed his *plein air* style, helping bring about what is called the First Great Awakening. He rocked. From a marketing point of view, this was a radical new innovation in supply. Whitefield's performance was such a revolutionary turn that it ushered in the great success of Methodism in America. This church owned exuberance.

The marketing principle of revival is simple. Any minister gets drab after a while. It's not easy stimulating a congregation when they've heard pretty much everything you have to say many times over. Having a Whitefield come to town to perk things up, to remind people of their sins and to "streak their faces with tears" is category advertising, yes, but as long as it increases the category in a controlled market, the individual churches are advantaged. In places where Coke advertises a lot, Pepsi sales also increase.

The revival impulse is deep in American consciousness. After all, what is more important than the belief that we can start over, do it again, be reborn? What the frontier is to geographical yearning, the revival is to religious. In the twentieth century, this marketing tool was spirited away from the itinerant Methodist in the field to the charismatic entertainer under the big top. The modern version of this religious speculator hails from the 1920s media ministries of former professional baseball player Billy Sunday and the radio songbird Aimee Semple McPherson. By the midcentury it was reformatted in the incredible career of Billy Graham, who made his movie star looks fit effortlessly on the TV screen.

Of course, it's no longer called a revival. Now it's *outreach*, but the inner workings and techniques are the same. A few years ago Franklin Graham brought his *crusade* (and, again, that's what he called it) to the campus of the University of Florida. Franklin is the spitting image of his father, Billy, and his show is a direct knockoff. When you see film of Billy's clockwork operation, you know that Franklin did too. The three-day revival was called "Festival 2002," and if you observe the tick-tock in slow motion, you can see humans yearning for rapture and the marketing machinery that is supplying it.

The routines of the Graham Festival have been repeated so often that you can set your clock by them. A month before, the advertising starts. A week before, the banners go up. On the day of the show, in come the busses. Essentially, the bus trip in from the hinterlands helps isolate and excite the crowd before they even come through the doors. The crowd revs things up. I stood in the parking lot as the busses emptied the believers. I felt just like you feel before a big football game.

The bigger the crowd the better, but the crowd has to be self-selected. This out-of-body sensation of welcoming the Holy Ghost depends on a bandwagon effect and as such depends on keeping dissension at a minimum. There were gatekeepers at the door carefully screening detractors. They spent most of their time turning back rowdy university students. To get the altar-call experience working, you must see your seatmates moving forward toward exultation, and you must not see any turning back. And although it doesn't hurt to have pickets outside to generate the sense of them against us, inside it's all us against them.

The show is worth studying if only because so many of its routines have been borrowed by the modern megachurch. In other words, ditch the doctrine, cue the percussion, turn up the volume, and run the video. We start with much music and witnessing. It goes on and on. While the entire event lasts about three hours, the actual sermon is over in what seems a finger snap. Thanks to television and the rock concert, everything is blown up to gargantuan size with sound amplifiers and massive JumboTron screens.

After almost two hours of praise and worship music, Franklin Graham appears. He knows he looks just like his dad. He is wearing an extraordinary outfit. On his head is a baseball cap with a red Ralph Lauren polo-pony logo. His shirt is blue denim, and over his heart is another bright red Ralph Lauren polo pony. Nowhere in the auditorium is there any imagery of religious affiliation: no crosses, no robes, no bells, no soaring imagery. In fact, the outreach is held in the University of Florida basketball arena, complete with the commercial logos of Gatorade and Nike hanging down from the ceiling.

Mr. Graham is not shy about commenting on his choice of sartorial affiliation. Yes, he proudly says, that's Ralph Lauren. And tomorrow, he promises, he'll be wearing the logos of the Fighting Gators. From time to time the television camera focuses on his baseball hat and his shirt, as if to say that there is something valuable, observable here. I have thought long about why Mr. Graham foregrounded the polo pony. Why both the hat and the shirt? His audience of mostly lower-middle-class country folk (about twice as many white as black) are not consumers of such upper-tier brands. They are more Wal-Mart, Sears, and JCPenney than Hilfiger, Gucci, and Lauren.

In fact, the audience is a hodgepodge of low-church Protestant denominations that have banded together to support the revival. They don't know one another, and they don't share the same denominations. During the week they compete for followers, but not now. The only things they have in common is football at the University of Florida and shopping at the mall. But they share the same yearnings. They are here to experience something, to become rapturous, to sense community, and then go home refreshed. They know the sensation they want, and they know Mr. Graham will provide it. They are wired, amped, and good to go.

While I could not recognize the various denominations of Christianity around me (although the logoed busses were all over the parking lot), and while Mr. Graham made it clear that God also would not recognize various denominations, it was clear that God did not care for non-Christians. "Muhammad didn't die for your sins," he says to enthusiastic applause. "Muhammad didn't die for your sins. Only one died for your sins, and that's the Lord Jesus Christ, son of the Living God." Mr. Graham is marketing the category.

So, while we didn't need to know competing denominations to find the Way, we all did recognize the commercial badge of arrival: the polo-pony brand. All in the audience had seen this at the mall as surely as they had seen the Nike swoosh on the uniforms of the football team and the visors of the coaches. Want to know what salvation feels like? Well, it feels like being able to afford this, which is what Mr. Graham was saying—the spiritualization of brands, the epiphany of deluxe.

I don't mean to have those little ponies drag too much weight, but it was so totally out of place to have the minister pimping a product; and yet the whole show had been so carefully choreographed that I knew it was not spontaneous. What characterizes the modern world of marketing is such syncretism, the layering of similar experiences, cobranding, product placement. Since there was no mention of denominations during the festival, the links are forged with commercial brands. If religion is a collectively produced commodity, so is shopping. Is there anything more eerie than being at an empty store? You need other believers. Material consumption is less restrictive than religious choice but no less articulate. Franklin can't tout a specific church, but he can invoke a common experience.

The show is very polished. To understand how polished, watch old film of Billy Graham doing the same gig. The sequences of Franklin's show are really Billy's. Same music, same sermon, same crowd choreography. The key is to get the sense of "don't be left behind." In advertising history, this approach was pioneered by P. T. Barnum and his

"I am coming!" says Barnum, playing on the apocalypse.

"Don't miss it; you'll never see it again" posters announcing the circus coming through town. Sometimes he even foregrounded himself as the main attraction.

In religious history, the technique, formally called "dragging the net," was perfected by Charles Grandison Finney (another Presbyterian) in the late-nineteenth-century revivals in upstate New York. A part of the crowd has been preselected to sit up front because they are ready to experience the conversion long before they come to the show. As they slowly inch forward, the pitch starts. Franklin intones, "Now come forward. The busses will wait for you to be saved. Your family will wait for you to be saved. Your God will wait." Then more music. Again the call comes forth. Be saved. Wait. Same refrain lines. More music.

This movement continues until it's hard to resist. It's very powerful not just because it's nifty to experience rapture, but because if there is one thing we all learn on the playground of youth, it's how awful it is to be left behind. We are herd animals, and watching the pack head out, leaving us in the lurch, is discomforting. The bestselling books, television shows, and movies are from a series called Left Behind for a reason. Look at any children's folktale: abandonment is a powerful theme.

The Messrs. Graham Show is compelling. And strangely *fun*. Marketing salvation may involve eternal damnation for the stayaways (and Muslims), but it provides an almost partylike atmosphere for the come-forwards. Step up to the register. Why shouldn't church business be like shopping? The tent revivals of the earlier awakenings sold cider and supplied musical entertainment along with salvation. At Methodist camps in the 1850s, young people roller-skated to a waltz version of "Nearer My God to Thee." In the 1980s two televangelists, Jim and Tammy Bakker, hawked a gospel of materialistic goods and rapture at the mall. For a short while, before the banks came a-foreclosing, they even had a gated theme park-cum-mall called Heritage USA near Charlotte, North Carolina, where you could shop in divine peace.

What the Grahams are doing is hardly new. Let mainline

churches arch an eyebrow, but if the revivalists find an audience with the hootenanny, some downtown church, currently losing parishioners, will sign up the next time the show comes to town. As R. Laurence Moore says, only slightly tongue in cheek, in *Selling God: American Religion in the Marketplace of Culture,* American churches invented fun, serious competitive fun. The minute you move forward, however, the fun is briefly interrupted. A member of the staff quietly takes your name and passes that name on to one of the sponsoring churches. Next week, your phone rings.

When Denominations Advertise

Anyone wishing to understand how commercialism works in modern life finds a provocative example in competitive denominational religion. For here we have essentially interchangeable suppliers (Protestant churches) of a perfect product (does everything, available 24-7, comes with a lifetime warranty) about which the only differences are in the narratives (brands). Thanks to what we know about narrative, we might guess that the supplier of the best story should, over time, be able to gain market share or, in the bafflegab of admen, "mindshare." But how to tell that story—that's the problem.

Historically, that story has been told in architecture, in music, in social preferment, in the service, and generally in all the accoutrements of what we recognize as "going to church." But now we have a new story-telling language: commercial advertising. What happens when this kind of speech for hire gets layered over denominational competition? What happens when churches become self-conscious brands buying time to hawk their goods in new plasmas like billboards, television screens, and on the radio? What happens when they start to *buy* attention in order to *sell* sensation?

As we have seen, with the exception of the revival, there is little reward in advertising the category. Why pay your dollar to boost somebody else's church? By the same token, there is little future in advertising the individual church unless it is a megachurch or uniquely sited like Marble Collegiate, simply because the CPM (cost per thousand impressions) is usually so expensive.

So what do you do if you are part of a denomination that has been spending the last forty years wandering in the wilderness of empty pews? You might well open your dog-eared copy of the Rev. Charles Stelzle's *Principles of Successful Church Advertising* and give it a try. And indeed that is what is happening. Hundreds of millions of dollars, perhaps billions before it's over, are pouring into the mainstream media, as denominations are simultaneously figuring out the puzzle in exactly the same way at the same time. This is the real leap of modern faith. The denominations have not paid attention to history, however. The Presbyterians were successful in the Progressive movement because they were almost the only ones flooding the commercial media. When everyone advertises, and advertises in a similar way, chances are it becomes a zero-sum game.

Who knows if the often-predicted demise of denominations is at hand? But we do know this: The very institutions that held commercialism in disdain are lining up to embrace it. Churchmen are skulking out from under the steeples and making a beeline over to the canyons of Madison Avenue. If you don't think the mainline churches are fully conscious about getting people in, if you think they are oblivious to marketing concerns, all you have to do is check the websites and calculate the amount of national advertising most of the mainline churches are now producing.

So let's look at how the mainlines are doing what they once did so well: sell their product. In the pages that follow, I'll glance at how the major denominations are spending millions of parishioner dollars and are becoming the salvation, at least, of their ad agencies. Then in the next chapter, I'll focus on one campaign in depth: the Methodist Church's "Igniting Ministry" campaign. (Meanwhile, with almost no advertising, the fundamentalists and the megas are still gobbling market share.)

- The Presbyterian Church (USA), which was such an aggressive force in the early twentieth century, has been running "Here and Now," a campaign it hopes will appeal to younger and more racially diverse groups. Before that, it ran "Stop In and Find Out." Few folks did. A helpful PR person from the organization told me that the most explosive ad in this campaign was an extended close-up of a woman grunting through childbirth. Many people complained. They are currently rethinking their spots. From a marketing standpoint, the Presbyterian Church has become an Oldsmobile; no matter what you say, it's still your father's church.

• The United Church of Christ had a blessed event in Adland. You may have seen the ad. It ran for a while in 2005, usually as a news story, not as a commercial spot.

> As church bells chime in the background, a burly bouncer works the velvet ropes at the church entrance. "No, step aside, please," he tells two men who—look carefully! as the camera moves in for a tight shot—are holding hands. They are turned away from worship. "I don't think so," the thug says to a young black girl, blocking her entrance. A Hispanic man and a person in a wheelchair are also denied entry.
>
> Fade to black. "Jesus didn't turn away people. Neither do we," intones a godly narrator in the name of the United Church of Christ. "No matter who you are, or where you are on life's journey, you are welcome here."

All hell broke loose in the secular land of network standards when this thirty-second spot was previewed. Two major networks declined to run it, deeming it "too controversial," presumably because it championed one side of the public debate on gay relationships. Both CBS and NBC cited longstanding policies against accepting what is known as advocacy or issue advertising.

The panjandrums of the United Church of Christ, its membership in free fall, expressed shock and dismay. Like the Claude Rains character in *Casablanca,* they were shocked, shocked, at how they were being treated. What about our theme of inclusiveness, they moaned to the news cameras, repeating "we're open and affirming" as many times as possible. What about our freedoms, our ability to speak?

In private, the UCC brass—and its ad agency—was thrilled by what had happened, for this ad took it straight to commercial Valhalla. Like the famous "Daisy" ad about Barry Goldwater from the Lyndon Johnson campaign during the 1964 presidential race (which invoked nuclear destruction if you voted for Barry) or Apple's 1984 Super Bowl ad (in which only zombies use IBM), "The Bouncer" got hours of play and tons of free press.

The television executives accused the UCC of seeking publicity by submitting an ad that was likely to be rejected so that the group could accuse the networks of censorship and get its message out as a news story. They pointed out that another UCC ad, featuring many of the same actors, had already been accepted for broadcast by both CBS and NBC, as well as the other networks.

True to the Madison Avenue code of conduct, the United Church of Christ said that the rejection of the bouncer ad caught it totally off guard. The UCC went on to run two radio spots that played off its contrived plight. One parodied a Christmas carol with lines like "O come, some of ye faithful, powerful and privileged," and then announced that "God invites all the faithful. So do we—the United Church of Christ." The other satirizes high-fashion worshipers, and then proclaims: "God doesn't care what you wear to church. Neither do we."

Did their gate increase? Well, not much, but the ad certainly built the brand. Thanks to the cauterizing power of homosexuality in American religious culture, the UCC is coming to own a share of the consumer mind—"front of mind"—as it is called in adspeak. They are owning an identification that other churches claim: they really are open and affirming, at least in their advertising. But to do it the UCC grabbed hold of the third rail of American religion and didn't let go. And this was done without making any verbal or printed mention of homosexuality, just a three-second close-up of hands holding and the predictable behavior of the news outlets.

"The Bouncer" came out of a huge four-year, $30 million–plus national campaign, the first in the United Church's forty-eight-year history, called humbly, "God Is Still Speaking." A problem is that UCC is a blended product, formed from the 1957 merger of the Congregational and Christian churches with the Evangelical and Reformed Church, so there is a real brand personality problem. The church is not as edgy in real life as its ads imply.

- The Boston-based Unitarian Universalist Church is edgy in real life, not just in advertising, and that's why it's doing well. The UUs, as they are called in the trade, are a religious community held together not by a creed but by a common set of politically correct values. That's a great brand personality, and the church has made the most of it. Small and proud—only about 175,000 members—it can say, at least for a while, that we're here if you need us, but we're not going after you. They have run some ads (often paid for in UU fashion by individual members), and the response has been to gather about a hundred new members. They now even have a campaign name, "Uncommon Denomination," so they are just like their brethren—at least in this respect.

- The Mormons and the Lutherans have similar marketing techniques, and they have been at it for a while. The Mormons are doing OK; the Lutherans not. To some degree, this is a function of spending and market placement. The largest single church advertiser in the 1990s was the Church of Jesus Christ of Latter-day Saints (i.e., the Mormons). For years they have been running boring and self-satisfied spots in which they attempt to own the idea of family. My favorite: a teacher is shown at home in an argument with her husband. We see her next at school, chastising a student in the hall for not doing a makeup assignment on the blackboard. The student tells her that someone else got to the blackboard first. Who? Inside we see the teacher's husband, writing "I'm sorry" one hundred times on the board. Well, almost humorless.

- Meanwhile the Lutherans (a church as complex as they come, in large part because of competing synods) continue to run *Lutheran Hour Ministries* from the communications arm of the Lutheran Church—Missouri Synod. These family-centric shows are pretty heavy and pious. The various synods are now pooling a three-year $98.7 million evangelism campaign in multiple media on topics such as parenthood, divorce, depression, and forgiveness. Supposedly there's talk that they are going to revamp the dour image and target the audience everyone else is going after—young adults—with their "Ablaze!" campaign.

• The Baptists, especially in the South, are by their nature and design independent entities held together only by the loosest of ties. To some degree, they have resisted formal campaigns, concentrating instead on the most effective advertising: word of mouth. And they have been successful, in part, because what they own is so provocative. *My way or the highway.* From a marketing point of view, what can match this: The Bible is inerrant, only we know how to read it; only one God, ours; salvation is available, with us; the Second Coming is at hand, we're your best choice.

Why should the Baptists advertise? One of the most important motifs in the so-called low-Protestant and even Pentecostal ranks is "We're growing," and the implication, "If we weren't right, would we be doing so well?" Attend a Baptist service (again, especially in the South), and you will usually see in the church bulletin the number of new members, and you will hear how the buses and missionary work are bringing in more and more members. You will also often hear the pastor extol the prospect that this growth is God's will. Would Wal-Mart be expanding if it wasn't selling good stuff?

But what happens when growth slows? Conversion has limits. So the sixteen million–member Southern Baptist Convention has begun a new campaign much larger than anything it has previously run. They are clearly targeting the niche du jour—youngsters—with the "Here's Hope" campaign, consisting of four different advertising spots. Typical is one in which a tough teenager wearing baggy clothes raps about the meaninglessness of life, calling it "hopeless, perpetual midnight." The shots are tight and fast, the music pulsing. The boy blows out a match. The screen goes dark. A sonorous voice intones, "There is a light."

True to the historical independence of the Baptist convention, individual churches, not the denomination, have to foot the cost of running these spots. For $1,200, any member church gets exclusive rights to show one of the four spots on local cable—as well as two radio ads and two print ads—for a finite term. So far, only a handful of churches have purchased the ads. Why should they? If you'll notice in all other campaigns, the denomination picks up most of the tab while the local church is along for the ride. If such advertising really worked, if it really upped the traffic, the individual churches would bite. The Baptist churches are savvy.

- A generation ago the Episcopal Church was at the top of the Protestant pyramid. It was the luxury brand. Its product was social status; the currency offered was cultural capital. Go to the top of banking, law, politics, or education, and Episcopalians would be there all decked out in gray flannel. In 1950 *Fortune* magazine reported that about one-third of CEOs were staunch Episcopalians.

  And the church as institution reflected the business model. It was organized from the top down, a vestige of the old Anglican system (which in turn was a mimic of the Catholic), based on the church-state unity featured in the concept of the divine right of kings. The head of the Anglican Church is the king or queen, although the archbishop of Canterbury is the CEO. So too in this country the bishops of the various geographical entities, under a presiding bishop, were responsible for the brand. They ran the show and, to a considerable extent, the country as well. More presidents of the U.S. in the twentieth century have been Episcopalians than any other denomination.

  At the end of the twentieth century, the Episcopal brand suddenly lost it. Although it's tempting to say that this is because of internecine squabbles over too much self-righteous liberalism or too much flaunted acceptance of homosexuality, the real problem is in the brand promise. What the church promised, it could no longer deliver: prestige, place, power. Meritocracy was the real enemy of Episcopal promise. Just one example: up until the 1960s, the church controlled an elaborate system of social positioning via education, and the promise of access to the upper echelons of political, legal, educational, as well as corporate life. Episcopalians were the gatekeepers at such prep schools as St. Paul's, Groton, and Middlesex. Why did they lose the gate? Not by politics or sex, but by talent. Hard to believe, perhaps, but the SAT did them in, as Nicholas Lemann argues in *The Big Test: The Secret History of the American Meritocracy*. The minute getting into elite universities depended on doing well on two hours of test taking, not on having two hundred proper ancestors, the game changed.

Although formal membership has always been small—from a peak of 3.6 million in the late 1960s to less than 2 million today—Episcopal strength was never in numbers but in connections. Like the Jews, with whom they share many similarities (small numbers, old traditions, and understood social codes of behavior), they could protect the brand best by concentrating it. But it worked only if they could deliver predicable access to this world rather than safe access to the next one.

Can they market their way out of this mess? The Episcopal Church of America (ECUSA) has established an ad collaborative from which individual dioceses can rent television and print campaigns, just like the Baptists. One question is which of the many splinter groups are going to use the denominational campaign. No matter: the decline of this denomination—pro-gay ordination or anti-gay ordination—is unstoppable. They can't deliver the goods. So the red-cross-on-the-shield decal on the rear window of the Jaguar subtly asserting "I am an Episcopalian (sorry about you)" surrounded by the decals of "St. Grottelsex" and Ivy League schools is the gasping of a brand in last rites.

While it would be foolish to count out the mainline denominations—remember, they have been in this slough before—commercial advertising has not proved effective in reversing the flow. Yet as ad agencies love to say when campaigns don't work as advertised, the sucking sound would be even louder without advertising. And it's true that advertising often makes current customers feel better about the product even if it doesn't generate new sales. Numerous studies have shown that the people who pay the most attention to specific ads are the people currently buying the product. But one should also remember the quip that advertising is often like pissing in a dark suit: it feels good, at least for a while, but soon. . . .

CHAPTER SIX

The United Methodist Example

Of all the mainline denominations, the most interesting to study is the United Methodist Church. Here's why. This church used to be smokin'! A few generations ago its religiosity burned over a huge section of New England. At the end of the nineteenth century, it was on fire with enthusiasm, with innovation, with camp meetings and music and preach-offs, and an in-your-faceness that the evangelicals and megachurches have commandeered today. The Methodists took it to the streets and were fierce and confrontational. Now they are like a weary bulldog nestled in front of the fire, gumming an old bone.

The Methodists were nowhere in 1776, they were everywhere in 1876, they were receding in 1976, and now they are slowly returning to nowhere. The United Methodist Church today is the result of the 1968 conjoining of the Methodist Church and the Evangelical United Brethren Church. As Rodney Stark and Roger Finke have observed in numerous books, the act of denominational mergers almost always presages a lack of zeal passed off in the name of economic efficiencies and ecumenical peacemaking. When you hear a denomination talk about becoming open and affirming, grab your coat.

Here's the result of their openness: in 1970 the UMC reported 10.7 million members in the U.S. It reported 8.3 million in the year 2000, a membership loss of about 77,000 per year. The drain continues. The Methodists are now the third largest Christian denomination and the second largest Protestant denomination, about to drop down another notch. In the U.S. at least, they had better rekindle the fire, and quick. Just their pension responsibilities and overhead are crushing.

As is typical of other franchises in distress, the UMC plans to advertise its way back to an increased market share. If ever there was a denomination set to run a national campaign, this is it. The Methodists are America's most widespread denomination, with at least one congregation in 2,997 of the nation's 3,142 counties. They have a huge campaign ready to spark the flame. Appropriately, it's called "Igniting Ministry" and results from a momentous decision in the 1980s to get back into the streets.

Logo of the United Methodist Church. (SOURCE: IGNIT-
ING MINISTRY CAMPAIGN VIEWBOOK, VERSION 1.2.)

As account planners are fond of saying, before you spread the Word, you need a wordmark. A wordmark is essentially a logo, but it's more than a trademarked image. It's a condensation of the product's values. Think the stylized signatures of Coke, FedEx, Ford, Disney, Nike, Kodak.

Here the Methodists have done well. On one hand, they have gone back to their history with the flame, the image of a belief on fire. On the other, they have used the shape of the cross. You now see this red-flame logo in front of every church. When the image appears in print, the "Open hearts. Open minds. Open doors." triplet follows, as well as the emphasis on people—not just people like you and the people of the church, but the people whose pictures are often part of the image. If you look carefully at these pictures, you'll see that they are the prospective brand switchers, the seekers, the people not currently in this church (not a seventy-year-old granny in the group). They are the people this church desperately needs if it is to survive.

After test-marketing the general concept, the UMC plunked down $18 million, followed by $25 million to launch the campaign. While this seems like a lot of money, the cost of buying media is huge. This is about what Coke Worldwide spends every two weeks. But that's not why it's important to students of marketing. What's important are the data the church is collecting along the way. Although these data are proprietary (I've asked), you can extrapolate a bit about how the campaign is working by watching what UMC does.

One of the most difficult parts of advertising to understand is this: does it really do anything other than, as they used to say, make the boss's wife happy? If it doesn't move the needle of sales, why do for-profit companies do it? The answer often has to do with the tax code. Money spent on advertising is a cost of doing business. Advertising is a deduction. Would you rather advertise or pay taxes?

That's one reason why nonprofits generally don't advertise. There's really no tax advantage. So when they do start spending money, you know there is a bit of desperation; a really tight market.

For instance, when you see hospitals or museums advertise, you know they're oversupplied with, you guessed it, too many items interchangeable with what other hospitals and museums offer. When there are too many CAT scanners in the neighborhood or too many Monets, you'll start seeing the ads: "Come visit us. We *really* care."

In addition, one of the hoariest questions in marketing is this: if advertising is effective, why is it the first expense to be cut when things go sour? In other words, if advertising worked as advertised, spending on advertising should increase during recessions. But just the opposite happens. The first person shown the door when markets contract is the ad guy. So what gives?

The Methodists provide some of the answers. Here's what they did. For $89.95, each participating local Methodist church got a "media planner," which included three CDs and two VHS tapes with previews of Igniting Ministry advertisements, as well as door hangers and direct-mail graphics, among other materials. The ads were easily customized for specific areas and regions. In fact, the United Methodist Church in Nashville would customize TV spots in-house, at no charge to the local congregation. Plus, if an individual church decided to cooperate, the main office paid the media bills, and it had an agency to titrate direct mail, newspaper, billboard, cable, radio, and bus-stop ads.

Better yet, the church headquarters, the ad agency (Buntin Group), and the testing firm (Prince Market Research) were all located in the same town (Nashville), so they could review the "overnights" together. And they could change ads at a moment's notice, as they did after 9/11, when they concentrated the entire campaign on a thirty-second spot featuring an empty bench in front of a waterfall and a godly voiceover asking viewers to join in prayer for the victims. (Plus, of course, they bought this airtime at a favorable rate, as commercial advertisers always flee during crisis times.)

But there was a hitch. The individual ministers were asked to track the flow after local saturation bursts of marketing. Did more people attend? Did they come the next week? How long did they stay? And the UMC hired a testing firm to do phone surveys to see whether the church's brand awareness had increased irrespective of attendance, and whether the advertising made the image of the Methodist denomination more favorable to viewers. In other words, did more people attend and did more people think positively about the product after the onslaught of ads? This kind of information is what all suppliers of fast-moving consumer goods (FMCGs) want.

What the UMC found from such specific targeting was that it could indeed "move the needle," at least for short periods. In a nationwide sample of 149 churches, it found it could boost first-time attendance by 14 percent and overall worship attendance by 6 percent. In some places, first-time attendance jumped an amazing 19 percent. They could, by shaking the stick, move the stay-at-homes back to church, but they still had real trouble getting newcomers. Brand switchers, they found, rely on word of mouth, are motivated by having someone actually come talk to them. What the UMC found was that the Pentecostals and Jehovah's Witnesses do it right. Knock, knock, anybody home? To paraphrase the old Smith Barney ad, the fundamentalists make Christians the old-fashioned way: they earn them.

Worse still, the Methodists found how quickly attendance trickles off as regression to the mean takes over. How much loss is yet unknown, because the campaign is still going strong, but "Igniting Ministry" does prove one of the tenets of advertising. Anheuser-Busch sells more beer on the Monday after Super Bowl Sunday. It's called the Super Bowl Monday Effect. But by Tuesday it's same-old, same-old. However, that's no reason to pull a campaign.

But the campaign has another positive effect. Brands work in two directions. The direction we usually pay attention to is the movement out into the market. We hear or see the ad and think perhaps about consuming the product. But ads also work in the other direction: back to the group already consuming the product. For instance, it's been shown that people who read car ads for specific models have just bought that model. In this case, the ads push you toward the buy hole; it comforts you after you've fallen through. It tamps down the postdecision dissonance that comes with making a major purchase.

So when nonprofits like universities, museums, or hospitals advertise, it is often to comfort their employees and current patrons. It's unclear how reassured current Methodists are by a campaign that they are paying for, or how comforted the worn-out ministry is by the responsibility to be "igniting," but the fact that the denomination continues to run the ads suggests that the congregants and ministers are not despondent. The denomination's legislative body voted in 2004 to extend the campaign another four years after research showed that more than 7 in 10 United Methodist pastors backed the advertising efforts. Two-thirds of the pastors said the principles of the "Igniting" campaign had helped to make their congregations more open and inviting to unchurched persons. But remember, they're only out of pocket $89.95.

There's another irony worth contemplating. We live in a world in which we often associate the value of a product with the fact that it advertises. That's why you see those little labels "As Seen on TV" in print and video ads, as if to say that if the product was no good, the producer would not be advertising it. In addition, once a company sees other companies in the same cohort buying advertising, the tendency is to think, "It must be working, or they wouldn't be doing it. I'd better buy some too." Maybe just the fact of advertising is comforting.

The Television Ads

When you look at the individual ads, however, you might well wonder what the Methodists are up to. The Buntin Group has created more than a dozen different TV advertisements that are grouped into what they call "Expressions." An Expression is ad mumbo jumbo that supposedly conveys the "different attributes of the United Methodist Church." Here are some of these Expressions: life to us is a journey, where do we look for information?, we like diversity, we do good works, love letters are nice, breaking news (a response to actual events, most probably disasters), and the old standby—rain. You read that right: just melancholy rain. This church has more rainy-day ads than anyone since Morton salt.

Methodists understand the melancholy meaning of rain. (SOURCE: IGNIT-
ING MINISTRY CAMPAIGN VIEWBOOK, VERSION 1.2.)

Each of the ads ends with the tag "Open hearts. Open minds. Open doors. The People of the United Methodist Church." I realize that every institution now thinks it needs a slogan even if it is totally vapid, but this one seems especially perplexing, at least to the one group currently roiling the ecclesiastical waters, namely, gays. The United Methodist Church has repeatedly voted to condemn homosexuality and has upheld a ban on the ordination of openly gay people. So perhaps the tag should end with ". . . Some of the people of the Methodist Church."

You can access the individual ads at www.mediawarehouse.ignit ingministry.org and see for yourself. A personal note: I have spent the last twenty years interested in advertising. I write books on the subject, teach courses on the subject, and consult with agencies and their clients. However, I still have no idea how a specific ad will "pull." I can tell whether I like the ad, how creative it seems to be, what its history is, and which other ads are similar. That said, I'm not impressed with these UMC ads. Maybe as an apatheist, I'm not supposed to be. But they seem so vanilla, so uninspiring, so almost dreary. In my advertising class, I show them to my students (who are the prime audience), and many of them have the same problems. They seem preaching to the choir. Well, maybe that's enough.

The two ads that have received the most media attention are

"The Gift" and "The Journey." In "The Gift" we see an attractive woman with a fancy package, all gift wrapped with a bow, leaving it anonymously for various poor people. Then, when she comes home, *voilà,* we see the same box, all gift wrapped, on her doorstep. What goes around comes around seems to be the message. Do good so you can get paid back? Is that the Christian way? Or is it Do good so you can be good?

The cheat sheet from the ad agency explains for those confused:

> We all receive gifts from God. We are called to share those gifts with others, and as we give, we also receive. What we get in return may not be tangible—or immediate. It may be as simple as the good feeling of helping others and the sense of satisfaction we get from responding to the call of God. Ultimately, we receive a giving, generous spirit and the eternal reward of knowing that by using our gifts for good, we have honored God and proclaimed our faith. "The Gift" television message offers the United Methodist Church as a spiritual community where the many forms of God's gifts are shared in service to others. In so doing, we can sense God's joyful affirmation "Well done, good and faithful servant!" (Matthew 25:21, NIV).

But that's not exactly the message I think most people would get. Had she returned home and been smiled upon by a grateful recipient or, better yet, by someone who had gotten a box from someone else, I would have understood. But I couldn't get past the fact that the box is all in fancy wrap, complete with a look-at-me bow, which implies that it is the kind of dead-weight gift of Christmas, a gift not of the heart but of the pocketbook. And, of course, it's exactly the same gift she gets when she returns home.

A still more confusing ad is "The Journey." This one is downright spooky. It's filmed to look like a high schooler's takeoff on a sci-fi film, with lots of weird cuts and angles. Was it shot by someone doing an imitation of Steven Spielberg's *Close Encounters of the Third*

Kind? Here for thirty seconds we see people following directional arrows, finding a path up what seems to be a hill. One man reaches the hilltop by following a series of arrows on Post-it notes. A young woman follows a trail of pebbles, while basketball hoops show the way for a young player in a wheelchair. OK, different people, different paths, get it?

But I didn't. I thought the United Methodist path should be well marked and get me to the hilltop safely. This ad seems to say, follow your passion. "Find your path. Share the journey," intones the omniscient voiceover as the disparate group on the hilltop grows larger, and the tagline materializes on screen: "Open hearts. Open minds. Open doors." Again, the cheat sheet explains. Or does it?

> We are all on a spiritual journey that leads us toward God. As we travel, our paths bring us to others who impact our journey. "The Journey" television message offers the United Methodist Church as a spiritual home where everyone can find their path and share the journey. By coming together in community, we understand more fully the God who loves us—and the paths God has for us. Thus we share the journey both with those who can help guide us and with those who look to us for support along their journeys.

Problem was, I didn't see a lot of people helping out other people. I just saw a lot of people struggling to read different series of sign markers. The goal of branding is to say, yes, there are lots of paths, but this path—my product—is one you should take.

The Print Campaign

The print campaign is less gooey, less vapid, and more focused. In the newspaper we see the earnest face of a young person staring at us solemnly. This face is surrounded by a flamelike pattern of other seekers, some older. The cheat sheet for pastors says that "this

Expression invites anyone to attend, wherever they are on the journey toward finding a spiritual home." Perhaps a bit more honest would have been to say "anyone *young* to attend," because we see featured a young African-American male, a rancher (he's wearing a cowboy hat), a late-teenage female, an Asian-American female, a Hispanic female, a Native American male (perhaps a counterpart to the rancher), and a physically challenged female.

Here, for instance, is the teenage girl. Below her picture are her beliefs.

"I believe you can tell a person's morals by the way they play golf," says a teenage Methodist girl. (SOURCE: IGNITING MINISTRY CAMPAIGN VIEWBOOK, VERSION 1.2.)

This is pure treacle. It is almost content free and hence totally nonconfrontational. It's also quite sloppy. Are we to believe that one of her six prime beliefs is "I believe you can tell a person's morals by the way they play golf"? Had she said, "I believe you can tell a person's morals by what's loaded on their iPod," I might have gone for it, but for this howler, I'd fire the agency.

In the body text at the bottom, we are told, "We may not all believe exactly the same thing, but the people of the United Methodist Church believe in God and each other." But it would be impossible not to believe in what the selected rancher, Hispanic, African-American, Native American, et al., believe in, given such unimaginative and uninspiring beliefs. No one argues with Hallmark cards, which is how this agency has positioned the church. But nobody really believes in what these cards have to say. We buy them because we prefer their dehydrated sentimentality to the complexities of truth. After all, we say, it's just a gift card, cheaper than a present, and easier than saying it ourselves.

Should you doubt this calculated insincerity, consider these radio and television ads presented as literal notes from God. As the cheat sheet says, this approach works best with "those who have lost loved ones, are divorced, new to the area, or are just trying to adjust to their course in life." One might also add, or for "those who haven't OD'd on nostalgia." Because we read in the almost unbearable words from God in typescript on the right, God is your junior-high-school sweetheart. Were I not an apatheist, I would be screaming blasphemy.

One of the most interesting parts of the UMC "Igniting" campaign is what are called in the trade "ambush ads." An ambush ad pops up when you least expect it. In a way, pop-up ads on the internet are ambush ads, as are ads embedded in movies or slid into video games as product placement. Here are some ads made to look like classified ads from your newspaper. The editorial comment for the pastor opines, "We know that those seeking spiritual well-being tend to look in all the wrong places, including the classified section of your local newspaper." Although the ad agency considers them "spiritual landmines," this is a category of nonexplosive duds. These are novelties, not ads.

I have focused on the United Methodist franchise because in many ways it typifies the denominational suppliers and the problems of positioning. Watch all the commercials and ask yourself, "What makes this Methodist?" Where, to use the jargon, is the brand *essence*; the *brand soul?* There is nothing in this "Igniting Ministry" campaign that makes *Methodist* mean something special in the way, say, that FedEx = overnight, Mercedes = prestigious, Pepsi = youthfulness, Porsche = speed, Gerber = baby, Gucci = glitz, or Volvo = safe. These ads don't condense anything about this particular denomination, don't separate it from another supplier, don't make it unique or compelling. All they

Fire the agency: love letters with God. (SOURCE: IGNITING MINISTRY CAMPAIGN VIEWBOOK, VERSION 1.2.)

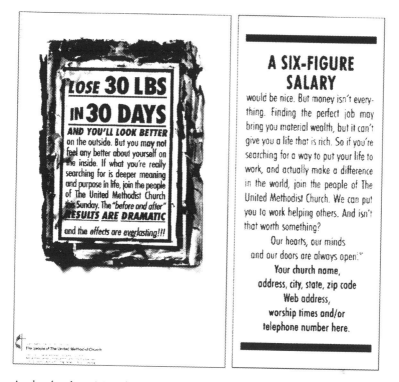

Ambush advertising from the United Methodist Church. (SOURCE: IGNITING MINISTRY CAMPAIGN VIEWBOOK, VERSION 1.2.)

seem to do is invoke the very cliches that have made the United Methodist Church anything but . . . igniting.

Left Behind: When Bad Things Happen to Good Denominations

So how have the ads worked? In 2004, while the campaign was in full swing, membership continued to drop just as it had in each of the thirty-six years since the denomination was formed through a merger. The latest total was 8.07 million, a loss of less than 1 percent from 2003 and a decrease of about 5.5 percent for the past decade. Despite the nationwide decline, however, tiny membership increases were posted by thirteen regional units in ten states. If the ads were run only in these venues, you could say they worked, but the campaign was nationwide.

By its very nature, advertising tries to get in your face. Once there, it tries to make a sale. To do this it has to promise something different from the competition. And that may be the problem for all denominations. You can have a nifty logo, a good slogan ("Open hearts. Open minds. Open doors."), and some good photographs of rain beating against the windowpane, but without some friction you can't generate a spark. You may be able to move the needle momentarily by blasting your name across the airwaves and through newsprint, but until your service, your product, makes people talk to one another about what they experienced, you will only be, for most people, a few lines on a marquee sign.

Alas, again in ad jargon, perception is reality. And nothing is worse than the perception of insincerity. I don't mean that the Methodists don't care deeply, but this campaign is so self-evidently an advertising campaign. The key to powerful marketing is that it not seem to be what it is; namely, a sell job. Often a failure to sell reflects a deeper problem, a loss of faith in a sellable message. Perhaps the "Igniting Ministry" campaign will prove that the company itself does not know what is special about its product.

CHAPTER SEVEN

The Church Impotent: What's Wrong with the Mainlines?

What I saw on Route 21 between the towns of Melrose and Keystone Heights in northern Florida was an almost perfect image of stagnant American Protestantism. There they were, side by side, offering services so similar that only an expert, if blindfolded, could tell which was which. It was like looking at the milk aisle in the supermarket—no product differentiation. Or worse, the water aisle.

Many of the churches were small but not particularly cozy congregations of about a hundred mostly white-haired members in rooms designed for three times the population. Everyone spread out, which made the gaps more pronounced. From where I sat in the back, furtively taking notes, it seemed as though I was looking across a half empty box of Q-tips. This was the world the Church Growth Movement forgot. Or perhaps this is where the Church Growth Movement is getting its membership.

Why were these denominations gasping for membership? Did the architecture provide a clue? Let the Catholics have their brick battleships, let the Jews have their single-story bunkers, these mainline Protestant denominations have markedly similar buildings: a little brick here, a little wood there, a little stucco, a few stained glass windows, an arch or two, three gradual steps up to the front door, grass out front, and the paved parking lot out back.

When you start seeing similar packages on a grocery store aisle, it often means the products are getting too undifferentiated to be branded properly. They are becoming generic. Lots of me-too products often means that some innovator is just about to transform the category. Think of Absolut vodka, Ben & Jerry's ice cream, Evian water, Starbucks, and the megachurch.

Many of these churches had the requisite marquee sign out front, thanks to Mel Stewart. But even there, where they could express distinction, they copycatted. Over a few months in north Florida I saw:

Don't give up—Moses was a basket case too

A Bible falling apart belongs to someone who isn't

A good place for the buck to stop is at the collection plate

The Easter Bunny didn't rise from the dead

Read the Bible. It will scare the Hell out of you

Free trip to heaven—Details inside!

Try Jesus. If you don't like him, the devil will always take you back

Give Satan an inch and he'll be a ruler

God's last name is not "damn"

The best things in life aren't things

No Lord = No Peace. Know Lord = Know Peace

Fight truth decay—study the Bible daily

Dusty Bibles lead to dirty lives

If you're headed in the wrong direction, God allows U-turns

Forbidden fruit creates many jams

Even here the suppliers were all reading from the same playbook of pithy sayings, literally. That they didn't attempt to localize their ads is a sign of a market in rigor mortis.

I often found myself feeling better for having gone to church, but when I looked around after church, I wondered whether others felt this. I saw hugging and handshaking, but when I went back the next week, the scene was almost exactly the same. After all, most of these congregants had been attending for quite a while, and the experience was neither new nor startling. It was for many of them not a chore but a way to set the clock.

As one who believes that most of what you need to know about midlife you can learn from country music, I'm aware of how important church is, at least in song. Country music, an oxymoron to some listeners, has been called "soul music for rednecks" and "blue-collar ministry" for a reason. If you listen to it carefully, you'll find the same anomaly I saw on Route 21. The singer, especially if male, is usually more concerned about getting out of church than in getting in.

Consider Craig Morgan's "That's What I Love about Sunday," which was a hit song for much of 2005, the year that I was church shopping along Route 21. What Morgan treasures about Sunday is seeing kids dressed up, the off-key singing of "Miss Betty," the swaying choir, "Momma's hands raised high," and then shaking the preacher's hand at the door, allowing Morgan to do what he wants— namely, go home, change his clothes, play football, read the paper, nap in the swing, eat some chicken, and go fishing. So successful was this song that a few months later Craig released "Redneck Yacht Club" explaining what Sunday is really about. Sunday afternoon he spends with his buddies out at the lake with their bass boats roped together "like a floating trailer park" and then they "pass out the jar" and get drunk. In other words, church is work you do with the women to be able to play in the afternoon with the guys.

After the service the congregants would often descend on me with church literature and sometimes hugs and ask me to sign the guest book and address form. They promised that if I filled it out, I would not be contacted. Alas, from a marketing point of view, they were true to their word. Only occasionally would someone look askance, as if I were an interloper. Well, I was. But they were invariably polite.

"I Love Jesus, and I Hate Church"

After a semester of churchgoing, I saw the problem. While the church leader in these country churches was male, the dominant audience was female, regardless of denomination. Nationally, the average for Protestant denominations is about 61 percent of adults in church are women. In addition, from what I saw, well over half of the pew occupants (at least on Route 21) were women over the age of sixty. As any advertiser will tell you, when you see this demographic, you are not looking down the barrel, you have already swallowed the bullet.

More interesting is that these older women were not widows attending alone or with a friend. Many of these women were currently married. Hubby was at home. Twenty percent to 25 percent of married churchgoing women attend without their husbands. At the Methodist church, an attractive woman of about my age came up to me with all the Welcome Newcomer paraphernalia, gushed about how good it was to see a newbie, and then, realizing that I was alone and that her attentiveness might be interpreted as coming on to me, immediately burst into a spirited explanation of where her husband was, and how much he had to do on Sunday, what with his golf foursome and all. When I went back a second time, she was still attending church alone.

In a review of David Murrow's *Why Men Hate Going to Church*, Marcia Ford, former managing editor for *Christian Retailing*, a trade magazine for retailers and suppliers in the Christian products industry, makes a telling point about wives who attend church without their husbands:

> I know those women well; I've been one of those women. They feel alone, abandoned, ashamed, embarrassed, angry, envious, ineffective, and guilty, for starters. Ask a woman where her husband is or why you never see him at church, and the guilt and shame rise to the surface. She may stammer, roll her eyes, and offer an excuse, but inside her head she's thinking, "I don't try hard enough to get him to come. I don't pray enough for him. I'm not a good Christian."

So, while a man may preside over the service, and the service may be primarily about males (God, Jesus, and, historically, the hierarchy of all surviving denominations is male), the dominant consumers are female. In a sense, they run the show. They choose the stories in the same way that any audience makes the bard toe the mark. They are also the ones who generally keep the enterprise afloat with volunteer labor, community building, and especially commitment.

The Victorians inadvertently codified this gender distinction by considering women the moral sex, the suppliers of moral sensitivity. Essentially, the Victorian view was that the women (only upper-class women, by the way; working women rarely attended), went to church, imbibed the ethical brew, and took it home rather like momma bird coming back to the nest to nurture the stay-at-homes. In the mid-nineteenth century, the English writer Frances Trollope reflected on America: "I never saw a country where religion had so strong a hold upon the women or a slighter hold upon the men."

At one level, the question of gender imbalance seems easily answered in terms of commitment. Men do not commit as naturally as women, for obvious sociobiological reasons. That's why in the great majority of cases, when marriages fail, it is the wife who files for divorce, blaming the man for failing to hold up his end of the bargain. Men shy away from commitment in religion as well. American women are half again as likely as men to say they are "religious" and "absolutely committed" to their faith. This commitment starts early. Some 70 percent to 80 percent of college students involved in campus ministry are women.

A recent Lutheran-sponsored study across the denominations concludes that young males may be spiritual, but "the church in its present expressions of ministry has failed to engage young men's attention and commitment." The study reveals that spirituality in young men today is most often only a vague expression of personal aspirations and experiences unrelated to church. "It has been the assumption that young men will return to churches when they settle down, get married, and have kids . . . But we are entering a time when young men have nowhere to go. They never were a part of a community of believers." Although 79 percent of young males profess to be believers, one-third attend church only once a year, or never.

Face it, the church event (as I experienced it) is not very appealing to men. The problem is clear enough: it's boooring. But it's also because our culture has addicted many of us to an expectation of excitement. The Bible has few chase scenes, and the pastor is not a guy's guy. I say this as a timid academic sitting in the back pew on Sunday wondering how much time I would like to spend with this guy. The problem is *not* sexual, but social. These pastors just don't seem to be very . . . manly. To be sure, part of the problem is that their social role is to "talk the talk *and* walk the walk," which essentially casts them as the high-school nerd.

Add to this the fact that most men do not like to be told what to do. These church services are all about taking instruction. Give money, sing songs from books with small print, stand up, sit down, stand up, sit, pray, go home. And men especially do not like to be told they are not in control of their fate. Remember the snake tossers in *Holy Ghost People*? In general, men like to be told they are explorers, masters of their fate, and good just the way they are. *They* won't get bitten by the copperhead. Most men don't buy self-improvement books. They don't pay attention to Oprah and Dr. Phil. The church tends to be from Venus, while men are from you-know-where.

Pastoral Personae Problems

In this context, it's easy to understand the long history of women falling in love with the minister, for in many ways he is exactly the sensitive guy their husband is not. The "reverend rake" is a fixture in American fictional culture, from Arthur Dimmesdale in Nathaniel Hawthorne's *The Scarlet Letter* to Elmer Gantry. From time to time he becomes famously real, as with Benjamin T. Onderdonk, the Episcopal bishop of New York whose real-life scandal kept the tabloid presses churning for almost a decade before the Civil War.

But no one compares with superstar pastor Henry Ward Beecher. Beecher was Bill Clinton in Billy Graham's clothing. In an age of public piety, he was far and away America's most influential cleric.

Even Abraham Lincoln sought his counsel. From a famous clan (his sister wrote *Uncle Tom's Cabin*), he became famous for his politics (abolitionist) and charismatic preaching (good news). Then in 1875 he was tried on charges of adultery, or "criminal conversation," as it was then called, with the wife of a famous protégé. For a year he stood at the center of a *National Police Gazette* maelstrom before the case was dismissed due to a hung jury. His parishioners were a better jury. Beecher was the confidant of several wives of his wealthy parishioners, and already by the early 1860s rumors circulated that his concerns had moved beyond the pastoral. Yes, these relationships had intense spiritual dimensions, but he may have persuaded the ladies that physical consummation was justified by a higher spirituality. They may not have needed much persuasion.

By far the most astonishing thing about these stories of adultery is that the husbands, as well as an inner circle of Beecher's friends, seem to have long known or suspected what was going on. In addition, the press would probably have passed the story by but that some of the leaders of the women's rights movement, including Victoria Woodhull, Elizabeth Cady Stanton, and Beecher's own sister, Isabella, came to his defense. And quite a defense it was. Woodhull, a radical feminist and an advocate of free love, answered critics by proclaiming that her ideas on sexual freedom duplicated the advanced practices of Henry Ward Beecher, who, she said, preached every Sunday morning to a dozen of his mistresses.

Although Beecher's escapades briefly outed the sexual dynamic of churching, the role of the pastor/confessor/lover is deep in the process. And with reason. For here is the tender, gentle, understanding man who will take time to listen to *your* problems. This man wants to be meditative, contemplative, concerned. He wants your affection and is willing to offer his own first. He will not always be itching to move on to his projects in the cellar or his foursome on the golf course. In fact, the pastor has no projects in the cellar, and if he's in a foursome, it's often more for show than for sport. *You* are this man's project.

To me, most of the pastors I saw along Route 21 seemed a bit too much Mr. Peepers and not enough John Wayne. The only exception to this hasty stereotype was at the Evangelical Lutheran church. In my notes, I called the pastor "Luther Stonecrusher" because he was the toughest hombre I've ever encountered outside the Western movies of my childhood. There were only a handful in the congregation, and he opined that low attendance was a good sign, because what he offered was tough. He was not in the business of "doing gentle." And he was right. I almost expected to see skid marks in the parking lot.

More usually, while churchgoing, I thought of George Bernard Shaw's quip that there are three sexes: male, female, and clergy. And the less generous quip: the church has become a place for little old ladies of both sexes. I'm sure that part of the reason Protestant denominations currently are having such a problem with gay ordination is that the pastoral persona is profoundly confusing to males. Gay ordination only exacerbates the unease. If the role is outed as gay, men rebel; if configured as nurturing, men find him dull. Women don't seem to care. They like a man who makes the effort to understand her life, her feelings, her concerns.

In a sense, this tension has always been present with American religious suppliers. While they may pretend muscular Christianity, may even strut and fret a kind of Elmer Gantry, they end up delivering feminine community. Looked at this way, you can see that Protestants go through long periods of almost feminine quiescence, then get roiled up as some new macho, in-your-face delivery system is installed. The pulpit suddenly becomes exciting, itinerant preachers appear, camp meetings, revivals, the anxious bench, the take-it-now-or-go-to-hell approach. What roils congregations is almost always the appearance of a new delivery system, and that delivery is usually aggressively masculine. Then it gets domesticated.

The Feminization of Church: How a Marketing Dilemma Was Made

Of the many insights into American culture gleaned from feminist studies none has been more enlightening than the role of women in storytelling. Moving off the pedestal and out of the brothel—the two splits of Victorian womanhood, saint or sinner—allowed modern women to become prime audiences for new kinds of out-of-the-home entertainment. By the late nineteenth century men were no longer the drivers of the marketplace of make-believe; women were opening their purses and essentially saying let's have some of these stories for us.

Two events, seemingly unrelated, occurred on the American cultural scene: the rise of competitive denominational religion and the creation of the sentimental pastimes—first the novel, then the movie. The sentimental novel was to Victorian women what television has been to us, part of their nervous system. And the stories that were the most successful were most often the stories that generated feelings women wanted; feelings of romance, nurturance, family, and community. Men dismissed these rules as tearjerkers or bodice rippers.

Thanks to the work of many feminist critics, we now realize that this inculcated sensitivity made its way from page to pew, or better yet, from pen to pulpit. Enough of the toughies, Luther and Calvin, and parsing the text. Victorian women wanted charismatic clergymen, not because they were leading us to theological purity, but because they were leading us to personal virtue and what are now called family values. They wanted heart along with head, heat along with light, feeling along with pondering, music along with exegesis.

Women wanted ministers who could feel their pain, who could make life interesting and refreshing and safe. If the menfolk wanted church as a call to arms, they got it. But if women wanted church as a safe place to congregate, a place where marriage and children were privileged, a place to sing together and dress up and hear family-affirming stories, they got it. The main themes of sentimental writing—female purity, male fidelity, religious devotion, the goodness of a child's heart, and family solidarity—became as well the stuff of church.

The history of American evangelical religion, however, seems so masculine, so in-your-face, so aggressive, so Burt Lancaster in *Elmer Gantry,* so Jimmy Swaggart sweaty, and so Billy Graham intense. In truth it is really so feminine, so musical, so entertaining, so safe, so sentimental.

Look back at the great innovations in churching—the so-called great awakenings—and you may see the female demand supporting new innovations in supply. In a sense, this feminization starts with John Wesley and Methodism back in the early eighteenth century. Read Henry Abelove's ground-breaking *The Evangelist of Desire: John Wesley and the Methodists*, and you'll see that Wesley's genius was the arousal of female passions, the same passions that were making a market for the novel. Women clustered in his services in part because it was a safe place to do the things otherwise forbidden: sing and dance, cry, and feel strongly.

As I've mentioned, in the mid eighteenth century, the charismatic English preacher George Whitefield, a Wesley protégé, took this highly emotional performance to the colonies. He attracted crowds too large for any building. But what did Whitefield do? He personalized the service, he storified it, made it juicy, made weeping and moaning not just acceptable but a sign of understanding, of being saved. People hugged one another. In public! His most famous American contemporary, Jonathan Edwards, may have been able to concentrate intellectual fury into print, to argue that we are sinners in the hands of an angry God, and to deeply scour chapter and verse, but Whitefield let all the other stuff loose.

Whitefield was a looker. He attracted women, some of them allegedly transfixed by his (literal) wandering eye. In this cartoon of Whitefield preaching in England in 1760, one woman in the audience is saying, "I wish his Spirit was in my Flesh," while another says, "His poor eye sparkles with Holy Zeal." Whitefield's delivery system, based on personal conversion and New Light excitement, produced the same kind of crowd hysteria as did Elvis or the Beatles. He made church safe yet exciting, daring, and, in a way, a place to feel sexy. A German woman from Pennsylvania walked forty miles to hear him preach. She reported that she had been spiritually awakened. She didn't speak or understand a word of English. Just his

Before Elvis Presley and Billy Graham, there was
George Whitefield. (SOURCE: POPULAR ENGLISH
SATIRICAL CARTOON, 1760.)

voice and presence were enough. She wanted to let loose, and, in the
cant of today, he gave her permission.

Not for nothing is dancing a never-ending concern of Protestantism. When you are inside the church, dance expression is acceptable—think Quakers and Shakers, names for groups, often women,
who found the physical experience joyful and full of movement. Go
into almost any African-American church today, and you'll see
women who lead the pew and aisle dancing. Pentecostalism depends
on this letting go. Meanwhile outside-the-church dancing is obviously sexual; men are involved, and hence dancing is tainted with

real danger. Church boogie is sex at its safest, and that is why White-field, the Tom Jones of two centuries ago, was so important in finding a way to mix hip action and birth control.

In the next shift in supply in the nineteenth century (often mis-nomered the *Second* Great Awakening, thereby implying that the audience, not the clergy, was sleepy), a new generation of minister revved things up. Again it fell to a new kind of supplier, the solitary circuit-riding itinerant, to make his way through the marketplace to excite the ladies. While it's hard for us, continually stimulated by electronic media, to understand how boring it must have been to attend the same church year after year, the unknown outsider really spiced things up. He appeared, preached, roiled things up, and then left town. Of course he was exciting. Had he stayed around for a few months, he would have become just like the minister who was putting you to sleep.

(Although itinerant preaching is usually considered an American phenomenon, such is not the case. All churches go stale with the same ceremony, and, let's face it, there are only so many sermons a pastor can give before dreary "been there, done that" sets in. The horseback riding, solitary, Bible-toting (and selling) Methodist minister was such a visual treat that we have considered him our own. But the Catholics got there first. As with many innovations, the Catholic mendicant orders were first to realize the dreariness factor could be lessened by having cameo performers. These were the *gyrovagus* (gyro = circle + vagus = wandering) monks who would pop in and preach from time to time. They were refreshing if only because they were different. And there is a closely allied French word, *colporteur* (col = neck + porter = to carry), from the image of a peddler carrying his wares in a bag hung around his neck. The modern version of this is the Seventh-day Adventist, the Mormon, the Jehovah's Witness, traipsing around your neighborhood with tracts and Bibles, no longer to sell but to use as come-ons for promised service. Does it work? These are some of the fastest-growing denominations. The best selling technique is so simple: it's the believer at your doorstep, looking into your eyes.)

Picture a Francis Asbury or a Peter Cartwright addressing camp meetings of thousands of people bent on generating excitement. Of course, it was a bit erotic, as well as a lot exotic. It was thrilling. Fun-loving sinners not just sashayed but barked like dogs, howled, squealed, flung themselves into a fury like the whirling dervishes they resembled. Religious dance fever had replaced the square dance. The aftermath of such revelries was called the "burnt-over" districts. They had indeed been singed.

Such campground religion was theater, wonderful and exuberant, the theater that Victorian women loved—melodrama. You watched the quavering souls totter and tip before you, as the pastor exhorted them to feel the devil, then cast him out. They were changing their lives not figuratively but literally. You could change yours. Get up! Move! And, as you watched them shimmy and shake as they cast the devil out so they could start over, you joined in. You too could be reborn.

Literature Shows the Role of Women

As might be imagined, this sensual, even sexual, aspect of rapture was not foregrounded either by the ministerial class or their acolytes, but by the active women and often passive men of the audience. Look carefully at this Methodist camp meeting from the early nineteenth century, and you see the delivery is coming from men (up on the lectern), but the excitement is expressed by the women (in the middle ground). Along the periphery are those well-dressed males presumably slightly bemused by the goings-on. And note too that four more male preachers are awaiting their turn at calling the tune.

Oddly enough, it is fiction that best captures the nature of these awakenings. Observe Mark Twain satirizing the process in chapter 20 of *Huckleberry Finn* (1885). Notice the demographics of the in-close crowd; no mention of adult men other than in the roles of trickster and duper—the square-dance caller of earlier days. Here,

At a Methodist camp meeting, men preach, women screech. (SOURCE: LITHOGRAPH BY KENNEDY & LUCAS AFTER AN ALEXANDER RIDER PAINTING, CIRCA 1835.)

from Huck's innocent point of view, the do-si-do-*without*-your-partner of revival:

> The preaching was going on under the same kinds of sheds, only they was bigger and held crowds of people. The benches was made out of outside slabs of logs, with holes bored in the round side to drive sticks into for legs. They didn't have no backs. The preachers had high platforms to stand on at one end of the sheds. The women had on sun-bonnets; and some had linsey-woolsey frocks, some gingham ones, and a few of the young ones had on calico. Some of the young men was barefooted, and some of the children didn't have on any clothes but just a tow-linen shirt. Some of the old women was knitting, and some of the young folks was courting on the sly.
>
> The first shed we come to the preacher was lining out a hymn. He lined out two lines, everybody sung it, and it was kind of grand to hear it, there was so many of them and they done it in such a rousing way; then he lined out two more for them to sing

and so on. The people woke up more and more, and sung louder and louder; and towards the end some begun to groan, and some begun to shout. Then the preacher begun to preach, and begun in earnest, too; and went weaving first to one side of the platform and then the other, and then a-leaning down over the front of it, with his arms and his body going all the time, and shouting his words out with all his might; and every now and then he would hold up his Bible and spread it open, and kind of pass it around this way and that, shouting, "It's the brazen serpent in the wilderness! Look upon it and live!" And people would shout out, "Glory!–A-a-men!" And so he went on, and the people groaning and crying and saying amen:

"Oh, come to the mourners' bench! come, black with sin! (amen!) come, sick and sore! (amen!) come, lame and halt and blind! (amen!) come, pore and needy, sunk in shame! (a-a-men!) come, all that's worn and soiled and suffering!—come with a broken spirit! come with a contrite heart! come in your rags and sin and dirt! the waters that cleanse is free, the door of heaven stands open—oh, enter in and be at rest!" (a-a-men! glory, glory hallelujah!)

And so on. You couldn't make out what the preacher said any more, on account of the shouting and crying. Folks got up every-wheres in the crowd, and worked their way just by main strength to the mourners' bench, with the tears running down their faces; and when all the mourners had got up there to the front benches in a crowd, they sung and shouted and flung themselves down on the straw, just crazy and wild.

One of the delights in such reportage is that not only can you see how sentimental reading prepared the audience for evangelical preaching, but also you can see how other authors viewed the handi-work of their brethren in cloth. Here now is Anthony Trollope, peer-less recorder of manners, dealing with the same pastoral interaction on the other side of the Atlantic. In *Barchester Towers* (1857), we dis-cover his counterpart to Twain's frontier revivalist. The evangelical

Reverend Obadiah Slope is limned with slightly more refinement, but his target audience of predominantly women is still in place:

> He [Slope] is gifted with a certain kind of pulpit eloquence, not likely indeed to be persuasive with men, but powerful with the softer sex. In his sermons he deals greatly in denunciations, excites the minds of his weaker hearers with a not unpleasant terror, and leaves an impression on their minds that all mankind are in a perilous state, and all womankind, too, except those who attend regularly to the evening lectures in Baker Street. His looks and tones are extremely severe, so much so that one cannot but fancy that he regards the greater part of the world as being infinitely too bad for his care. As he walks through the streets his very face denotes his horror of the world's wickedness, and there is always an anathema lurking in the corner of his eye.

The great literary text explaining the American experience of distaff ecstasy is Sinclair Lewis's *Elmer Gantry*. Again the focus is on the rogue male who plays the ladies into conversion by promising sensuality on one hand and eternal damnation on the other. He is the insinuator of sin and the redeemer of the sinner. He dances them into epiphanic frenzy. How? Lewis leaves no doubt. Gantry understands how to wrap his arm around the pulpit and minister to exactly those he earlier wrapped his arm around and seduced.

Elmer Gantry lit a firestorm of disbelief, but critics often overlooked how perceptive Lewis was of an interaction between unfulfilled women and a charismatic man with plenty of concentrated libido to go around. Lewis spent weeks going to camp meetings, interviewing attendees and observing the interaction of sensuality in the service of abstention. Is there any fruit so tempting as that which is forbidden? And any Adam so charismatic as the man who professes higher belief? What Lewis captured in the early twentieth century had been brewing in the American pot for the previous two centuries.

The Warner Sallman image has become an identification character to brand objects, literally.

If you want to *see* this feminizing of the pastoral persona, consider the midcentury image of the ur-pastor, Jesus. The God-as-man may have been the rough Semitic carpenter in earlier times, but He was becoming the delicate, sensitive ideal of Victorian women written about by the likes of Elizabeth Stuart Phelps and soon gushed over as Valentino on film. For many of us who grew up in the 1950s, this was the Christ bequeathed to us by our grandmothers. There He was in the chromolithograph on the front page of presentation Bibles; He was there for our father's wallet-sized image to be tucked into combat gear; and, until the Supreme Court took it down, He was there over the blackboard of almost every American school. There were two portraits at the front of the classroom: Gilbert Stuart's George Washington and Warner Sallman's Jesus Christ. If ministers ever sought an image of their perfect form from the female perspective, here it was.

Man-made Problems

From time to time in the delivery of religious experience, the male service provider simply steps aside or even disappears. It doesn't last long, but it does show what's lurking behind the curtain. Mother Ann Lee, founder of the Shaker sect, was an innovator in stressing female "fun"—the "heavenly banquet" of Christ, without the nuisance of coital sex and all the uck! that follows. The superfluous male also evaporates in the Holiness movement of the New York sisters Sarah Lankford and Phoebe Palmer in the 1830s, as well as in the Seneca Falls Convention on women's place in society in 1848. Men need not apply.

In the late nineteenth century, church was becoming women's space, and the service was becoming women's churchitainment. Along with new ways of receiving the Word, the formation of tract and Bible societies, foreign and home missions, Sunday schools, education societies, potluck dinners, and temperance groups were the innovations of women serving women. Not surprisingly, men lost interest.

So it's not happenstance that suffrage movements such as those of Susan B. Anthony and Lucretia Mott came from this church space. Entire denominations like Christian Science and Seventh-day Adventism came from powerful women (Mary Baker Eddy, Ellen White) as well as workers movements, like the Catholic Worker Movement (Dorothy Day), women's rights (Elizabeth Cady Stanton), and the Women's Christian Temperance Union (Frances Willard). In no other part of American culture did women take such an entrepreneurial, even commanding, role.

Church slowly became woman's space for a number of other reasons. Immigration, and migration of freed slaves, drove all kinds of single women into the cities. Churches (Salvation Army, Nazarene, Wesleyan, Seventh-day Adventist) found a ready source of volunteer labor in harboring these single women. The fact was that these churches were often more social movements than theological movements. They were primarily concerned with the sisterhood, especially the sexual habits of this new parishioner—the single woman with money, a job, and no man to tell her what to do with it.

New images of community were foregrounded. No longer was Christianity the movement to save the world against impossible odds; now it was becoming a movement to introduce relationship—not only with the sisterhood, but with a wonderful man. Christianity was increasingly portrayed as a passionate relationship with Jesus Christ. Here comes the problem: a personal relationship with Jesus is not only not compelling to men, it is also profoundly confusing. "Jesus wants to have an intimate relationship with you" is more likely a turnoff than a turn-on to men. Replacing "A Mighty Fortress Is Our God" and "Onward Christian Soldiers" with "draw me close to you" and "your love means so much" may resonate with women but not with men. Religion was becoming personal and emotional.

Men wandered away. They went to clubs, bars, deer camps, fraternal organizations like the Moose and Elks, even the office, where they could fantasize about saving the world against impossible odds and most definitely *not* have a meaningful and personal relationship with Jesus, especially not Warner Sallman's Jesus. Most men have no desire to fall in love with another man, let alone one with cascading Breck Girl hair and a sticky-sweet smile. This barely sublimated sexual configuration developed precisely because women often went to church for the a-man-who-cares-about-me sensation that men find repulsive. Should you wonder why homosexuality is the most explosive issue in a group that considers itself organized around forgiveness, this may be why.

In this context, consider the countervailing pressures as males fight to take back not the night, but the church. The Southern Baptist Convention and Promise Keepers enjoy lighting this fuse by announcing the dominance of men, first in church and then in family. Most people roll their eyes at such adolescent assertions (if you have to repeatedly announce it, how confidant can you be?), and certainly this male reaction is eerily descriptive of past chauvinism. Witness the names the Promise Keepers give their "Power Up" rallies: "Stand in the Gap," "Live a Legacy," "Choose This

Day," "Go the Distance," "Turn the Tide," "Storm the Gates," "Uprising," and "Unleashed."

If Promise Keepers currently shows the desperate straits of men in church, think only of the Oneida community of John Humphrey Noyes or the rumbustious behavior of Joseph Smith. These men brought radical products back to market—*really* muscular Christianity. They weren't huffing and puffing, they really were unleashed. Noyes took phallocentric community to the nth degree, and Smith moved his community over the frontier into the hinterlands. Both men were seat-of-the pants pastorpreneurs who generated sects (in this case pronounced *sex*) protected from censure by distance. And that's how they got away with what women would never support: complex marriage and polygamy—also known as plenty of partners for the male leaders. This was the male version of restoring potency to church.

Far more common was the via media, the stay-put church consisting of a performing male up front and a predominantly female audience below. Commanding the pulpit were Henry Ward Beecher, Norman Vincent Peale, and Billy Graham, or the electronic versions that amped everything up and produced such testosterone-loaded parodies as Oral Roberts, Jimmy Swaggart, and Kenneth Copeland. Backstage, however, supporting these men with their hands on their checkbooks was the same audience I saw arriving for church with hubby back at home. That is until the new generation of pastorpreneur like Joel Osteen, Bill Hybels, Rick Warren, et al., appeared with a revolutionary new marketing plan to make church safe for males—the male-friendly megachurch.

CHAPTER EIGHT

Out of the Ivory Tower and into the Missionary Fields

Because all this history and culture of the feminized church was made real to me on Route 21, I decided to spend time at the one church on that route that seemed to be outstripping the competition: Trinity Baptist Church, in Keystone Heights. Did ontology recapitulate phylogeny? I wondered. Will the individually successful church recapitulate the traits of the successful denomination? What exactly was the role of men? And the force of women? So I went to talk with Dr. James Peoples, the pastor.

I had spent some time on his website www.trinitybc.org and could see that what he wanted to create was exactly what I wanted to understand. How do churches grow? How do they compete when the product is essentially interchangeable? Trinity Baptist's motto was "Reaching North Central Florida and Beyond." I assumed that the "beyond" didn't refer to the hereafter but to the geographic region extending east from the center of the state to the Atlantic Coast.

Pastor Peoples was positioning his church squarely in the middle of the next burst of Florida growth. The church's master plan includes an increase of seating capacity up to 1,400, twenty-four more Sunday school classrooms, and greatly expanded facilities for children. When you see this kind of aspiration, you know that this

The fund-raising brochure promises that Trinity
Baptist Church will look just like a junior college.

little country church, which had only a few hundred members a
decade ago when Pastor Peoples arrived, wants megachurch status.

Pastor James, as he likes to be called, was nothing if not forth-
coming about the centrality of growth. That meant, first of all,
expanding the physical plant. The church now has a country school
look to it, cinderblock and brick with a sign out front announcing
Bible school. Another sign nearby asks, "Does Your Life Have Purpose?" When I asked about the expense for expansion, Pastor James
said that people have to see big to believe big.

On Sunday the place is packed, cars all over the place. Out front,
under the portico, is a converted school bus that makes its rounds
gathering parishioners too poor or feeble to drive. The bus is emblazoned with "Trinity Baptist Church." The bus is an interesting

development in churching. As Pastor James told me, there is a delicate balance between how many people you want to bus in relative to how many drive in. Too many bussed believers may make the congregation uneasy because the congregation becomes older and poorer. But the act of bussing says "we care." This church has a base of nine hundred members, so one bus will do. Two would upset the balance. And three would be trouble.

I had heard Pastor James preach, and he's eager, sincere, often shrill, and usually on point. Better than that, however, he's helped out with all kinds of equipment that I didn't see in the neighboring churches. He's wired, literally. On either side of the pulpit are two large drop-down projection screens, a miniorchestra to his right complete with horns and drums, and a sound system so accurate that I could hear him perfectly in every corner of the sanctuary. The wireless mike has made churchgoing as easy as watching TV. Many of his parishioners were a little deaf, but I never saw one of them straining to hear, as I had seen at other churches.

James said that his church was called a "blended church" not because it mixes age groups or racial ones but because it incorporates the new technology with the old-style organization. By "blended," he meant that his parishioners sat in pews and had hymnals in front of them. But the hymnals were never used. The lyrics were flashed on the screen; they were easy to sing, easy to understand, and best of all, bouncy. The band was jazzed-up with preformatted CDs. All the audio boosts and stage lighting made James's role bigger than life.

The electronic version of Pastor James is impressive. He knows how to work the AV stuff. Trinity Baptist has spent about $75,000 on it, and he's been to school to learn how to make the most of it. James keeps an eye on the back of the church, where there is another drop-down screen that is seen only by him, the choir, the band members, and whoever is looking back over the top of the congregation. Below this screen in a glass-walled booth is the control room. Here James has an engineer who makes sure that the system is properly cued up and working.

James could do it all himself, but the backup is just to be safe. The church uses a software program called MediaShout that lets him put a lyric, a Bible verse, a video sequence, or a graphic up on the dual screens with just a click. Pastor James can display texts over full-motion backgrounds, add soundtracks, create animated announcements, show pictures of new members, or double back over earlier scenes for emphasis. And, as we both agreed, it's so much better than what I sometimes use in class: the dreary, emotionless PowerPoint.

James's monitor is linked to the engineer's console, so that if he makes a mistake, it gets corrected. All the song lyrics, passages from some fifty-two versions of the Bible, preformatted videos, even external feeds from the web can get arranged in the matter of a few moments. OK, it's not television in the La-Z-Boy, but it comes close. A major difference is that it's Pastor James's finger on the remote.

The equipment transforms two events that men don't like. First, men don't like to sing. At other churches along Route 21, I would often hear a woman really getting into the hymn, but rarely a man. The men would hold the hymnal and mumble. After all, most of the famous hymns come out of the eighteenth century and are essentially poems set to music. They certainly don't rock. But in this church you watch the lyrics on the big screen, and you can belt it out à la karaoke just as if you were in a country and western bar. In fact, sometimes a church member sings a hymn in pure karaoke style with accompaniment provided not by the band but by MediaShout.

And, second, men don't like to pray out loud in public, especially while being watched. By and large, men are ashamed to ask for help, especially in front of women. But with MediaShout, when you pray, it is to the accompaniment of soft Lawrence Welk–type music. Sometimes the keyboardist plays the background. It's almost like rapping. In old-style church, the minister said, "Now let us pray." In the new style, he says, "Join me in prayer but only if you want."

Trinity Baptist is growing. Although Pastor James has never heard of the religious economies theory of church competition and arched an eyebrow when I invoked competitive amenities, he's fully aware he's mixing it up with other suppliers along Route 21. And, although he is clearly dedicated to growth—not just because of his mission but because of the debt load of his future expansion—he is very cautious about discussing what some might consider poaching and what he calls "transfer growth." He feels better about finding the nonbeliever or the lapsed believer than the brand switcher.

Pastor James did admit, however, that Trinity was picking up members from another Baptist church across town, which has a minister under investigation for making sexual advances on a teenage member. That wasn't poaching; it was rescue. Ironically, he mentioned that the other church was fast-growing partly because the minister was capitalizing on the fact that he was a sinner, yes, but one who has been saved. That didn't seem fair, but it is the Baptist way, and, having attended the other church, I knew Pastor James was telling me the truth. Every time I attended, the accused molester wanted us to know that he had done wrong (and who hadn't? he queried) and he had found forgiveness. This is Christian jujitsu.

I mentioned to Pastor James that the only industry that admits to wanting transfer growth is the tobacco companies, who make the opposite claim; namely, that they don't want new users, but only those already hooked on another brand. Pastor James smiled. He assured me that there were quite enough nonmembers for him to meet his growth targets without disturbing his neighbors. Later he was kind enough to email me a quite sophisticated mapping of demographic trends that the church had commissioned to predict future growth. He assured me that it was not out of line or inappropriate for growth to be a primary goal. The goal in becoming a megachurch is not just to be big, it's to do God's work better.

Pastor James certainly has thought of the necessity of bringing more men to the church, or, in his terms, more men to Christ. He has about ten women working almost full-time for the church. The "almost," he admitted, is because of the added health insurance costs of full-time employees, but, yes, women do most of the organizational planning and arranging. He nodded understanding of the problems of men but said there really was nothing more that he could do other than try to make them comfortable. And sponsor a golf tournament at the local course.

While the great Freudian question is, What do women want? Pastor James is going to have to ask the great denominational question, What do men want? And he may find an answer where other pastor-preneurs have found it: in the vulgar world of getting and spending.

Entire industries are dedicated to selling stuff to those who live on Mars and those on Venus. In many respects, speculators in religious supplies are no different from car dealers. Not only do the sexes like different objects, they respond differently to the process of selling. Women are more attentive; they respond more by smiling, giving verbal feedback, nodding their heads. Men often presume that women are agreeing with them when in fact they are not. When men nod, however, it usually means agreement. Men respond to business jargon and its supposed authority. They converse with more directness and authority and use fewer qualifiers. Men interrupt more frequently than women. Men do not like to be told they should do something and especially do not like to be told they have done wrong. Ashamed men are quicker to fight than to pray.

Levels of assertiveness are variable, but usually the male responds quicker and sharper to aggression. Body language shows this. As little girls, women are often encouraged to use powerless signifiers: more closed body language, less use of space, more compliant skills. I was always surprised in church to see the response to the pastoral "Now let us pray." Women tended to dip their heads; men's often bobbed straight back.

Men don't like to be lectured to, and they hate to be shamed. Don't call them sinners. Call them strivers. The very thing that women may like—namely, a safe, predictable environment—is boring for men. Men like the idea of seeking, of leading, of doing things, of engagement, of danger. Call it "Bible study" and they won't appear. Call it "Iron on the Forge," and they may. Forget the pancake breakfast and annual retreat. Remember that nothing is more important for anxious men than bonding under the leadership of the father figure. Sports are based on it. So is war.

While I realize that this observation is as true as it is trite and smacks of the psychobabble of the 1960s, I was about to see what happens when church becomes a bit aggressive; when it starts not to challenge masculinity but to pander to it; when the more traditional—and female-oriented—calls for conformity, control, and ceremony are dropped; when singing, lectures, and never-ending programs are put aside; when a new kind of fantasy is promulgated, a fantasy of saving the world, of *step aside, we're coming through* is not just believed but acted upon. Religion becomes ta-da: *purpose driven.* To follow my purpose in church shopping, I was going to have to look at the next big thing in churching: the megas. And to do that I was going to have to leave the county and go to the sprawl.

The Church Aggressive: The Importance of Sprawl

Pastor James is at the edge of making a marketing transformation. Just to the south of him lies Orlando's famed Interstate 4 corridor, and to the east is Jacksonville. If you like it, call it the "exurbs." If not, it's "sprawl." No matter what it's called, it's the promised land of churching; thousands of unaffiliated believers seeking instant community. America's population is decentralizing faster than any other society's in history. In a sense, these are the new missionary fields filled with the new seekers.

These clusters have broken free of the gravitational pull of both the farm and the city. They exist in their own worlds; communities with no community, or what I call "mallcondo" land. Mallcondos can grow huge. Mesa, Arizona, for example, has more people than St. Louis or Minneapolis. Very often they're known by the county name, as in Loudoun County, Virginia, or Polk County, Florida. These places are just *out there,* with little civic life, and hence just right for fierce and innovative religious competition—fertile ground for the megas.

Growth westward from Jacksonville, which already has the greatest number of megachurches in Florida and bills itself as "Where

Florida Starts," and growth northward from Orlando, which runs a close second in megas and calls itself "Where Florida Vacations," is the sprawl Pastor James is trying to adopt. He would like this part of Florida to be the place "Where Florida Prays."

The national distribution of megachurches reveals the importance of mallcondo sprawl. Over 75 percent of these huge congregations are located in the Sunbelt states, with nearly half of them in the southeast region, where a history of evangelical growth supercharges the mix. California still has the highest concentration of megas, followed by Texas, but then there's Florida, Georgia, and the Carolinas. Sprawl cities, such as Houston, Dallas-Ft. Worth, Los Angeles, Atlanta, Phoenix, Charlotte, and Oklahoma City, sprout megachurches almost as quickly as malls and almost in the same places: at interstate cloverleafs.

Off to Orlando

There's probably no better example of a sprawl city than Orlando, Florida, home of the infamous I-4 corridor that swung a historically Democratic state over to the Republican Party during the 2000 presidential election. There really is no *there* there; rather, it was the sudden sprouting of DisneyWorld that drained the swamps, settling the ground for the massive landing of northern snowbirds. Downtown doesn't exist in any traditional sense, only a bursting of mallcondo pods in every direction. As the city advertises, "It would take more than sixty-five eight-hour days to visit all of the entertaining offerings in Orlando," by which it inadvertently means that there's no downtown. If ever there was a sprawl ripe for supplying order on the fly, it's Orlando.

And so one Saturday in January 2006, my wife and I were off to Orlando to see the future of "doing church." Auspiciously, just as we were about to start our pilgrimage, we were stopped by a family of Jehovah's Witnesses, who must have sensed our mission. Since I was

In a leaflet, we see the promise of the New World of Jehovah's Witnesses: we become friends with the grizzlies.

in something of a hurry, I accepted a little tract, "Live in a Peaceful New World," in lieu of a little conversation. On rice paper was a colorful scene that could be understood around the world. A happy brown-skinned family is bringing in the harvest. The foreground is filled with happy harvesters, the middle ground is a lake scene surrounded by greenery, and in the distance are snowcapped mountains.

But what struck my eye was a mother and daughter patting an American black bear in the right foreground. That seemed to me such a foolish act that I wanted to warn the Witnesses that the bear might bite, but too late. They were gone, and we were speeding south to visit other suppliers of the peaceable kingdom. Later when I went to the Jehovah's Witnesses' website, I found:

Even in this troubled world, you can gain happiness from accurate Bible knowledge of God, his Kingdom, and his wonderful purpose for mankind. We do not provide for exchanging electronic correspondence (email), but if you would welcome further information or would like a free Bible study, please fill in the form below or write to Jehovah's Witnesses at the appropriate address.

It occurred to me that maybe the Witnesses were savvier than I thought. Perhaps the bear was there exactly to pique my interest. If so, the marketing was successful.

On the drive down Interstate 75, I noticed how much of my travel time was being interrupted by religious suppliers who were attempting the same connection. We passed some eight billboards asking us to be concerned about the condition of our souls and those of our unborn children. The marketing was appropriate to high-speed travel: "Are you on the straight and narrow or on the crooked road to hell?" one of them asked. "Never too late to follow Jesus," said another. Most of the billboards wanted me to know that the unborn child has a heart that beats at three weeks and a brain that operates in six—"Life begins before birth." What a marketing coup that pro-abortion groups own "pro-choice" while the anti-abortion groups own the far more resonant "pro-life." Who cares about choice when life is at stake?

There were also signs for the Holy Land Experience, a theme park in Orlando that promised "a Visit to Jerusalem in Orlando." It was right next to the Prime Outlets, a huge outlet center, that promised "The POWER of Passionate Shopping."

But I had megachurches on my mind, and, thanks to the Hartford Institute for Religion Research's website www.hirr.hartsem.edu, I knew them all. The Hartford Institute, with a contribution from the Lilly Endowment, has an ongoing study of the church growth movement and generates a database of congregation growth, denominational affiliation, and incidental information. Without it, I would have been lost. The Hartford survey warns, however, that its guide depends on the integrity of churches to self-report the numbers accurately. As I was to learn, rather like some schools polled by *U.S. News & World Report* for its annual college survey, integrity is sometimes in short supply. After all, if growth is what you're selling, exaggeration is an occupational hazard.

As I learned, if you ask someone where the big churches are in a town, they often draw a blank, maybe listing one or two. Ask them for the cineplex or the mall, and it's like you're on MapQuest. They can give you accurate directions. After checking around, I decided on visiting Northland, Calvary, First Baptist, First Baptist of Central Florida, Discovery, and FaithWorld. Each of these churches had well in excess of the baseline two thousand attendees, and so I had planned a Gray Line–like tour of what it means to be on the expanding side of the American religion business, on the Disney side, as it were, of conglomerated rapture.

Since megachurches, like the retail centers they often imitate, seem to operate 24-7, my plan was simply to drop in during the weekend, attend a service if possible, look around, chat up the staff and parishioners, and then see if I could get a sense of the enterprise. The one thing I did not want was to have to attend the midweek services where things "get down to business." What with my problems simply reading the Bible, I didn't want the men's study group. I wanted the megachurch experience in Orlando without having to pay the piper.

I started at the southernmost church and worked my way north. Discovery Church looks like a reconditioned warehouse, a Safeway grocery store undergoing conversion, complete with open girders and half-installed floors. In fact, the parking is next door at a nameless strip mall. The sanctuary, called the Auditorium, was done up in stylish black, jammed full with high-tech equipment. Big cables were all over the place. Next to it was a coffee house–styled room, also loaded with AV equipment, appropriately called the Acoustic Cafe.

Discovery was brutally spare, not a whiff of religion, no iconography; instead digital clocks that presumably count down to service time. Also up on the walls in Helvetica type were the directions to the family entrance, the office, the gift shop, and rest rooms. Things were chaotic, what with work still being done and a new service added this Sunday to accommodate the increased gate.

As with many exploding megas, Discovery is more like two churches—that is, it has more than one location, linked by a "feed."

So there is a second outpost at Olympia High School, which has Sunday services fed by satellite. Apparently there are more outposts in the offing, as my informant said there was no stopping Discovery now. I was at the primary campus at the intersection of Orange and Holden avenues, where, I was proudly told, on Sunday the traffic backup forces overflow parking into the strip malls on every side. Traffic doesn't lie. This is the place to be.

As I learned, megas depend on disrupting traffic flow. There is no better advertisement in mallcondo culture than an attraction so powerful that car traffic jams up before it. Very often the church even makes a display out of hiring local police, complete with flashing blue warning lights, to direct the flow, as well as having parking attendants wearing headsets like air traffic controllers. To an audience that grew up on rock concerts, nothing is more powerful than a little jostling at the gate.

I chatted up the attractive and vivacious wife of the pastor in charge of evangelism. She had been with the church when it used to be called Baptist, twenty years ago. Now it was all business, all "purpose driven." She said those words in almost a conspiratorial whisper, as if she were telling a secret. Discovery she said—as if I had missed the point of all the Helvetica—was all about discovering yourself, about discovering God, and that's why, she said, the church was doing forty days of *discovering your purpose.* Although she was unfailingly purposeful in asking my wife and me to attend the upcoming Saturday afternoon service for the kids ("It'll knock your socks off"), I had other discoveries to make. While I'm sure Discovery knocks off socks, I found it oddly dreary. I think it's because I associate all that Helvetica with hospitals.

Next was the First Baptist Church of Orlando, a monster of a junior college campus complete with its heavily advertised Payne Stewart Athletic Fields. Mr. Stewart, the golf pro, had been an active member of the church, and his death in a private jet crash was memorialized in many places around the church. It was a macabre yet apt analogy. He had God as his copilot en route to a far more important tournament.

The parking lot was huge and had nifty signs like Goodness, Gentleness, and Faithfulness to help you get back safely to your car. In between the lots was a little sugarplum chapel that looked like something out of the Disney classic *Snow White and the Seven Dwarfs*. It was the only thing at First Baptist that looked like a church, and it was a confection, a folly—the wedding chapel in the dale. Doubtless, that was its use.

Looming over it was the megachurch, all windowless brown stucco and crawling with couples who were attending a "Song of Solomon" conference on marriage. I couldn't help but think that their wedding chapel was closed and the work-on-the-marriage part was beginning in earnest at the Big House. Everything inside the First Baptist Church of Orlando was hospital mauve. There was nothing, absolutely nothing, that looked uplifting or aspirational or churchy. This place certainly didn't soar; it hunkered down. If architecture were the judge, its concerns were clearly of the here and now. Play it safe.

We went into the sanctuary, a mix of high-school auditorium with cineplex seating, set deep underground. The pews were upholstered and rose up some fifty rows to ground level. The impression was that we were sunk in a bunker, with external light coming in only from the window slits above us. These windows could be curtained off so that the circus lighting could take effect. I could see all the strobes and spotlights hanging from the ceiling. Was that a disco ball light at the apex? It was.

While we were padding around, Pastor Tommy Nelson from the Denton Bible Church in Texas was leading the not-inexpensive conference on introducing Jesus to your marriage. Everyone was looking a little glum. Up in the control booths, oddly enough at the ground level, I chatted up the lighting guy, who, along with the video crew and the sound guys, really put on the show. They had just come back from doing the *son et lumière* at a Texas megachurch and were rightfully proud that the stuff here was exactly what they use in rock and roll shows. No, the lighting man said, even better. First Baptist has more movable lights than even the Rolling Stones had on tour, and, if his console was any indication, you'd have to be a jet pilot to flip all the switches and watch all the dials without crashing. He was more than willing to show me around the cockpit, but I had seen enough.

Outside was a kiddie playground called Noah's Park, the rival of anything you could find in a city playground. But I was itching to get over to the Payne Stewart Athletic Fields. Here was a first-class football stadium, a running track, and a baseball diamond. I suppose it made sense. Athletics were not just a way to attract the most important niche of believer—the highschooler—but also a way to signal how important kids are to the community. No wonder the church was pulling in the young marrieds!

Only later, as I tried to understand the attraction of the megas, did I realize how important this was in terms of combating the old-style church. These were all *boy* sports. When we had entered the church and gone to the visitors' welcome area, I had seen a big cutout of the golfer Mark O'Meara, all decked out in his golfing outfit, complete with his commercial endorsements in place. The cutout was a promo for an upcoming inspirational talk from Mr. O'Meara on how his religion has helped his life, and I must say I was attracted. All this athletic stuff was getting to me. This was a place that knew how to make men feel at home. The men's ministry is huge, as is the annual golf tournament at Bay Hill, the signature course of Arnold Palmer. Later I would realize that this is exactly what is called in Advertising 101 the Unique Selling Proposition.

This place is something that I was not seeing on Route 21. Remember the nice woman at the Methodist church who was concerned, and perhaps a little angry, that her husband was out playing golf? At this church Mom didn't go to service while Orlando Dad was out on the links. He went along with her to church, talked a little golf around the service, and then played in the afternoon. After that, maybe he went to the Mark O'Meara talk.

If this was the First Baptist Church of Orlando, with some four thousand members, one of whom was O'Meara, then I was all fired up to see what the First Baptist Church of Central Florida had with a reported ten thousand members. Maybe Arnold Palmer. Alas, this church was not much more than an imposing sign next to Lowe's on one of the many stop-and-go highways of commercial sprawl that make up the I-4 corridor. I didn't see how it could be providing the Hartford Institute for Religion Research anything like accurate numbers.

Not only did the First Baptist Church of Central Florida look run-down and shuttered, but it had little Burma-Shave signs around the parking lot announcing that if you got some kid to attend its school, you'd get $500 off your kid's tuition. I spoke briefly with a woman in a pickup truck who had come to fetch her kid from a basketball event. I asked her if she attended. No, she said. She had to work at Lowe's. Then why was her kid here? She pointed over her shoulder to the big-box store.

Every megachurch I'd seen was spotless; in fact, the cleanliness is almost oppressive. But this establishment had airborne flotsam blown about in the corridors, and a coating of dirt everywhere. Later I wondered how quickly megachurches could do the growth thing in reverse: shrink overnight. I suspect it can happen in a month. If what you go to church for is, in a sense, the sight of something rapidly growing and hence screaming *shoppers' value,* what happens when that shouting stops? What happens when you attend and more and more pews are empty? Now I thought I knew. This place was a mega going micro.

There wasn't anyone around to tell me what had happened, so off to Calvary Assembly of Orlando, which hands-down won the prize for architecture. We saw it from miles away. This was no Safeway on steroids, no exploding junior college, and certainly nothing like any church I had ever seen before. Calvary glistened in the bright sunlight, literally. Most megachurches have given up the medieval attempt at generating awe through soaring architecture, stained glass, and big marble steps. So they usually ape the mall and try to up the ante with the rock concert AV systems. But Calvary Assembly is a piece of art. It looks like an office building with the top third wrapped in tin foil. In fact, it looks like a fortress with a diamond plopped on top. When you are cruising I-4 at seventy miles an hour and coming in from a distance, it looks a little like the star of Bethlehem. Well, as you get closer, maybe a pillar of salt.

Inside in the cavernous auditorium, I got a chance to see what I had long heard about: the smoke machines. The stagehands were preparing an evening show called "Yo Soy Tu Padre." There were wires and cables everywhere. Smoke was puffing up the back walls. I was warned by a stagehand that "the liquid nitrogen presents a serious hazard to civilians," so be careful. Happy to say that Calvary knew how to use this powerful effect, having "experts in cryogenics on the staff." Not only are smoke machines strange to see in church, but I was a little put off by the big canisters of liquid nitrogen being off-loaded from a truck with all kinds of hazmat warnings flashing. Better living (and religion) through chemistry.

Calvary knows what to do. It is a franchise operation. So there is a well-stocked gift shop with logoed stuffed animals and T-shirts as well as a coffee shop called Wholly Grounds. Calvary, as I had been forewarned, is one of the most politically edgy churches in Central Florida. It houses Exodus International—the group that wants to make gays straight by introducing them to Jesus. I looked around for their offices, but, alas, they were unfindable. Perhaps wisely. Time was drawing nigh. We had a service elsewhere to attend.

The last stop of the day was at Northland, a new church growing like gangbusters with the steel I beams cutting across the old church, and bits and pieces of the new church still linked with the old. Northland calls itself "A Church Distributed," and it seemed to be meant literally. Out in the street was the standard scene of megachurch marketing: the blue lights of the rented local police cruiser announcing to all that Something Important Was Happening Here. We didn't worry. Invariably these churches have special parking for first-time visitors right up front next to the handicapped. If you ever wonder who's really important, check out the reserved parking spaces. The newbies get the best. After all, we're the ones who build the brand.

Like Discovery, Northland was an interesting name choice. To be sure, it was on the north side of Orlando, but it was also a comforting name to the snowbirds. It was like home. And the fact that it kept repeating its slogan, "A Church Distributed," reminded me that perhaps many of the parishioners might feel that they too are part of a vast distribution of modern family. Away from home, this is the new home.

Much is made at Northland of the children's space, again as part of the replacement of what's missing in your uprooted world and as well as part of savvy targeting to young adults. The kiddieland was designed by Wacky World Inc., an offshoot of designers who had worked for Disney. Essentially, it's a standard classroom building with a foyer of 3-D cartoons coming off the wall. As you enter, the space is cartoonish and exaggerated, like something you would see at a carnival. But when you move farther into the school space, it looks like the usual blackboard-and-chairs world of elementary school. Except that there were plenty of signs telling you the Lord was watching. Wacky World's concept was a bit too Brave New World for my taste, but the design company is currently doing a booming business with megachurches. The kiddie playground is becoming the necessary loss leader to attract young seekers.

Crossing the construction site, I felt right at home. I had spent considerable time in my office watching the stop-action camera film the act of construction on Northland's website. Your tithe at work. On the far side of the mammoth new building was the current church building done in early shopping mall: sloping roof, electric doors, hotel furniture, hospital check-in.

In the entrance, eager-faced women were handing out leaflets that looked like a blown up version of *My Weekly Reader*, a throwaway I used to get in grammar school. It had ads from local organizations, church information like the operating budgets (we need more money was the lesson to be learned by the side-by-side pairing of income and expense columns), space to doodle, and a nifty centerfold that laid out the service you were about to attend complete with a précis of "The Big Points." Men appreciate that. A section called "In the Spotlight" displayed this quote that kept me busy when the service dragged a bit: "We can't find God for the same reason a thief can't find a police officer." I'm still not sure what it means.

No matter, I wasn't there to quibble over analogies, I was there to observe. The Church Distributed (they kept repeating it) never pulled me in. The fourteen-piece band and singers were passable; the pictures of new members flashed across the ubiquitous drop-down screen were interesting, as was the ersatz marriage ceremony in which we all said "I do" and made our promises of fidelity to Northland; the standard skit was predictably ironic and gave vent to how men feel being dragged to church, but the sermon was confusing.

In his sermon, Pastor Joel C. Hunter admitted that we were off to "a bad financial start" and that this was especially bad because we are a "double-tithing church" (meaning 20 percent of your gross). He reported that he had spoken to a friend who does income-tax returns for ministers, and this CPA friend said that of his sixty-six pastor clients, only four were tithing properly. Needless to say, none of them was double tithing, as was Pastor Joel. Forgetting the fact that his friend needs a little pastoral care from the Church of Accountants for blabbing his clients' confidential information, this seemed confusing. If pastors don't tithe, is the product not worth buying? That's how I read it. I thought I was going to be shaken down, but after all this money talk, there was no mention of any offering. No golden bowl was passed beneath my nose.

"We need money badly, yet we're not asking you" is my idea of manliness. No tears, no whining, no pleas, just straightaway guilt for a brother in distress. We're lying on the battlefield all shot up, but we are not yelling "Medic!" Maybe that was the sense of a Church Distributed.

And when I looked at the small group meetings, I saw events directed to just us guys: AMEN (A Meeting of Men) offers a new subject each week that is relevant to men; there's flag football, soccer, tennis, ultimate Frisbee, martial arts; guy groups to deal with fear, anger, and anxiety; special interests like "Links Fellowship, which connects golfers throughout the world in Christ"; the motorcycle ministry ("all styles are welcome, must own a motorcycle and have a valid motorcycle license to participate"); the Faith and Science Group that "meets to discuss scientific facts in light of the Bible"; the various over-thirty-five and over-fifty singles groups; and then the one I won't be attending: "Word Weavers, a writers' critique group." If only *critique* hadn't been included.

So again I could see that the magnetic poles of gender had been reversed. The welcome mat was out for guys. Northland is guy friendly. But not entirely. In some respects it was just like that Methodist church on Route 21 with the woman bemoaning her errant husband and praying for his return to the fold. Here's why I say that.

In the attractive fund-raising brochure that I picked up in the foyer, I learned that Northland is a bit more sophisticated in its moneymaking ways. It knows who holds the purse strings. The church can get men to come, but can it get men to give? In the four-page, full-color, glossy come-on (which looks like something a hospital would produce for fund-raising), is this full-page letter from Cynthia L. Heinz to the membership:

> When Northland handed out the "Together We Can" building information, I made it a point to attend one of the information meetings Pastor Joel C. Hunter hosted . . . I felt the Lord tell me to pledge $10,000. I prayed and prayed again, and always the same number came to my mind. I didn't tell my husband what the number was, but only asked him if he was interested in praying about contributing. He basically said over and over that the Lord had not moved on his heart to contribute. I was confused. Was I to wait for the Lord to move on my husband's heart, or just pledge on my own? I prayed more and reminded the Lord that I didn't have any money and am a stay-at-home mom with no means of coming up with the money. I told God that if He wanted me to pledge it alone, then He had to provide the money through me, and not go through my husband or our household budget. So I acted in faith and pledged it on my own in private. I decided not to worry about it or wonder where the money would come from. If God had truly spoken to me about the

pledge, then the money would come. If not, it wouldn't! Either way, I was off the hook. Some people might think I was wrong to pledge alone. They might think there's a lack of marital unity. Others may think that it's not proper wifely submission to pledge separately. I don't know. I just decided to step out in faith.

Recently my father, who is 80 years old and lived in New York, sold his home. Out of the blue, he decided to give his eight children money. Guess how much he sent me? It was a little more than my pledge amount! There is something you need to know about my father. He believes in God, but frequently puts me down because of my outspoken relationship with God and because I believe the Bible. He thinks I live in the extremes because I quote Bible verses in my general conversations. He believes God is only to be a private part of one's life and tells me I should not talk about God with others because of the principle to render unto Caesar what is Caesar's, and unto God what is God's. What is ironic here is that he was being used by God in my life to render unto God what is God's! I can't take any credit for this. God is showing me He's in control of all things, and He is more than able to accomplish through me what He wants done. My earthly father's extravagant gift will be used to bless my heavenly Father's heart and, in turn, will bless so many lives, including those of my husband and our five children. How cool is that!

With that Mrs. Heinz signs off, secure that she has been part of a miracle and not the recipient of the annual gift tax exclusion of $11,000 from her dad. A word of warning to Pastor Joel: better not promulgate that letter to the various men's groups.

FaithWorld, the Exception that Proves the Rule

I encountered no such subtlety in the last megachurch I visited in Orlando. That's because its roots were not in the megachurch movement but in the televangelist eruption of the late 1980s. The place was called FaithWorld, and, refreshingly, it was all about money. It might be better called Gimme Money. From the street, FaithWorld looks like a prison, complete with high fences and gatehouse. But inside it had all the trappings of a TV studio: industrial building with double-decker tiered amphitheater, gift shop on one side, on the other side those nice women handing out church literature. TV cameras were all over the place.

As soon as I parked, I realized, whoops! This was not what I expected. I was one of the few white faces. On the data sheet from the Hartford Institute for Religion Research, FaithWorld was rated as nondenominational with an average attendance of five thousand per weekend. On the FaithWorld website, there was something interesting, however, that I should have read with more care. Usually the church website will be the name of the church with a *.org* at the end. The site for FaithWorld was a domain name: clintbrown. net. The .net is a reference that explains intended use. For instance, *.com* is commercial; *.edu* is educational; *.gov* is governmental; *.org* is organizational (generally nonprofit), but *.net* means a network-based organization. In other words, *.net* is an operation that has a number of other components feeding into a central electronic clearinghouse.

Before becoming FaithWorld, this place was the headquarters of Pastor Benny Hinn, the white-suited, soft-talking faith healer of the upper television tier. For years I had watched Benny cure people of the most debilitating diseases, and then he just up and headed west. In so doing, he sold his shop to Clint Brown, who was then doing business on the other side of Orlando. Clint had been running an empire of music and book publishing, an internet video service, a radio network, and a media production outfit, all presumably under the tax-favored umbrella of a church. In fact, on the website, visitors are cautioned:

> Please keep in mind that [our] studio is not a commercial facility. It is an extension of Clint Brown Ministries and is used primarily for the growing musical and multimedia needs of our ministries.

It is during the "down time" of our in-house projects that Tribe Studios may become available for certain outside projects.

Clint, a white man, is the impresario of an empire of African-American praise-and-worship music. In fact, the service I attended was about as close to rapturous as this milquetoast Yankee has ever experienced. The place rocked. There were no golf groups for men, no support groups for anxious writers, no ultimate Frisbee tournaments, and no getting in touch with your lost Cub Scout. This place was for shakin' your booty and then paying the piper.

Up on stage, for almost an hour before Clint appeared, a group of singers, mostly women, holding microphones, belted it out, while behind them in a sunken pit was a band that had two huge drum sets and lots of horns (I couldn't see everything because there was a huge electronic keyboard obscuring my view). Behind that, standing on bleachers reaching almost up to the rafters, was a veritable wall of the chorus. The experience was rather like being in Edgar Allen Poe's "The Pit and the Pendulum," where the walls are coming in at you. Only this wall was all acoustic, and it was getting louder and louder. You vibrate, whether you want to or not.

The minute we walked in, I knew the rapture train was in the station. Usually in church I'd sit scribbling my notes, but not this time. Everyone was vibrating, and the music hadn't even started. I was shaking too, if only as a contact high. These choir members were no supernumeraries on the stage; they were no background mood setter; they were a central part of the excitement. I could see in them the supercharge of ecstasy that was to be mine for letting myself go. Their hands were up, their eyes were up, their backs were arched. They were exactly like the images I had seen in Steven Katzman's *The Face of Forgiveness: Salvation and Redemption*. I couldn't slouch and pretend to be small.

(Certainly music is a crucial element to religion. Almost every religion starts its services with chanters of some sort. Then instruments. Now amplification. Just consider the impact of the introduction of the pipe organ into church services in the mid-Victorian times. We forget that it was rare for a church to have an organ before the mass-production of keyboard, pedals, pipes, couplers, stops, and bellows. By the early twentieth century, most American churches had the wherewithal for a proper booming sound, and the churches that were successful retrofitted the organ into the apse. Before that, the organ was a concert hall experience, then an accompaniment to film. In every case, the blasting of air through the pipes corresponded to the blasting of emotion through the listener. Like the bagpipe, which it eerily resembles, the pipe organ doesn't ask for attention, it commands it.

Once the components could be miniaturized, you find the explosion of the electric home organ, an object that takes up pages of space in old Sears and Montgomery Ward catalogs, along with the upright piano. For a while, before it went bankrupt, the Wurlitzer Organ Company made the process electronic, and now, of course, the organ is fit inside the computer chips of synthesizers.)

FaithWorld is a crucible of sound. There is no escaping it. To make this experience still more rock-your-world-'til-you-say-uncle (or at least open wide your wallet), the place was filled with television cameras. Not just the podium camera and two stationary cameras in the center of the crowd, or the up-on-the-wall camera, but a camera on a huge boomstand that moved back and forth across not just the entire stage but across the audience as well. In the trade this is called the "eye of God" camera.

And where did all the captured images go? Who knows? Not to any television station that I could locate. Presumably they are fed to Clint Brown's internet streaming video (by subscription only). But I don't think that web viewing was the real purpose. The real excitement was that up on the JumboTron screens on either side of the stage were pictures of . . . us!—the hand-waving, jitterbugging, singing, and gasping us, the stars of the show. At last: on Dick Clark's *American Bandstand,* where I always secretly wanted to be.

I wasn't alone. The group that seemed most connected to jump and shout was a dozen or so white folks up front, who were activated by the least provocation. The predominantly African-

American audience didn't seem to mind their presence. In fact, everyone was having a good time, except for a young gentleman to my left who was a little glum. I know this because at regular intervals we had to say hello to our seatmates, put our hands on their shoulders, look them in the eye, and say something affirming, like they were going to inherit money. Once we had to hold hands with our pew mates, and at the count of three—if we wanted to accept Jesus—we had to give a squeeze. Plus, if we did this, more money might be coming our way. I didn't reach for his hand; I grabbed hold of his girlfriend's. She was clearly having a time jumping up and down, but, strangely, when it came time to squeeze, she went limp.

When Clint finally appeared, we had already been assured that God had a big surprise for us. If we wanted the surprise, it would help if we would just stuff what money we had into the little envelope in front of us. "Only give if God has blessed you so you know what you're doing," we were instructed. I should have read the envelope carefully because it had a number of boxes to check, only one of which was "tithe." The others were for the building fund and the special contribution, all of which were to come.

No matter, Clint had arrived. Much was made of his coming by the stagehands wheeling out his personalized Plexiglas podium. There was no sermon as such, but a litany of short stories dealing with providential reward. Clint had been having visions. In one of his visions, he'd seen some of us becoming very successful. And he'd seen a lot of sick people getting well. And people were going to die and leave lots of stuff to some of us. He'd seen that too.

Then Clint says it's time to give again. Here's a helpful story: Years ago a young man had nothing to give the church, so he gave Clint the tie he had from working at Popeyes, the fast-food place. Lo and behold, years later an older couple came to see Clint. They had retired from the Midwest and just wanted to thank him for helping them. How? Well, it seems that the older man owned a clothing store and had been told at the Mayo Clinic that he had eight months to live. He had no heirs, only his nephew living in Florida, working at Popeyes. He gave the nephew the store, and the nephew had done great things with the store, and the Mayo Clinic was wrong and, *whew!* In a few years who do you think comes driving up to the church in a Mercedes-Benz SL class (the entire congregation gasps, as they seem to recognize the nameplate) but the selfsame nephew.

Story over. Time now to fill out that little envelope again. God will pay you back, with interest.

And remember my own story, says Clint. The audience knows, because he must have been repeating this every Sunday. He started with nothing. He came to Orlando with $800 in his back pocket, which he had to spend on rent, so he only had a few sawbucks to his name. And now he has a recording studio, a book publishing outfit, song licensing royalties, a website, and, well, you know the rest. He's a .net millionaire just like .com Bill Gates.

Not quite. If you google *Clint Brown,* you'll find that he had a bit of trouble with his ex-wife, and in the divorce filings the *Orlando Sentinel* found that the Browns used large amounts of church money to finance what it called an "extravagant" lifestyle. Clint owned a $1.4 million home with a $7,000 monthly mortgage paid by Faith-World; seven cars, including a $95,000 Mercedes Benz SL class for business travel; credit-card charges at stores like Neiman Marcus that totaled more than $450,000; and an annual salary exceeding $500,000. One of Clint's credit-card expenditures, according to his wife, was $70,000 worth of women's clothing—none of which went to her or her teenage daughter.

Admittedly, it's unfair to link Pastor Brown and FaithWorld with the other Orlando megachurches. FaithWorld is such a Happy Meal of deceit. But it does open up what other megachurches do to prosper, what museums now do, what universities and philanthropies do, what department stores do, what all for-profit entertainments do. Before all else, if they want to succeed, they must first put on a good show. They may pretend not to be looking, but the successful ones are watching the customer with an eagle eye. You may think that you are watching them up there in the pulpit, but, in truth, they are watching you closer. Say what you want, an aspect of modern competitive churching is now, as it has always been, *show business*. If not, they're out of business.

What I saw budding on Route 21 with Trinity Baptist and in full flower in Orlando is a new kind of theater, the emerging church, the postdenominational church, the Wal-Mart church, McChurch. These were efficient, tidy, expeditious, eager, intensely consumer-sensitive churches. They were open for business 24-7, and, little by little, they were taking market share from those comparative sleepy-heads who were open for only two hours on Sunday and who were performing a ritual not really relevant to a young audience eager for excitement.

This shift in suppliers is happening in almost any medium-sized city of today. In almost every mallcondo sprawl over 200,000, there is a specific church growing like kudzu, doubling every few years. These new churches are the result of a strange confluence of market-ing, pastorpreneurs, population shift, consumer demand, AV equip-ment, consumption communities, entertainment economy, and good old-fashioned yearning for a feeling of epiphany and the bandwagon effects that generate it. But they are also there because, as Pastor James has seen, we now know they are possible. Build it, and they will come.

So where did all this new marketing know-how develop? How did those Orlando churches learn how to put on this show? What makes Pastor James think his *Field of Dreams* approach is possible? To find the answer, we need to observe some of the most innovative marketing in American culture, the rise of doing church like a rock show, and the trial-and-error approach of a handful of religious speculators who understood the human yearnings for rapture and community and the new ways religion could deliver it.

CHAPTER NINE

The Megachurch: "If You Are Calling about a Death in the Family, Press 8."

What I saw in Orlando—and what I may see in Keystone Heights if Pastor James builds his dream house—is a new kind of delivery system, a much more efficient experience of what we go to church for: communal and individual sensation. And the reason for this shift in churching is not complicated. In the last generation, our collective nervous systems have been rewired, thanks to electronic media. To be sure, movies, radio, and television have been around for generations, but only recently have some churches realized that they could integrate the technologies and turbocharge their product. In truth, they got there second; the rock concert did it first.

Ironically, and to their detriment, mainline churches, like their cultural cousins the universities, fought this onslaught of electrons. They were a bastion of print against video, hymns against hootenannies, aesthetica against vulgaria. They were lineal, print based, historical, and hierarchical. More than that, they were private and exclusive. Getting in was difficult. You had to read.

The old-style delivery system was up front, coming down from the pulpit, and predictable: enter, be humbled, hymn, pray, hymn, sermon, pray, hymn, exit, go back to being yourself. As a matter of fact, it cared more for the security of repetition than for the excitement of innovation. Stay in line. It was run by old people. The emotional transfer was weekly, short (a little over an hour), and scripted. Church, especially for the young, was a chore.

We Will, We Will, Rock You

Then in the 1960s, the mainlines found that they were losing part of their audience to the excitement of doing religion in new ways (New Age, Wicca, Eckankar, Tibetan Buddhism) and to pop psychology, both of which took feeling good as a birthright, not an internal manifestation of external grace. Emotions were becoming an end in themselves (Esalen, est, biofeedback, meditation, massage, spa culture). Listening was foregrounded—not as in listening to the pastor but to your inner self. Or to music, figuratively, *soul* music. By the late 1970s, this was seeping into church. Encounter groups would meet in church basements, and guitar services would take place upstairs.

Oddly enough, it was rock concerts that showed not just the yearning for community and elevated experiences, but that the adaptation of electronic culture could amp up these sensations. Those growing up in the 1960s were called the Woodstock Generation for a reason. Huge JumboTron screens, advances in mood lighting, stage hijinks, and especially the developments in sound amplification could make the out-of-body experience almost commonplace. You could drown in sound.

And if that didn't do it, pharmacology could help. A tablet of XTC or Ecstasy (3,4 methylenedioxymethamphetamine) was often part of the concert experience. Ecstasy removes inhibitions. Users report feelings of being suddenly happy, confident, energetic, social, silly, and relaxed soon after ingestion. Circumspection is lowered. Compare pictures of attendees at rock concerts and evangelical revivals; you'll see a similar affect, hands up, eyes rolled, neck arched, mouth open—rapturous.

Turn on, tune in, drop out. No one said it like this, but what if the sensations of Sunday morning could be like what happened Saturday night? In retrospect, coupling the church experience, which promised rapture to only a select few, with the excitement of the rock concert, which delivered the goods to the many, presaged a new kind of church experience. What the church needed was more *mass,* not in the sense of a religious service, but of attendance. It needed greater numbers.

Size Matters: The Sociology of *Mega*

The first thing to notice about these new churches is that they are . . . big. By definition they have a rather arbitrary baseline of two thousand *consistent* weekly worshipers. But even this number is now dated, and a new term, gigachurch, having ten thousand is coming into use.

The largest mega-gigachurch in the world, the Yoido Full Gospel Church in Seoul, South Korea, is simply beyond comprehension, with a reported seventy-five thousand members. So too is the Lakewood Church in Texas, which claims over thirty thousand weekly attendants. But below these mega-gigas is a churning market in which growth is equated with value.

The actual number of megas is uncertain; as mentioned earlier, self-administered questionnaires are the standard means of gauging church size. Churches often estimate their attendance based on the number of people their sanctuary—whoops, auditorium—holds. This is relatively easy to do if the space has individual seating, but pews complicate the process. Often megachurches report a cumulative attendance for multiple services based on the assumption that no person attends more than once. And sometimes, like universities, they simply juice up the numbers to improve their comparative rankings.

But here's a reasonable guess. In 1970 there were about 10 megachurches; in 1980 there were about 50; in 1990 about 250 fit the description; in 2005 about 1,210, almost twice what there were in

2000. As I write this in 2006, there's a new church reaching mega status in this country every few days.

Why did they appear so suddenly? For a number of reasons, perhaps best described by Malcolm Gladwell in *The Tipping Point: How Little Things Can Make a Big Difference*. Herd mentality is at the heart of fashion, rock concerts, teenage smoking, war, best-selling books, and numerous other endeavors that spread like the flu. Gladwell coins three rules of epidemics (the Law of the Few, the Stickiness Factor, and the Power of Context) to explain geometric explosions in what is essentially human taste. Consumers move in trickles, then droves. The trickle became a stream in the 1970s, a tsunami in the 1990s.

Growth itself is a powerful selling tool. As any student of Branding 101 knows, being able to say you are the fastest growing has pulling power. It implies leadership. Leading is not a measure of quality, however, but of consumption. Take beer, for example. There's the leading light beer, the leading imported beer, the leading Mexican beer, the leading German beer, the leading microbrewed beer, and so on. Where taste is hard to measure, the invocation of leadership often substitutes for the real thing, even if leadership is in an unimportant category.

No church ever claims to be the best, to get you safe passage quicker, but almost without exception a church claims leadership of some sort. Touting growth and size is one of the few ways of asserting this. If the product was not so good, why would so many people be buying it? Growing churches, like growing businesses, have learned the importance of generating "business at the door." Shoppers equate crowding with value. Read church marketing literature, and you'll find it littered with terms like "market segment," "niche," "satisfied customer," even "ROI" (return on investment). Such phrases trip easily off the tongues of pastorpreneurs. Sometimes you'll even hear that increasing size is not just a natural by-product of righteousness, but a harbinger of the apocalypse.

If the religious economies observations are valid, these standalone suppliers are going to have the effect of Wal-Mart on local retail. While they claim they target the unchurched, they are really harvesting brand switchers up and down the denominations. At the macro level these churches are now ministering to four million weekly attendees and possibly as many as eight to twelve million. Yet megas currently make up only three-tenths of 1 percent of all congregations. Consider this: the largest 10 percent of mega-congregations contain about half of all churchgoers.

Look at it another way. See all those little churches on the side of country roads like my Route 21? These churches have more pews than flock, and unless they change, they'll have more past than future. Little congregations of fewer than a hundred at worship, in rural communities and inner cities, are shutting their doors at the rate of fifty a week.

Rather like Wal-Mart, the megas have almost no brand personality, and, ironically, that's a selling point. Physically they are laid out with eerie similarity, and doctrinally there's little product differentiation. They have almost no denominational affiliation; in fact, the greatest number of megas are nondenominational (more than one-third), followed by those loosely tied to Southern Baptist, then the Assemblies of God, the Presbyterian Church (USA), and the United Methodist Church.

You can see this purposeful lack of denominational identity in their names. In Orlando I saw Discovery and Northland, but consider these: Woodale Church, Over the Mountain Community Church, Mountain Valley Community Church, In the Pines Community Church, Saddleback Valley Community Church, Willow Creek Community Church, Lakewood, the Fellowship of Las Colinas, Mariners Church, Calvary Chapel, the Church of the Open Door, Community of Joy, House of Hope, Gateway Cathedral, New Life Fellowship, Seneca Creek Community Church, Cedar Run Community Church, Sea Breeze Community Church. As opposed to their brethren who proudly proclaimed their competitive presence by posting small signs on the outskirts of town notifying all passersby that a Methodist or Episcopal or Presbyterian church is nearby, these places have something in common: they whisper no word of a denomination. But note the reiteration of *community* in their names.

And in the true spirit of capitalism, if you follow the money you will see that the real genius of the megachurch is that little of that money escapes. As with the Las Vegas city-state casinos, a not inappropriate comparison, what happens here, stays here. There is no far-off headquarters to support, no unfunded pensions of people who live in Timbuktu to pay, no notes of someone else's profligacy to come due. What this means is that when you are asked for money, and, believe me you are, it is almost always in the name of fostering home-base growth. Tithing, which seemed subtle or at least talked about in hushed tones at the mainline churches, is touted at the megachurches. But passing the plate is understated, sometimes even neglected. Megas are not after pocket change.

The method of collection by the dollar instead of the dime is successful. Income at the average mega is about $6 million a year (all megas combined gather $7.2 billion a year), and you can see where it goes: in those steel girders, in the new sound system, in the expanded parking lot, in the school addition.

Better yet, much of that income is tax free. True, the churches do pay an unrelated business income tax on activities not substantially related to the church's religious, educational, or charitable purposes. Megas do pay payroll, sales, and, often, property taxes. But as with Pastor James, megas often escape employment taxes by hiring only part-time staff, depending of volunteer labor for the rest. Sometimes off-loading jobs on the private sector can even build brand value. For instance, paying the traffic officers (who, as mentioned, are often off-duty cops using city police cars) can run a church almost $100,000 a year. The compelling visuals make it more than worthwhile.

The Allure of Anonymity in Generating Community

The bane of old-line churches is the freeloader. In the trade he's called a CEO (Christmas and Easter Only) or a CME (Christmas, Mother's Day, and Easter). You pay his overhead, but he contributes little. Worse, he shows others that church can be done on the cheap, without sacrifice. If you want regular contributions, if you want the idea that tithing is something important to do, if you want commitment, the one member you want flushed out of the group is the eleventh-hour empty-pocket drop-in. Church is an intentional community, and so the freeloader—the face you see only on holidays—is a danger to all around him. He demonstrates how little intention is needed.

Not so to the megachurch. In many ways, exploiting the freeloader is what this church is all about. The mega does not depend on intimacy. Just the opposite. It thrives on big-box anonymity. This is a bandwagon, not a quilting bee. In a sense, the hanger-on is not just welcome but necessary. Not only is he part of the "live studio audience" that we associate with the hit show, he's also part of the buffering that provides the safe place for the anxious and circumspect who are, after all, the core constituency.

The megachurch generates a social plasma that gives both the moocher and joiner a chance to interact with each other. As we will see, the mega depends on generating hundreds of connected social cells. Under the seeming sea of faces are intense clusters of various levels of believers who sort themselves over time and weave the allegiances that make community possible.

Sociologists say that most people know about sixty people by their first name. That is true whether they belong to a group with six hundred or six thousand members. This interior cell-group system, called by such terms as "fellowship circles" or "friendship circles," is an analog to the kinship circles that earlier denominations depended on to generate the sense of belonging. In a sense, freeloaders are like the second cousins at the family reunion; they allow families to interact without feuding.

So big congregations, far from being a deterrent, are a marketing asset and a stabilizing force. They provide the anonymity that allows newcomers, the curious ("seekers," in the parlance), to feel comfortable while comparison shopping the church against other entertainments. Just as in the mall, window shopping and shopping around are central and important parts of the final purchase experience. Drive to the mall. Go inside. Look, dream, maybe buy. Maybe not. But seeing plenty of shoppers bustling about gives a sense of connection and purpose without the countervailing sense of responsibility.

As well, size generates pools of excited and committed volunteer labor. A church really needs only a minister and a flock. Everything else is day labor. So megas concentrate on what makes the brand powerful: growth. What you sell is the perception that *whatever* it is that you are selling is in demand. People milling about does exactly this.

Why Megas Look the Way They Do

Another way to understand the megachurch paradox is by its looks. They don't look like churches; at least most of them don't. Remember how banks and colleges used to look like gothic churches? Think Yale, University of Chicago, or Princeton. Megas now look like junior colleges—the revenge of mass marketing. In fact, most of the megas I've seen look rather like Pastor James's church on steroids: like a small office complex exploded into a small college campus.

This is not to say that some of them don't mimic the denomina-

What do you get when you cross a community college with a church?
Willow Creek Community Church.

tional husks they strive to subvert. Sometimes they look like overblown Norman Rockwell confections, as if nostalgia were mixing it up with the department store. Some megas self-consciously mimic the town center complete with the town square—the *commons*. People milling around is crucial. And sometimes, like Calvary Assembly of Orlando, they go downtown-high-tech as if to say "we're like works of art, please." But rarely does the architecture say "we're one of them," referencing the standard-issue brick and mortar denominational church.

In the 1970s Rev. Robert Schuller, a widely televised preacher, went to the New York architects Philip Johnson and John Burgee and asked them to design a modern cathedral suitable for his brand of big-box Christianity. The result, a huge, angular form of reflective glass that became known as the Crystal Cathedral, opened in 1980, and is probably the most talked-about building in Orange County after Disneyland. Far more usual is Lakewood Church in Houston, which takes the commercial auditorium concept to the nth by actually being one. As Pastor Joel Osteen jokes, the Astrodome is next. A joke, yes, but it makes one wonder if perhaps skyboxes and in-seat television monitors will be the next megachurch innovations.

The mega's inside is more interesting than its exterior. What you see is usually a flat and squat stage space at the base of a tiered bank of stadium seats. Over the stage, where the crucified Christ belongs, is often a scrim curtain. Video images can be projected on this backdrop. Joel Osteen's Lakewood Church features a huge slowly rotating golden globe, implying what?—a certain worldliness, perhaps. But the gist is this: the altar is no more.

The worship space, the old "sanctuary" is now an *auditorium*. In fact, the down-front space looks suspiciously like a high-school stage before prom night, and, in fact, that's precisely what it becomes. Skits, band, video, and pastor share the same territory. One week the New Life Church in Colorado Springs, Colorado, uses this space in the traditional manner, the next it's completely transformed. For Easter the church celebrates with a full-scale staging of the life, death, and resurrection of Jesus Christ—with a cast and crew of 750, mostly coming from the church's membership of 11,000. You never know what you are going to see when you go to church. That's part of the attraction and part of what separates it from "your father's church."

Not only is there no altar, there's no pulpit. The pulpit, that enclosed platform for the dreaded "talking down," is more usually a Plexiglas stand for a few pastoral notes. Notes? *Fuggedaboudit.* Sometimes the pastor consults a teleprompter on the back wall high over the audience's head. Organ? Stained glass? Dim candle lighting? Not on your life. Instead, synthesizer, unadorned wood panels, and pinpoint spotlight on the pastor is the megachurch way. The front of the megachurch is performance space, not bully pulpit; the real control is the electronic keyboards in the engineers' bunker directly in front of the pastor and behind the congregation. The audience seating is most often of the cineplex variety, comfy and tiered either in pew form or individual seats, carpeted floors, and plenty of legroom.

It makes no difference how large the auditorium stage is because most attention is not focused on the minister but—again, as it was in Pastor James's church—on the screen image of the pastor. After all, we've learned to prefer the simulacrum to the real in any number of other places; why not here? We watch the JumboTron, not the performer. Over to the side, where the altar used to be, is often a digital readout announcing information before the service begins, and then during the service there's a running subscript carrying special announcements. You know a kid is throwing up downstairs when you see creeping across the screen like a news ticker, "Will parents of #4536 please come to the reception area."

Just as country churches all seem to have the same marquee sign out front, the megachurches all have the same electronics inside. I was jokingly told that the real power behind the megas was the technical staff, and I have come to appreciate the observation as truth. Event staging has always been a central aspect of great awakenings, now more than ever. Appropriately, the Technologies for Worship Conference, where this trade is taught, is a constituency of the National Association of Broadcasters. When you look at their conference program, you can see how they have lifted the rock concert apparatus and set it down in the traditional apse. Here, for instance, is just a bit of the subject matter covered at the 2006 Las Vegas convention:

The Power of Personal Branding
Worship Software to Expand Your Media Presentation
How to Set Up Internet Broadcasting
Getting the Best Purchases for Your Worship Facility
Enlisting and Training for Your Broadcast Ministry Production Staff
Lighting Techniques for Church
How to Use In-ear Monitors
Reaching the Masses over the Internet
Microphones and Religious Applications
Introducing Change in Your Church without Offending Almost
    Anyone
High Definition Video: Up Close & Personable
Loudspeaker Applications for Houses of Worship
Relationships & Burnout
Creative Uses of Broadband Distribution for Worship
Creating an Intimate Worship Space

As these churches have learned, it's all about the show, and the show is seamless. No embarrassing pauses, no mistakes. If I had to characterize the megachurches I've seen, I would say that they are awesomely clean and cleanly unawesome. You don't see a crucified Christ but neither do you see dirt. No missteps, pratfalls. In fact, in many ways they are as antiseptic as a hospital, complete with industrial rubberized flooring, handrails, and that dreaded Helvetica type. All that's missing are the color-coded floor lines taking you to where? The coffee shop, the weight room, the men's conversation pit?

In my two and a half years of church shopping, I saw plenty of howlers in denominational churches, none in the megas. True, this was partly because I was usually attending the Sunday services, so possibly the Saturday shows had ironed out the kinks. In the megas'

Divine inspiration via woofers and tweeters. (SOURCE: *TECHNOLOGIES FOR WORSHIP MAGAZINE.*)

determination to eschew traditional religious symbolism, they have much in common with Quaker meetinghouses, and in their desire to remove any hint of amateur showmanship, they have much in common with MTV. That's an oxymoron I never imagined confronting in church shopping.

Upon entering the church on a day of service (Saturday, Sunday, Wednesday evening), you are usually greeted in the traditional foyer with floral arrangements and bulletin-bearing hand shakers in business suits. The entrance is quite similar to what you see if you go into a luxury car showroom, only minus the car. There are lots of doors and no main portal. In the churches of my childhood, you were funneled through a compression entryway that essentially announced "Main Entrance: Abandon Hope All Who Do Not Enter Here." Instead, the megas offer the easy entrance of a modern business— lots of doors to everywhere. The doors themselves are a giveaway. In the place of a great Lorenzo Ghiberti sculptured slab of bronze on ancient hinges, you are more likely to find the electric sliding doors of Target.

Go inside, and you will find not an ounce of old-time religiosity. There are few, if any, wall icons, no little telltale signs of stained glass or covered dishes, or polished silver or gold that one associates with the Don't Touch, Be Careful! Be Quiet! Act Devout! He May Be Watching! Everything works. No burned-out lightbulbs or carpet stains. The megachurch makes a fetish of having everything operational. Showtime. Ready to go. Just like the mall.

What the megachurch does is an exercise in awe substitution. In the old-style church, the sense of impending epiphany, of rapture, was built into the architecture. Your neck was snapped by looking upward and then jolted by looking sideward. All that iconography conspiring to take your breath away. Until the railroad terminal, the cathedral was a scientific marvel, and by far the biggest enclosed space a person would go into. Now even houses have "cathedral ceilings," not to mention what we routinely see in shopping malls, government buildings, and sports arenas. So the mega creates awe by lowering the lights, flipping on the AV system, and giving the place over to those who have attended the Technologies for Worship Conference.

In old-style churches, you can't see the show. What's happening? You are never sure. No wonder the fidgeting kiddies were sent away. The main event is happening in some enclosed sacred space far from view. In the megachurches, the show is on the stage and at the end of your nose on those huge screens and stuffed into your ears as if you were wearing earbuds. You see and hear *everything* with precision, from the breathing of the pastor to the logos he's wearing. No blur. No black robes. No muffled sound. Awe is still inspired by the senses, yes, but only because all of them are plugged into electronic amplification. The pastor's image is the size of a Macy's Thanksgiving Day Parade balloon; the sound from his hidden body microphone and wireless transmitter is iPod sharp; and, as I previously described, there is all manner of *son et lumière,* thanks to smoke machines, scrims, streaming video, and theatrical lighting.

In many megas you can buy a video or audiotape of the exact service that you have just consumed. While this might make sense in the old-style church where you miss a lot, here you miss nothing. Rather, it seems a testament to our belief that if it's on tape, it must be good. Is it live or is it Memorex? means that the experience has such depth that it needs to be revisited as well as stored away in the home library. I had a chat with a man at Willow Creek Community Church who told me that he had almost "a full set of Bill Hybels." I have a colleague who collects the novels of Laurence Sterne for almost the same reason. Not to read but to have.

Not only are there taped copies of the exact service you attended, but the weekend services—often four of them—are almost perfect copies of each other. I know. I went to an entire weekend of the same four services at Willow Creek. From time to time I teach two sections of the same course, and I often have trouble remembering whether or not I have covered this or that point. These pastorpreneurs are pros, but in the mega experience, the sermon, the skit, the music, the video, are all so short and punchy that they really can't lose their way.

Megachurches all have kiddie playgrounds that rival anything you'll see at Junior's school. Rule number one of modern marketing: if the kids want to go somewhere, Mom and Dad will follow. Why do you think that McDonald's and Burger King have those elaborate jungle gyms? The care of tots, from these elaborate play centers all the way through adolescence with state-of-the-art electronic game rooms (with a Christian motif, of course), is standard megachurch fare.

And rule number two of modern marketing: you are only as big as your parking lot. The mega parking lots are huge. The traffic jams on the highway prove that you are en route Somewhere Important. Once parked, you can take a shuttle bus to the various doors of the church just as you do at Disney World. Needless to say, the lot is spotless, as is the rest of the campus.

Discover the Champion in You: The Language of Doing Church

As an English teacher, I was struck by not only how the megachurch has co-opted university lingo (*campus, enrichment classes, study groups, pastor* called *doctor, mastery learning*) but also how it's changed the way we talk about doing church. Most obvious, of course, is the category itself. How long has it been since we created a form of church that merits a distinct new name—like *megachurch*? Denominations come and go, picking up and discarding names, but there hasn't been a neologism to describe the physical church since the late Renaissance. So we have *chapel, basilica, monastery, oratory, cathedral, collegiate, abbey,* or *parish* to describe size, importance, or placement. But *megachurch* is the first noun to use the number of parishioners as a standard and that, in itself, is noteworthy.

When megas talk about themselves, the terms used are often *emerging church, discovery church, purpose-driven church, full-service church,* or simply *faith community.* These terms give a sense that cultural accommodation is going on, a sense of conjunction not with the world beyond but with the here and now. In fact, the word *religious* is often dropped in favor of *spiritual.* Megas are visionary, all right, but the vision is of the world around. They are evangelical, all right, but the crusading zeal is more to increase the gate than to spread the Word. Doctrine takes second place to filling up the house.

As mentioned, the name of the individual megachurch reveals these social concerns. The Over-the-Hill-and-into-the-Vale church name has become the standard, bleeding out all the denominational associations like The Third Methodist Church of Your Father's Hometown. The megachurch is, as you are repeatedly told, "not your father's church." In fact, when I asked Pastor James if he intended to change his church name from Trinity Baptist after the major expansion took place, he hesitated and said that he had nothing to hide but that, sure, he would consider it. If he wants to increase growth and separate himself from the rest of Route 21, he will do more than consider it.

The megachurch resettles the language of the human potential movement to refer to itself as *refuge* or *safe place,* almost as if it could post those yellow signs of a baby safe in mommy's hands. This new church is a *shelter* for the battered (or for those who consider themselves to be), not in the ancient sense of being beaten by sin, but in the modern sense of being wounded by life.

Go on to the websites, and you'll see this identity foregrounded. The Lakewood Church of Houston, Texas, has a vision of itself as an "oasis of love in a troubled world." The Valley Cathedral in Phoenix, Arizona, portrays itself as "a forgiveness center, and not a guilt center, a city of refuge, where many who had been injured by the organizational machineries and other religious groups could gather and be healed." Willow Creek Community Church is self-described as "a place for those who have given up on religion, seekers who have been turned away or turned off by old-time religion." The founder of the Vineyard franchise of affiliated churches used the term *second-marriage church,* which is not just self-descriptive but again appeals to contemporary categories of disruption restabilized.

The genius of the megachurch is that it has copycatted the language of therapy and applied it to itself without the least hint of vulgarity. This is a place to get in touch not with the eternal ineffable but with the daily effable. That's why it's in business all week long. From pastor to parishioner, this is a church in the business of coping, adapting to modern life, finding your place here/now, not there/then.

First you deal with getting on with this life, then with getting on to heaven. Just look at the list of Willow Creek sermons for the last decade (they are listed on the church's web page), and you'll see an almost chicken-soup-for-the-soma-not-soul inventory of subject matter. Adjustment is key: adjusting to your children, to marriage and job, to a spouse having an affair, to apathy, to abortion, to debt, to divorce, to drugs, to competition, to being lonely, to not measuring up, to repetition, to sloppiness, to lust, to anger, to being passed by, to racism, to growing older, and, well, to just about everything that you would prefer not to speak about in public. Especially if you are male.

Look still closer, and you'll see that the megachurch has adapted the language of addiction therapy and the 12-step method of recovery. Hurt is the power of Satan, Jesus is the power of positive thinking. Bad habits are misplaced addiction, and addiction is a disease, yes, but one that can be overcome in steps. You are tired of being weak; you go here to be strong. Every week Joel Osteen tells his Lakewood audience, "God believes in you more than you believe in yourself . . . God sees you as a champion . . . God sees you as a victor." We shall overcome not just sin and guilt but also credit card debt and troubles with Timmy. The sermons (and they are not called that; they are called *messages*) are invariably encouraging and easy to swallow, sugarcoated with optimism and affirmation. No one is called a sinner, they're just someone with a broken part. In this context, the megachurch called the Landing Place in Columbus, Ohio, makes perfect sense.

Knowing this, it's understandable how one strain of big-box religion has gone straight to the cash register to express its vision. Cue

Clint Brown and FaithWorld. The "prosperity gospel," or "name it and claim it," as it is also known in the megachurch trade, celebrates materialism, yes—of the pastor, to be sure, but really of the congregation. Joel Osteen of Lakewood Church, T.D. Jakes of the Potter's House in Dallas, and the wonderfully named Rev. Creflo A. Dollar of World Changers Church International in Atlanta all preach that God wants you to be prosperous. In this world. *Now.* Sure, their endorsement of material success is in striking contrast to the teachings of more traditional Christians, but they are also addressing an obvious area of adjustment and adaptation. Manufactured things have shared meanings. Almost as if to demonstrate the power of deep-pocket grace, Pastor Dollar drives a Rolls-Royce and travels in a Gulfstream jet.

Once inside the church, there is often a special lingo to define the congregants that reiterates this gospel of adaptation. As a general rule, the weekend drop-ins are called *seekers,* not believers, and *vision and mission* are what they are seeking, not belief and faith. These weekend freeloaders are "church shy," which gives a telling sense of church as a venue for those with low self-esteem. You don't believe not because you are resisting but because you just haven't felt centered in church. Yet.

Often the mega will confer on this seeker a clubhouse nickname. So at Willow Creek he's "Unchurched Harry" and at Rick Warren's Saddleback Church, he's "Saddleback Sam." What better way to put the target audience at ease than with the lingo of the neighborhood treehouse? Car salesmen often greet you as "buddy." Why not the pastor? Sam and Harry are raising young families, recent transplants into the neighborhood, just trying to make it in the workaday world, in the family world, and quite possibly in the church world. Why not treat them as fraternity pledges?

So forget the language of fire and brimstone, or a dictate to serve the poor, or an admission of shame. Who wants to feel bad when there are suppliers who can make you feel good? Don't bring me down. Just as grade-inflating teachers make all kids slightly above average at school, the megachurch pastors make their parents feel the same way at church. In my years of church shopping, I was sometimes called a "work in progress," giving me the nifty feeling that I was still being created and hence not an object for criticism. I was not called "the mess you've made." Or "the mess Satan made of you." Megas flourish by making the people inside feel good about themselves and their search for success. Why not? When you realize that there are competing services for attention on Sunday, the tough grader will soon find his classroom empty. Just over the hill from the mega is Lake Wobegon.

Ka-Ching! Words

Three other words, used both in the services and in the general conversation of those doing this kind of church, are: *born-again, evangelical*, and *purpose-driven*. As with *megachurch,* they announce a new configuration not just of language but of religion's place in American popular culture.

Born-again used to refer to a small cluster of aggressive believers, or zealots. At one point, born-agains were passionate, transformed believers who colonized the Protestant extreme. In the beginning of the last century, they were part of the tiny Pentecostal movement. Now born-agains are all over the place, and, although the Pentecostals are still only a small fraction of the over three hundred thousand churches in the U.S., they are arguably the most important influence on contemporary American Christianity. Imitation is indeed the sincerest form of flattery.

Born-again has come to mean any member of a church that uses the term. For instance, at the end of Joel Osteen's sermons, he says, "If you can pray this: 'Lord Jesus, I repent of my sins. I ask you to come into my heart. I make you my Lord and Savior.' If you pray just this, we consider you born-again." In other words, *born-again* means, "I am a churchgoing Christian," but it sounds like, "I have been saved." It's such a powerful coinage not only because it plays into the American belief that you can start again, have a "second act," move on to the next frontier, but also because it implies that the Pentecost has *already* happened. *Born-again* also has a certain bumper-sticker aggressiveness to it: "I'm saved (too bad about you)."

Meanwhile the ministering message of *evangelical* has incorporated political and social positions to become a portmanteau term. At one level, *evangelical* simply means marketing, that is to say the act of selling the *good news*. But *good news* has overflowed its religious banks to seep into politics. *Evangelical* has packed in the conservative political agenda of the religious right, so it now includes opposition to abortion, stem-cell research, and same-sex marriage. In the 2004 presidential election almost 80 percent of self-described evangelical Protestants voted for President Bush.

And then there is the church word du jour, *purpose-driven*. When I was in Orlando, almost every church was using it, sometimes as an organizing tool of sermonizing, sometimes as a product promise, sometimes simply as a catchword adjective. This is a product claim that can't be beat. What tops it? No wonder Pastor James has "Find Purpose in Life" on a banner flying in front of his church.

As we know, such catchwords are at the heart of branding. They don't have to be true, but they have to be evocative. So if Maytag is dependable, if FedEx is fast, if Volvo is safe, if Coke is the real thing, then the megachurch is purposeful. Thanks to the marketing genius of Rick Warren, who unleashed a blitz of buzz when he published his not-all-that-innovative book with the title *The Purpose Driven Life*, the megas now have all manner of purpose-driven this and that. There's purpose-driven youth, purpose-driven coffee mugs, purpose-driven music on CDs, purpose-driven calendars, purpose-driven screen savers, purpose-driven Bible covers.

The subtitle of Warren's chapbook that goes with the text is even craftier: *Scriptures and Reflections from the 40 Days of Purpose*. As admen from Claude Hopkins to David Ogilvy can attest, nothing is more compelling in making a sale than talking about using some number of the product for some length of time. "Take two of these at bedtime for three days." After all, it's step-by-step addiction therapy applied to salvation. The 12-step program.

Rick Warren's invocation of *40* is an act of marketing savvy in that numbers imply not just sequence but precision. He begins by stating that the number God uses whenever He wants to prepare someone for His purposes is—you guessed it—40! Noah's life was transformed by 40 days of rain; Moses's was transformed by 40 days on Mount Sinai; the Israelites spent 40 years in the desert; David made himself strong by Goliath's 40-day challenge; Elijah became emboldened when God gave him 40 days from a single meal; the

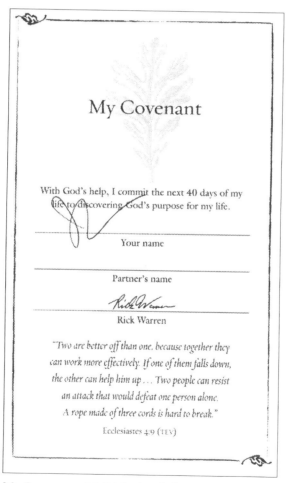

My Covenant with Rick: the pledge page from *The Purpose Driven Life*.

entire city of Nineveh reversed its decline when God gave the people 40 days to change; Jesus was empowered by 40 days in the wilderness; the disciples were convinced by 40 days with Jesus after His resurrection; and, well, you get the point. If you don't appreciate the way numbers work on the brain, spend a few minutes watching their invocation in the infomercials of Tony Robbins, Ron Popeil, or Jack LaLanne.

And what will happen in 40 days is, of course, just what the modern penitent wants: a little purpose, reason, explanation, order and 40 other such words explaining why. Lest you doubt this will happen, the book has 40 chapters so if you just take one-a-day you'll be thinner, richer, healthier, sexier, or, in this case, *born-again*. In another act of virtuoso salesmanship, on page 13 (alas, not page 40) there is an author/reader Covenant (an inspired word choice) committing the reader to using the next 40 days to "discover God's purpose for my life." As you can see, after I bought the book I signed on. I swear I signed it in good faith. Alas, my dedication started to flag and I was unable to finish the full 40 chapters. I didn't so much renege on my part of the covenant as run out of purpose. But Warren's book will doubtless have sold close to 40 million copies by the time you read this.

The Market-driven Church

If you pay attention to the language, and the human potential movement from which it comes, you'll soon see how the megachurch has revolutionized the church experience. It repositions the product and, by extension, the consumer. Old-style church was meant to encourage soul searching, introspection, private experience, inner contemplation. The old-style building, like the service, had plenty of space for solitary moments. It was run from above—not necessarily from the heavens but from the pulpit.

The mega, however, is a public place. It's for performance, moving around, milling about, seeing and hearing things. You couldn't find an out-of-the-way place in it because the whole point is to be in the crowd. Sure, you can be alone in the bookstore, alone in the cafeteria, alone in the souvenir shop, alone in the weight room, but there is no place to be alone in contemplation. It's run from below, from the seats.

Knowing what the seat holder wants is the insight of one of the visionaries of church marketing, Willow Creek's Bill Hybels. Here's his epiphany. In 1975, as a 23-year-old, Hybels wondered why so many people claimed belief, yet so few went to church. What was wrong with church *as a place?* For eight hours a day, six days a week, for six weeks, he and some members of his youth fellowship went door to door in the environs of Chicago asking questions worthy of George Gallup. The questions flowed into one another so that he could follow the concerns of his respondent upstream to the spring of concern.

WILLOW CREEK SURVEY 2002

Thank you for completing this survey! This information will be used to understand our church and to closely evaluate ministry opportunities. This is anonymous, so please give us your honest and thoughtful responses to the questions. If you have already filled out this survey at a previous service, do not fill out another one now. Use a pencil or pen; an usher can provide one for you. At the end of the service, please place your survey in one of the baskets located in the lobbies. Thanks again!

SECTION ONE

Please tell us about your church involvement

1. How long have you been attending Willow Creek (including Axis and Willow Creek Wheaton)?
   - O_1 I'm visiting for the first or second time
   - O_2 One year or less
   - O_3 2–3 years
   - O_4 4–5 years
   - O_5 6–10 years
   - O_6 11 years or more

2. What *most* influenced you to attend a service at Willow Creek <u>for the first time</u> (including Axis and Willow Creek Wheaton services)?
   check one option
   - O_1 A friend or relative brought me to a service or an event
   - O_2 I heard about Willow Creek from a friend or relative
   - O_3 I drove by the church and decided to visit
   - O_4 I moved to Chicago and someone recommended Willow Creek
   - O_5 Media coverage caught my attention
   - O_6 I was attracted to a particular program or ministry here
   - O_7 I heard about a special event or service
   - O_8 I learned about Willow Creek through the web site

Client-centered selling: the Willow Creek questionnaire.

The Route 21 conundrum was on his mind. Do so many sports fans stay away from the games they claim to follow? Do so many shoppers avoid the mall? Why the disconnect between religious claim and church attendance?

At the time, the answer was surprising. The impediment to family attendance was, in a word, *men*. They balked. Here's how he discovered this. Hybels started his questions with: "Do you actively attend a local church?" If the answer was yes, he politely went on to the next house. Why waste time? If the answer was no, however, he asked "Why not?" and charted the responses. Here are the common refrains: "Churches are always asking for money." "Church services are boring, predictable, routine, and irrelevant." "All you do is stand up and sit down." "I don't like feeling ashamed."

And when Hybels could speak just man to man, he found out the secret. Men don't like being religious in public. It's not that they are not eager for the born-again experience, rapture; it's that they prefer it not be displayed in front of women. Promise Keepers, the fundamentalist Christian group that fills football stadiums with just men, has been hectored for its sexist policy, but it has understood male yearning and reticence, and capitalized on it. In the company of women, men don't want to be seen as being told to sing, to say stuff, or to give anything. They don't like ceding control, which is, after all, the essence of feeling rapturous. They like the sense of voluntary activity, of doing something, of questing, exploring the edge on their own. Again, that's why the woman I met in the Methodist church along Route 21 (who prays for her husband to accompany her to church) is guaranteed solitude.

If there is one marketing secret Hybels learned, it is this: Men are the crucial *adopters* in religion. If they go over the tipping point, women follow, children in tow. But men are exquisitely sensitive to the very thing women seem to like in church: namely, authority. When men have to cede too much control, they won't budge. And Hybels knew exactly how to comfort them. He gave them a new name: *seekers*. And he gave the service a new subject: *felt needs*. "Now let us pray" is not as man-friendly as "join me in prayer," which is not as successful as what I heard at Willow: "I'm going to pray, and you may want to join in." And he gave men something that had become progressively difficult to find in the modern world: a chance to be in the company of other men. His church was built over a web of special-interest groups, all for and about men.

The Role of Unchurched Harry

Hybels mined this niche market. He cleverly renamed his target "Unchurched Harry." As the owners of professional sports franchises have learned, if you can hold the men together, keep them feeling that they are important, allow them to bond to one another while maintaining the sense that everything is voluntary and unforced, they will form a nucleus of furious energy. They commit. Just look at the season ticket prices charged by the professional ball clubs, and you can see that this is the inelastic demand of commitment. Just look at the martyrs. Rent the video of *Holy Ghost People,* the documentary of Pentecostal snake handlers in West Virginia, and watch those men tossing poisonous snakes around at one another all in the name of divine evidence, and you'll see what sociologists call "rough camaraderie."

Robert Bly's *Iron John: A Book about Men* is not an unconsidered term, for men in groups will go through blistering fires to be forged together. These are the guys who charge the hill to blow up the pillbox or drill down the well to rescue someone trapped. Men in groups are superpotent (and superdangerous). The special men's sections of Willow are called "Iron on Iron." All right, all right, the forge of Iron on Iron is in reality a group of guys who get together to talk over breakfast, but this shows what it takes to get men to congregate. When women want to talk, they pick up the phone and go out to lunch. When men want to talk, they make a production out of it.

What Hybels understood is that while men may retire in private, they seem to crave the public company of other men. They like it when it's organized for them. So Willow Creek has group seminars on subjects like "How a Man Grows in Christ" and "Building Purity"—always without women. Usually the groups meet in clusters of six to eight men, but there are occasional meetings of upward of one thousand. This move from squad to battalion is the key to male affiliation. As the brochure says, Willow is "committed to turning irreligious men into fully devoted followers of Christ" because, as any political leader can tell you, the conversion experience is far more potent for males than for females. A converted male gets in your face.

If you want to appreciate Hybel's talent with men, just observe this on-the-fly note sent to the listserv of those lightly affiliated with the church:

Dear Enews Friends,

Sorry for breaking into your day, but I just had an idea that I thought you might be able to help me with. This weekend I will be continuing with my series "Life at the Boiling Point." I will describe how serving people in the name of Christ adds heat to our spiritual lives and gets us closer to the "boiling point." I would like to end the message with some true-life stories from people who have experienced significant spiritual growth as a result of putting on a serving towel and volunteering in the name of Christ. Would you be willing to write a brief paragraph describing the spiritual benefits that have come your way since you decided to put on a serving uniform and get into the game? Your story has the potential to inspire many thousands of people. I will protect your anonymity, as well as be sure to give God all the glory in the deal. How about it?

Thanks!
Bill

P.S. Our enews communiqués have had to be one-way up to this point (so that I can do my day job!). But this time I would really appreciate hearing from you, so please just click on reply and let it rip!

There is such a sense of muscular and manly Christianity to this query. The male recipient is being asked to help a fellow in need, the subtle shift from "putting on the serving towel" to the more manly "serving uniform," the allusion to "getting into the game," and the invoking teamwork, as well as the final "let it rip" speaks, to me at least, of guys helping guys. It's hard to resist.

The care of men is megachurch job number one, and I have not seen a single mega that doesn't focus on getting him in its crosshairs. Young men are, let's face it, almost nonexistent in the old-line denominations. They were simply not to be seen on Route 21. In fact, young men are disappearing from many places where they used to congregate, preferring instead such places as the internet, the car, watching television, the job, and the video arcade.

It has not always been this way. In the late nineteenth and early twentieth centuries, the average young man used to spend upward of twenty hours a week in the single-sex company of other men. Often men would spend almost 5 percent of their disposable income on such things as uniforms, clubhouses, initiation, and trips. That's what clubs such as the Elks, the Masons, the Moose, the Loyal Order of Redmen, as well as the Grange were all about. Many of these organizations were church related, as with Knights of Columbus and the Salvation Army.

For various reasons, these male-only organizations have mostly dried up. Even barber shops, fire departments, gyms, and pool halls have gone unisex. And that's why such voluntary assemblies of men like deer camp, strip clubs, NASCAR pits, cigar bars, old-style poker games, bass fishing, and motorcycle gangs have become so interesting for ethnographers. Often men go to such places not to hunt, smoke, gamble, or even ogle women, but because they know they will be in the company of other men. It's why paintball is so popular and why country clubs have been so slow to admit women. Car pooling works for women, not men. If you could promise that only men would be in the car pool, perhaps it might be successful.

Once men start thinking that church is a woman's space, they stay away. While it is far too simple to say that this is a reaction to the women's movement, the yearning for male bonding seems constant and transcultural. Men hunt in packs. For many men the locker room, the garage, the steam room, the cellar, the hunting shack, and the cigar bar are places of retreat and relaxation. Sociologists lifted a term for such male-only places from animal husbandry: "loafing sheds." Loafing sheds used to be built into the male groups of church life like elders, deacons, or the ushers as well as affiliated groups like Cub Scouts and Boy Scouts. As the process of running the church has become pastor-directed women's work, many men have wandered off to do church at the electronic altar of the home temple of television.

When you look at Willow Creek's men's groups, you find that along with divorce, self-help, marriage and job counseling, singles groups, and ministerial and evangelical clubs, there are meeting places for men to be with just men: loafing sheds. Here are some of the groups. Accounting Groups do the books; Campus Operations manages set up, parking, cleaning, and tending the grounds; a section called Cars deals with maintaining, detailing, and repairing cars; Faithful and True for Men offers "support and encouragement to men seeking to maintain sexual purity and integrity in a sexually charged world"; Pastor of the Day offers "a listening ear and spiritual direction to those who call or come to church with spiritual questions or concerns," as well as the more predictable Sports Ministry (basketball, volleyball, football, golf, and 5k runs); Men's Ministry (talk about life); Front Door Team (tours and greeting); and Production & Programming (sound system, staging, camera, lights). There is also a Cross-Roads group that meets to ride motorcycles.

The sensitivity of Willow Creek to male concerns is at the heart of the brand. Most churches can deliver the redemptive feeling, forgiveness, and the promise of a better life. Some churches focus on generating rapturous feelings. But few can provide lasting community for men. A poster hangs outside Bill Hybels's office. It says: "What is our business? Who is our customer? What does the customer consider value?" These questions are lifted not from St. Peter but from Peter Drucker, the patron saint of management, and they affirm the reversal of the usual gatekeeper/dispenser mentality in favor of a consumer-sensitive response, with a special concern for men.

"Put Me In, Coach"—Promise Keepers: The Megachurch on Steroids

It is the desire of men to separate from women and safely bond with one another that lies behind one of the more interesting extensions of the megachurch: the aggressively men's-only intentional church group called Promise Keepers. Although it claims to be nondenominational, PK is drawn primarily from the evangelical born-again Protestant movement, the megas, and, to a degree, the very churches out there on Route 21 that have eased anxious men out of participating. This audience is indeed huge, for a while in the millions. And it is easily panicked; PK dispersed almost as quickly as it had congealed, but since the turn of the century, it seems to be re-forming.

Started in 1990 by Bill McCartney, a burly University of Colorado football coach, Promise Keepers surged along with the megachurches. The group made no secret about who was excluded—women—but the exclusion was in the name of revitalizing the family. The promise was that the committed male would replace the casual husband. What woman could argue with that? Or, in one of the most repeated quips, a PK's wife said proudly, "I sent a frog up there, and they sent me back a prince."

From a first meeting that drew ninety-one men, in a few years PK was filling up football stadiums with seventy thousand plus. By the mid 1990s the promises became a bit clearer. And scarier. More than a million men were eager to "promise" not just to return home but to "take back" any number of institutions that had been hijacked by "liberals," aka feminists. These men were coming home all right, not as helpmates but as God's apocalyptic horsemen.

In the late 1990s the balloon burst, partly because its self-dealing agenda was simply so transparent: so antigay, antiabortion, antifeminist. What also hobbled the organization was that in a desire to draw a more diverse (read African-American) crowd to show that it was not also antiblack, the high attendance fees (almost seventy dollars for a two-day session) were waived. Unmotivated spectators, such as myself, poured in. The freeloaders came for a look and passed right by.

In other words, Promise Keepers had the temporary fate that some megachurches are now having: the distance between the front door and back door is too short. You come, you look around, you beat your chest, but what happens next? Once finished swelling the crowd, boredom sets in. Many of the men who joined the march in Washington, DC, in 1997 (shades of the 1995 Million Man March of Minister Louis Farrakhan's Nation of Islam) just kept marching—back to the television, the office, the Barcalounger, the garage, the golf course.

But after the turn of the twenty-first century, with the reelection of George W. Bush and his idea of family values, Promise Keepers started showing modest signs of reinflating. This happened in the so-called red states. The organization had scaled down from a high of about five hundred full-time employees to about one hundred, but slowly hired more. In 2005 the group bumped up the number of tour stops to twenty, including the eighty-thousand seat University of Arkansas football stadium, its largest venue since 1999.

Putting so-called family values aside, holding in abeyance the often repugnant subterfuges of PK (like the selective reading of scripture), and bracketing the passive aggression of a group that is forever claiming that it must "take back" this or that role that has been co-opted by women, how important is it that this group has provided a secure lair for men in a world increasingly devoid of men-only space?

I think it's crucial. Promise Keepers is all about what the religious sect foregrounds and what the megachurch carefully nurtures: male bonding. However, now following the model of 12-step programs, these dispossessed men are expected to find a male "faith partner." Supposedly, each Promise Keeper shares his deepest fears and secret sins on a daily basis with this mentor/compatriot/sponsor. Obviously the purpose is to make each man accountable to another for keeping his promises. Less obvious is that this dialogue mandates separation from spouse and bonding with the faith-partner buddy. And since it takes a year for most men to develop that trust, the time frame is open ended. Then these male partners are to form small male-bonding groups in order to spread the movement through local churches. PK thus forms an easy synergy with the megachurches, encouraging and reinforcing greater male participation in congregational life while at the same time giving the men carte blanche to private space.

The group even has a seven-step mission statement called "Seven Promises of a Promise Keeper." Along with promises to love Christ, be pure, support marriage, help the local church, practice racial tolerance, and make the world Christian, is this, promise number two: "A Promise Keeper is committed to pursuing vital relationships with a few other men, understanding that he needs brothers to help him keep his promises."

The invocation of brotherhood, the idea of sacred promises to be kept, and the sense of separation from the Other (in other words, the female) is crucial. These men are on a *mission,* and woe to whoever comes between them.

When you attend the stadium meetings, you can see this sense of Us-versus-Them being inculcated. Like football cheering in which each section competes to yell loudest, so the individual brotherhood groups compete by cheering "We love Jesus, what about you?!" or "We are the brotherhood, we are connected!" or just "Jesus, Jesus, Jesus!" From time to time the men are asked to hug a neighbor and promise to "watch his back." Sections do the wave, just like the undergrads at football games, although the Promise Keepers are doing it for the glory of God and the salvation of the family. And there is a lot of high-fiving, as in all male conviviality rituals.

As with the megachurch, the JumboTron screens and super-amplified music not only allow the men to lose their inhibitions about raising their hands and gyrating their bodies, but also encourage them to dance—if not *with* each other then at least *near* each other. It's strangely like the high-school prom complete with the football coach leading cheers. And, after all, the exuberance of bonding is being done for the glory of God. So here are men who might wince at the sweatlodge rituals of Robert Bly doing exactly the same kind of chanting and prancing that might be considered a little girly.

There are no girly men in the eyes of God, however. They are all Arnold Schwarzeneggers. The Jesus of PK is not the Warner Sallman Jesus of Presentation Bibles. That image of Christ, you may remember from chapter 7, results from the feminization of denominational Christianity. That neurasthenic Christ was passive in the onslaught of adversity. He's the Christ of Route 21. But the Christ of the Promise Keepers is more like the Terminator. Certainly he's the star-quarterback Jesus. He's take-charge, take-it-back, make-it-mine Christ.

The stadium meetings have such high-falutin' titles as the "Stand in the Gap" rally or "Uprising: The Revolution of a Man's Soul."

"Like getting a high-performance tune-up for the soul":
Promise Keepers Unleashed.

There are no women around to arch an eyebrow and opine, "Where did *this* Christ come from?" or "How come you guys are dancing with each other?" The purgative of mass confession (we have made a mess of things) combined with the elixir of not just forgiveness but divine selection (we are the champions) makes even the most repressed and uptight male into a dervish.

So who are these meek men made dynamic dervishes? According to a survey conducted by the National Center for Fathering and cited in *U.S. News & World Report*, the median age of Promise Keepers attendees is thirty-eight. Though 88 percent are married, 21 percent have been divorced. Fifty percent report that their own fathers were "largely absent" when they grew up (65.7 percent of these said this absence was because of work). Fifty-three percent said they knew what their father felt toward them, and only 25 percent were satisfied with themselves as fathers. Thirty-four percent attended Baptist churches. Eighty-four percent were white. These are the men who are not attending church along Route 21. They may be the ones playing golf on Sunday.

These are the same guys who used to be the core of the Masons: middle-aged, middle-class men yearning for connection not just with one another but with the Imperial Potentate, the Grand Poobah of the Frat, with a distant and maybe even disapproving dad. The group language of PK is not the secret voodoo of a fraternal order or the psychobabble of therapy, but, as one might guess, the jabberwocky of sports. Not for nothing was this movement started by a man still called "the coach" and it's not happenstance that the meetings take place in football stadiums and are held together with the cheers and rituals well-known to the weekend warrior.

These men of PK are NFL-tough. They can envision life as a football game. They've even seen this game, hundreds of times. They know the broadcast patter: how much punishment he can absorb; great second effort; he bulls his way for extra yardage; you can't stop him—you can only hope to contain him; it's decision time—they're knocking on the door; the defense is tough in the red zone; this game is being won in the trenches; he's slow getting up;

they have to stop the big play; they're marching down the field; it all depends on where they spot the ball; they've got to punch it in here; and the litany of win one for the Gipper. In this world, women are cheerleaders. They are on the sidelines. They shout, Go team! I heard none of this language along Route 21. Pastor James did encourage his male parishioners to wear their team jerseys on Super Bowl Sunday, but his heart clearly wasn't in it.

Admittedly, the sports trope is hardly new. At the turn of the century, Billy Sunday, a former baseball star, rallied "back-slid" Christians with robust sports metaphors. Billy Graham, who felt equally at home in a stadium and on a golf course, assured audiences that "Jesus was the greatest athlete who ever lived." His son and evangelical heir, Franklin Graham, does the same thing, even decking himself out in the sports jersey of whichever team/town he's converting. But the intense PK focus on football lingo is startling. This is the stuff of muscular Christianity, literally. Put me in, Coach.

Joining this particular Fellowship of Christian Athletes not only makes you a player but also allows you to spend bench time with your pals. You've shown yourself to be a man's man; now you can just kick back and relax. You've confessed, you've cried, you're vulnerable; now you can be left alone for a while. You made the team. No one can touch the Godly Man. Do not disturb. Maybe now you're even ready to attend church with the wife and kiddies and sit still.

All the liberal criticisms of Promise Keepers are true enough. *The Village Voice* attacked its "sanitized multiculturalism" and called its "policy of racial diversity so overt that it reeks of insincerity." *GQ* (*Gentlemen's Quarterly*) hardly known for having an opinion on anything more complex than a Windsor knot, did a major piece on Coach McCartney called "Triumph of His Will," a reference to a famous Nazi-inspired movie of almost the same name. *GQ* calls the coach "a lop-eyed loon" and "a raving lunatic." *New York Times* columnist Frank Rich, who can be counted on to lower the boom on this kind of rabble-rousing, sneers at the group and its "Robert Blyesque hunger to overcome macho inhibitions." And this is tame compared to what the National Organization of Women has to say: www.now.org/issues/right/pk.html.

While it is easy to take potshots at such men and their smiley-face approach to the complexities of their discontent, it may be that what we see in the megachurch and Promise Keepers is something embedded deep in organized religion: not just the creation of gendered space but the protection of such space. In the mainlines, men have been eased out, inadvertently, to be sure. This recent surge, this time to the megas, like the series of other great awakenings in this country, may be just another of the periodic resettling of the sexes. Except that this time men seem to be the crucial consumers, and the contested space is the church itself. If privileging men is the price of repatriation, some women seem to be saying, then it's worth it. After all, it's more effective than praying for their return to the fold.

CHAPTER TEN

And This Too Shall Pass: The Future of Megas

If we look at Promise Keepers as one amplification of the megachurch, it may help explain part of the revival of aggressive Christianity in America. As with previous awakenings, this one is happening partly because of a new innovation in supply—the church of electronic enhancement. As fictional rock guitarist Nigel Tufnel says of his amplifier in the mock documentary *This Is Spinal Tap*, this is religion turned up to eleven. This manly-man religion, this boom-box Christianity, this in-your-face religion, this wanna-make-somethin'-of-it religion, may be the masculine response to so much of what has caused the male to distance himself (and feel distanced) from the world around him. In a sense, the megachurch has become a safe haven for men, a place to find respite from what he takes to be the woman-centered, baby-centered world at the turn into the twenty-first century.

This is church as heroic performance and safe haven. And you can go to the Saturday twilight show or the Sunday matinee. There's plenty of parking outside, no dress code (the only people in suits are visitors), no "let's be meek and ashamed," and, most important, there is plenty of camaraderie. Inside church proper there are all the technologies men appreciate: the sound system, the magnifying screens, and the comfy seats. The service is nonthreatening, the band is better than the dolorous organ music, there are plenty of slick music videos to make emotions easier to sense, the hymns are follow-the-bouncing-ball, and there's no "kneel down you miserable sinner and be ashamed." Best yet, there are none of those grayhairs of Route 21 threatening to pray for this and that, including you.

To further reiterate, when the pastor (although that term is never used—first names suffice) delivers the sermon (and that word is never used—*message* is the term), you can see him from different points of view on the various screens, just as you can with the new DVD technology that allows you to shift angles of vision while watching football. In the megachurches I've attended, there may be sermonizing about felt needs, but more often it's about building projects, about adding a wing, about installing new technology. I can't recall a mega I've attended where the sermonizing has lasted much longer than a half hour.

But best yet, there's plenty of stuff for a guy to do while the wife and kid do their things. Successful megachurches have all manner of entertainment from the guy side of the street. I have often wondered if there was a direct ratio between the number of flower arrangements and male comfort. Flowers are profuse on the denominational altars but almost never seen at the megas. Instead, here are weight rooms, fast-food franchises, touch football, bowling alleys, golf trips, racquetball, and plenty of Iron on Iron. In 12-step fashion, there are support groups galore, although never called that. There's a group to help *you*. Oversexed. Undersexed. Philanderer or philanderee. Drug recovery. Single parent. Divorce recovery. Fix your car. Fix your slice. In addition, there are groups that help you with your finances, your career, your motorcycle, your parenting, the way you feel.

The City (Downsized and Decentralized) on the Hill Inc.

If you were looking for an apt analogy for the megachurch, you might consider a medieval hillside fortress château like Les Baux de

Provence in southern France or the hilltop multitowered town of San Gimignano in Tuscany, Italy. These fortified dukedoms were like extended families, all hunkered down behind their gates. You ventured out during the day to till the soil, harvest the crops, do your trading, and then you skedaddled back inside at night and pulled up the drawbridge.

These gated communities were intensely aware of threats from outside and willingly huddled together under the rule of a charismatic leader, the overlord. Unlike earlier city-states of the Roman Empire (Florence, Venice) or later northern German counterparts (Bremen, Hamburg), nothing much came out of these enclaves. They were almost completely self-enclosed, in part because there was no fissure between political and religious life. They were essentially theocracies, yes, but they were also highly adaptive to the surrounding cultures. They were in many ways the beginnings of the modern corporation.

Before all else, the megachurch is megabusiness. It has the heft to harvest the economies of mass production and just-in-time inventories. It's all-encompassing. It runs all the time and provides almost all the social services of a town. Church care and school care and community care get reunited. A few megas even self-consciously mimic the *Mayberry R.F.D.* town center, complete with the town square—the commons. People milling around is crucial.

Although much is made of missionary work outside the church, it's usually as a way of getting money in. I've never seen accurate numbers on exactly how much is really spent on missionary *outreach*. The general rule is that a church may tithe 10 percent of its income, which leaves plenty to spend on itself. When I mentioned to Pastor James that in every church I'd attended, especially the megas, they made almost a fetish of some faraway place where "we are doing such good missionary work," he arched an eyebrow and told me that all the churches are now saying this. Actions, he said, often don't follow words.

As modern philanthropies have found, if you are trying to get people to contribute, it's easier to do it if you position the goal far outside the core organization. If you watch ads for groups that are raising funds to help children or victims of disasters, for instance, you'll often see faraway scenes of help being proffered rather than on the other side of the tracks. Actress Sally Struthers poses with potbellied kids in Africa, not Alabama. It's often easier to raise money for AIDS victims in Sudan than for those next door. The exotic not only captures our attention, it deflects our guilt. By writing the check, we're doing all we can.

Much of this religious activity is happening in Latin America and Asia, far from the eyes of the Western media. But the place you always hear about in church is Africa. Very often a specific village is invoked, and we are given specific updates on how well our ambassadors (who used to be missionaries) are doing making bricks and converts. Patch the cellphone call into the church's PA system, and you are there, making a difference.

To be sure, Africa is not just the battleground of Protestant denominations duking it out for converts but also the contested ground with Islam. As well, Africa is in our minds as the home of slavery. What is more compelling than the photograph of the kindly, white soldier of Christ with the black skeletonic child, blown up to gargantuan size on the JumboTron? I saw many of these images at the megas I visited. Is it easier to help the black child in Darfur than in Detroit?

(Skeptics of the effectiveness of this missionary effort abound. An International Monetary Fund study released in 2005 found that $1 trillion in assistance has been spent in Africa in the past fifty years without much to show for it. I suspect the same conclusion might be drawn about church monies, except that conversion seems more important to them than bricks. Plus how do you combat AIDS without at least discussing population control?)

Megachurch pastors seem to be forever going off to the missionary fields to observe the dollars spent and reporting back on the need for more. But, in truth, many of the dollars raised for such projects seem to be spent nearby, on the music studios, the food courts, the basketball courts, the playgrounds, the weight rooms, and expanding the parking lots. *Outreach* often means "taking in." So, while raising thousands every week in the name of missionary work, the Fellowship Church in Grapevine, Texas, employs a chief technology officer and spends 15 percent of its $30 million annual budget on new AV delivery systems.

As is often the case when money is to be made, consultants make it. For instance, Willow Creek employs two MBAs, one from Stanford, one from Harvard. Megas hire MBAs to hedge their monies and marketing experts to organize their email, direct mail, pamphlets, videotapes, audiotapes, books, and the like. The efficiencies of the city-state approach to church is that no tribute, no protection money, is paid to higher-ups. What comes in, stays in.

In 2005 both the staid *BusinessWeek* and the cheeky *Economist* decried in cover articles ("Earthly Empires: How Evangelical Churches Are Borrowing from the Business Playbook" and "Onward, Christian Shoppers," respectively) that the megas are becoming the new tax-advantaged behemoths. You could almost hear them gasp as they pointed to the new industry of faith-based consultancies, the number of chief financial officers, chief operating officers, and church leaders with MBAs. But what the business magazines really marveled at was the cash flow. After all, the Lakewood enterprise in Houston brought in $55 million in contributions in 2004, four times the 1999 amount. They are one step away from becoming hedge funds. One church even provides mortgage brokers and real estate agents. But that's precisely the point. Here is the nostalgic village re-created in its most aggressive form, the gated community, descendant of the ancient city-state.

There is another marketing aspect of the megas that is now being appreciated by commercial interests. The mega is a wonderful *consumer aggregator*. That is to say that it's one of the few social groups made up of affiliated people who voluntarily gather together. Such homogeneity is ideal for microtargeting. And indeed companies like Chrysler have experimented by providing cars out in the parking lot for postservice test drives. In exchange for mentioning the cars, the company contributes to the church's charities.

But far more intriguing is the application of product placement to the service itself. As a way of plugging the Disney film *The Chronicles of Narnia,* ministers were offered a chance to win a free trip to London along with $1,000 cash. Here's how it worked. The minister sent in the text of his sermon in which he plugged the movie (honor system, of course) to the Outreach Media Group. In so doing, he secured a slot in the sweepstakes. Whether or not the *sermo-mercial* will catch on is anyone's guess, but it's not much of a stretch to contemplate logoed coffee cups or brief adverts on the drop-down screens. After all, think how another consumer aggegator, the local cineplex, has been transformed.

As might be expected, with so much money swirling around, many from the corporate world are eager to lend a hand to the new church-as-business. At the end of the 1990s, there was even a publicly traded company humbly called Kingdom Ventures. KV's sole mission was to help churches like Pastor James's maximize its investment in generating growth. The company operated (or claimed to) twelve subsidiaries to work with ten thousand churches on everything from fund-raising to event planning (it provided speakers and artists for events) to upgrading technology (it helped decide which new audio and visual equipment was right for your church). Alas, Kingdom Ventures now seems to be on its way to corporate purgatory—not because of its business plan but because of a subpoena it received from the U.S. Securities and Exchange Commission relating to its stock transactions.

What makes Kingdom Ventures interesting is that for a time, at least, it was really in business and really making money. It was even listed on the NASDAQ. The industry of helping stand-alone churches industrialize is clearly replacing the old-line denominational staff who helped with day-to-day matters. A new breed of PR firm is sprouting, the most famous of which is A. Larry Ross Communications of Carrollton, Texas, which positions your church for "proper exposure." A few advertising agencies have positioned themselves for "proper exposure" as being faith based, the most famous being Artistry Marketing Concepts, not by happenstance also in Texas.

But the most interesting outsourcing is to independent impresarios like Luis Palau. Palau learned the trade running Graham-style revivals. In the 1980s he realized he could tie local churches together and employ the synergies of mass production and cross-marketing. If you want to get your church noticed in a hurry, you hire Luis. His events, really imitations of rock festivals, last a few days, energize the consumer base, and provide a sense of overflow excitement. In so doing, they eerily mimic the nineteenth-century Methodist camp meeting.

Palau has done the old-style revival one better by realizing that he can externalize his costs by renting the captive religious audience to commercial interests. So he has now trimmed his festivals from a handful of days to two, sought corporate sponsors instead of donations from participants, brought in Christian rock bands and extreme sports like skateboarding and BMX riding, and put up a food court in the middle of all the activity. All selling branded products, naturally.

When I was in Orlando, I saw his handiwork. Just like the old P. T. Barnum posters advertising that the circus is coming, Palau had posters everywhere announcing the upcoming show. The Luis Palau Orlando Festival was coming to town in the service of a few churches, and "affinity sponsors" were all in place. These sponsors even fit into various groups like "Presenters" (Chick-fil-A, Regal Boats); "Platinum" (Clark Consulting, Z88.3, a radio station); "Gold" (State Farm Insurance, Rosen Centre Hotel); "Silver" (Westin Grand Bohemian, My Neighborhood Storage Center); and "Bronze" (Evangelical Christian Credit Union, GMAC Real Estate). Palau even worked out arrangements with a number of retailers such as the Gap and Best Buy so that a percentage of your purchase there can go to the Luis Palau Evangelistic Association, of which an undisclosed percent goes to missionary work.

What the advertising failed to mention were the names of the sponsoring churches. No mention of either God, Jesus, or rescuing your eternal soul. Although the festival carries a slogan of "Great Music! Good News!" that's as religious as the posters get. For someone unfamiliar with the Christian meaning underlying the term *good news,* Palau's festival could easily be mistaken for some other feel-good, yet nonreligious, gathering. Palau and his organization hope to draw people in by deemphasizing religion and playing up the fun. At least Billy Graham told you what was going on under the canvas big top. Ditto Barnum.

One other bit of megachurch marketing that merits comment is *The Shepherd's Guide,* a buyer's guide for Christians wanting to patronize other Christians. These guides are often passed out at megachurches (I got one at the First Baptist Church of Orlando). They have the look and feel (including the nontrademarked walking fingers on the cover) of the yellow pages. So if you want a God-fearing CPA, plumber, dance instructor, locksmith, or optometrist, here's the place to look. But, as we learn on page 5, "Please do not ask for a discount from any advertiser because you think that Christians should give discounts to Christians." The demurrer continues into a thicket of confusion; "Stop and think about it this way—who of you would be willing to pay twice the price of 25 percent more for a product or service. Then what sense does it make for you to expect or demand a discount?" As far as I could see from the Orlando *Shepherd's Guide,* the most common advertisers were attorneys. There were also quite a few God-fearing marriage counselors. Coming and going.

It's only a short step, and a very alluring one, for the megachurch to post its own internal *Shepherd's Guide* just for members of the congregation. Here one really sees the value of the gated-community/walled-city approach, especially from the male point of view. The church not only provides a place to meet with guys interested in your views on the meaning of life, but you can also find the guy to cut your lawn or get rid of your crabgrass. Better yet, he can find you.

After all, the very qualities that make the huge church attractive to a mobile society also resolve the day-to-day problems in the style of huge corporations: they endlessly network. So if you go to megachurch websites, you can often find the link for help around the house and in the life. Try the Community Church of Joy in

Selling to the choir: *The Shepherd's Guide.*

Glendale, Arizona, as an example. Click on the business directory, and you'll find listings for cleaning the pool, car, carpet, office, and marriage. You'll find someone to get you in a new job, in the new house, in a new frame of mind, and even, finally, in the cemetery.

Merchants in the Temples: Pastorpreneurs

The overlord of these little city-states is always a man, and a very affable man blessed with organizational skills. Often he's the son of a minister. Just as a disproportionate number of early advertising men came from the ranks of the pastorate, so too with these marketing men. They grew up watching their dads. They knew the product and how to sell it. They knew the power of sincerity and promise. They knew what growth meant and, more important, they knew what the opposite of growth meant. They learned from an early age that you keep one eye on the front door and the other one on the side door. Whether you like it or not, you are in the religion business. Before you made a sale, you gathered a crowd.

In no way are these pastorpreneurs the sleazeballs in sharkskin of televangelism or the hose 'em down hucksters of tent revivals. Nor are they the right-wing politicos like Pat Robertson and Jerry Falwell. This new man of the cloth is in pinstripes and just at the edge of celebrity culture. He is, in the best sense, a merchandiser, or better yet, brand manager.

The paterfamilias of this group is the ever-self-effacing Bill Hybels (just call me Bill) of Willow Creek Community Church. Hybels is an authentic marketing genius who got kudos from the likes of Peter Drucker and Harvard Business School. In fact, in the 1990s, Harvard dispatched a troop of MBAs to look at the Willow operation. They were converted not by the faith but by the numbers: yearly revenues then topping $12 million (today it's more than double that) of which barely half goes to staffing and operations, about 30 percent to operating costs and part-time salaries, 12 percent to debt reduction for the $34 million building, 2 percent to miscellaneous, and the rest to the cash kitty. No corporation throws off that kind of cash unless it is an oil driller atop a dinosaur death pit.

Hybels has not been slow to play on his Cambridge connection. He knows the value of cross-branding. In one of his emails sent to those affiliated with the church, he writes:

Dear Enews Friends, 3/17/2006

I am writing this to you from a hotel room overlooking the Charles River in Cambridge, Massachusetts.

Since 1991 I have been representing Willow at the Harvard Business School as the second-year MBA students debate the case study done on our church. The professor (who has not only become a good friend, but has also agreed to speak at the Leadership Summit this August) leads a robust class discussion for about 45 minutes and then allows me to address the class and have questions and answers for another 45 minutes. I wish you could all be "flies on the wall"! To listen to some of the brightest and best students in the world bantering with each other as to why a church that began in a rented movie theater has grown like it has and wields the global influence it does is almost illegally fun for me. I keep wanting to blurt out the two word explanation . . . Only God!

Part of his entrepreneurial genius is that while Hybels clearly basks in his Harvard connection—after all, what affiliation is more powerful in the seeker world?—he invokes both the aw-shucks humbleness at the same time as "I got into Harvard." While the buffoon Pat Robertson has to continually remind his viewers that he went to Yale, Bill Hybels positions himself as the man Harvard goes to when it needs expert advice.

Having watched Hybels in operation, I was impressed with his offhanded ease in the pulpit. As an apatheist, I know I am his niche market. I am Unchurched Harry. And it wasn't that I went to scoff and stayed to pray; Hybels had a wonderful way of including the unchurched in a sense of togetherness. He's a study in contrived self-irony because he clearly knows how important he is, but he never comes across as lording it over the congregation.

In fact, Hybels claims to be amazed that people study him as a motivator. "I'm an incurable team player," he says, and his staff agrees—as long as he's the quarterback. What compares with the Willow team? The Salvation Army, the Girl Scouts, and various paramilitary organizations. All in all, concluded the Harvard study, Willow Creek is a tribute to "knowing your customers and meeting their needs."

The pastorpreneur with the hottest hand has been Rick Warren of Saddleback Church in southern California. Like Hybels, he has mastered gee-whiz, but his reach has been far greater. Hybels's Willow Creek Association has almost twelve thousand affiliated churches, but Warren's Pastors.com ties him in with one hundred thousand pastors worldwide each week. He has email forums, archives of all of his sermons, and a place to post prayer requests. He also sends a free weekly newsletter, *Rick Warren's Ministry Toolbox,* to pastors. In his Hawaiian shirts and his I-can-look-straight-into-the-camera style, he oozes sincerity.

As a backhanded tribute to Warren's success, two books attacking him have been published by Christian presses. What his critics complain of is his incessant marketing. But what I find particularly noteworthy is that when one of his marketing acolytes, Greg Stielstra, wanted to use Saddleback as an example of buzz marketing in his *PyroMarketing: The Four-step Strategy to Ignite Customer Evangelists and Keep Them for Life,* Warren complained to their mutual publisher, HarperCollins. He didn't want to be seen as a marketer. How ironic. That's like Bill Clinton not wanting to be considered a politician.

Warren has launched a massive movement—built around his blockbuster best-seller, *The Purpose Driven Life*—in which more than thirty thousand churches and other organizations have conducted programs. The gist of the *PD Life* is bumper-sticker simple: "God made you to do His work. That's your purpose." Want details? Here's how it breaks out:

1. You were planned for God's pleasure (worship).
2. You were formed for God's family (fellowship).
3. You were created to become like Christ (spiritual growth).
4. You were shaped for serving God (spiritual service).
5. You were made for a mission (evangelism).

It just so happens that this purposefulness all happens at your church. You can see why his fellow pastors have signed on. Under all of this is really the voice of Norman Vincent Peale's *The Power of Positive Thinking* filtered through Bruce Barton's *The Man Nobody Knows.* Adjustment through Jesus. Although Warren claims to hold the "self-help" approach to Christianity in disdain, arguing instead that only God's Word can reveal what the true purpose of life is, if you read closely you'll soon see that *purpose* is a catchphrase for fitting in, for finding community *in church.* No wonder in front of Pastor James's church along Route 21 flies the banner "Does Your Life Have Purpose?" Want it? We got it!

A bit more complex is Joel Osteen, if only because he's seemingly so simple. Again, he can look straight into the camera eye and make you think he's the son you never had. He looks suspiciously like a fishing lure, all shiny and coruscating under the lights. He puts on a show of endless sincerity and promise, preaching it, as he says, "not sad but glad." He's so carbonated that he's hard to resist.

Osteen has made himself as ubiquitous to television viewers as Warren has to pastors. That's because he's bought up time in the top twenty-five markets and moved out of the Sunday morning ghetto into the edges of prime time. It costs Lakewood about $14 million a year to get this exposure, but it's worth it. Joel and his very attractive wife, Victoria, can now be seen in 92 percent of the nation's households, in addition to live in front of some thirty thousand worshipers in Houston.

Not to put too fine a point on it, but he's not much of a deep thinker. If you read his book *Your Best Life Now: 7 Steps to Living at Your Full Potential,* you'll see that everything good is a sign from God. So, for instance, years ago, when he was upgraded from coach to first class, he opines, "That's the kind of thing that happens *naturally* when we live favor minded. That's why we should get in the habit of consistently speaking God's favor over our lives." This is providentialism carried to the level of parody.

What makes this ironically entertaining is that on December 19, 2005, he and Victoria were on a Continental flight to Vail, Colorado. This time he was paying for first class, not praying for it. According to press accounts, Victoria stormed the cockpit after a spill on her tray wasn't cleaned up quickly enough. She made such a scene that the Osteen family was asked to leave the plane, which they did, holding up the flight for almost two hours while their luggage was removed. Putting aside the class (first) and destination (Vail), and the behavior (a "hissy fit"), one wonders if this was as well the favor of God. But the wonderful thing about Osteen is that you don't have time to contemplate; there's always something happening next. Something good. Something just for you. Favor God.

And then there is Ted Haggard. Pastor Ted gained national

exposure as the head of the National Association of Evangelicals and
as a semiregular on Fox News's *The O'Reilly Factor*. He was also the
focus of a cover story in the May 2005 *Harper's* magazine that declared
his two-thousand-member-strong New Life Church to be "America's
most powerful megachurch." For a while Haggard was the go-to guy
whenever the networks needed a sound bite (even though he had not
written a best-selling self-help book—unless we count his *The
Jerusalem Diet: The "One Day" Approach to Reach Your Ideal Weight—
and Stay There*). On camera, he exuded a school-boy enthusiasm, especially while attacking the sexual proclivities of others.

And then he blew up. In 2006, he resigned after allegations of
homosexual activity and drug abuse (appropriately, Ecstasy) were
made by Mike Jones, a former male prostitute. After the requisite
hemming and hawing, Haggard stepped aside only to announce that
after three weeks of intensive Christian counseling he was now completely heterosexual and presumably good to return to the pulpit.

What makes Haggard such an interesting case study in pastor-
preneurship is not his flirtation with what he supposedly found
abhorrent, but his intense narcissism and his ability to connect that
inappropriate self-esteem to that of his parishioners. His love affair
with being filmed is clearly a yearning to be seen, yes, but so is
theirs. Like the parishioners at FaithWorld, they too want to perform. So, for instance, preblow-up when his parishioners appeared
a bit too rapturous on camera, he gave them a little heads-up on TV
decorum via the church's listserv. His words:

Here are a few tips:

1. If a camera is on you during a worship service, worship; don't
dance, jump, etc. Secular people watching TV are touched with
authentic worship, but jumping and dancing in church looks too
bizarre for most to relate to. Remember, people watching TV
news are not experiencing what you are experiencing. They are
watching and thinking. Worship indicates sincerity, dancing and
jumping looks like excessive emotionalism.

2. If reporters want to interview you, talk with them, but use words that make sense to them. Speak their language. Don't talk about the devil, demons, voices speaking to you, God giving you supernatural revelations, etc. Instead, tell your personal story in common sense language.

3. Don't be nervous. Be friendly and open. Reporters typically don't have an agenda, they authentically want to know what we do and why we do it. For example, Barbara Walters is working on a story about heaven and will interview me and get some supporting shots from the church. She might not use any of it, but she wants to put together an interesting story. Since we believe in heaven, we are, in fact, a good source. So, if she talks with you, don't be spooky or weird. Don't switch into a glassy-eyed heavenly mode, just answer, "Heaven is real. It's the place where God will be fully present with his people. He will reward people in heaven. Heaven is better than Colorado Springs." Say it straight and clear. Don't worry.

When the email leaked out and it seemed to some as if Haggard was trying to orchestrate how people in the church behave, Rob Brendle, associate pastor, glossed his boss's email thus:

This email was to let our congregation know of some of the week's happenings, and coach them a little bit on communicating effectively with the media. Every subculture is a world unto itself, with its own traditions, expressions, and norms; evangelical Christianity is no exception. When we become aware that our meetings are gaining a wider audience, we want to present our faith in a way that is understandable to as many as possible. We believe the media is a friend and great asset to the church, and we want to work together well.

An even more provocative example of choreographed behavior is to be seen in Alexandra Pelosi's HBO documentary *Friends of God*

(2007). Pelosi spends much time with preblow-up Haggard, letting his overlarge grin fill the screen like a cartoon beaver. In one scene, after Haggard opines that, "Surveys say that evangelicals have the best sex life of any other group," Pelosi expresses the requisite amazement. Without missing a beat, Haggard turns to ask a pair of young male parishioners how often they have sex with their wives. The comment seemingly comes out of the blue. Yet the young men don't beg off. They've been coached. Or so it seems because one of them quickly responds, "Every day. Twice a day." Then Haggard asks the man how frequently his wife climaxes. "Every time," the man says, again without missing a beat. Leaving the subtext of Pastor Ted's own behavior aside for a moment, you can see what is being confected. This is a wonderland in which ecstatic performance is not just constructed, but relentlessly marketed. The church has gone from being an institution providing safe passage to a world beyond to an institution providing rapture in the here and now.

Little wonder that the next step in megachurch development is the gated-community housing development—literally the city-state. Although Haggard's mega is currently in free fall, not too far away in Longmont, Colorado, LifeBridge Christian Church is planning to develop 313 acres into residences, a community college, and a senior center. With a brand promise like that, who wouldn't want to establish residence?

Danger of Celebrity

For better or for worse, what all these pastors have in common is celebrity. Etymologically, a celebrity is one who is celebrated, *celebratus*. The condition of being celebrated is ancient, doubtless one of our most central socializing devices as it separates leaders from the tribe. In all cultures certain people are capable of being honored, not just for what they have done but for what they can continue to do for us. This recognition is not always a function of the individual's specific acts. In fact, the elevation of certain people—celebrities—is often dependent on their ability to perform certain rites. In the church we still honor the role of the priest in "celebrating" certain events like baptism, the Eucharist, marriage, or the last rites.

The pastor often projects a version of Christ that is similar to the denomination's brand identity. So on one extreme the Unitarian minister promulgates a cerebral Jesus, while the Pentecostal uses a hyperactive Jesus. As well, if you look at the famous pastor-celebrities in church history, men like Martin Luther, John Calvin, George Fox, John Wesley, Roger Williams, Jonathan Edwards, you will see that they generate a mirror Jesus. If the churchman is sacrificial, intolerant, and belligerent, so too his Jesus. The further away from cult status, the more tempered the ministerial persona, but successful denominations attempt to match their minister, their celebrator, with their version of the savior.

The modern pastorpreneur celebrity is not a stern taskmaster but an accommodater. In an entertainment economy where alternatives continually exist, Hybels, Warren, Schuller, Osteen, et al., portray adjustment, making peace, an Oprah/Dr. Phil persona. The template is Norman Vincent Peale. And when you listen to them preach, you get a sense of "yes, you can" and very little "no, you can't."

I'm certainly not the first to notice that this is the application of the human potential movement, of the modern application of emotional adjustment techniques, to religion. The mega Jesus is the Jesus of Bruce Barton, the Jesus of this world, the Jesus of growing a business and prospering. Rotary Club Jesus. Behind Joel Osteen is a huge slowly spinning golden globe, not the crucified Christ. At the extreme, this is the Jesus of the so-called prosperity gospel, the Jesus who helps you get stuff. But at the more tempered level, this is the Jesus who, like the pastorpreneur, considers congregational and personal *growth* an end in itself. In a sense, growth is a surrogate of salvation.

The Mega as Timebomb

The centrifugal qualities that make the megachurch so powerful as a city-state will sooner or later work against it. That's because of a centripetal force. The yearning for pushing out, or in church terms, expanding the missionary fields, is to gather new converts. What happens when there's nowhere to go? How the pastorpreneur equilibrates these opposing pressures of "stay close in," "us against them," and, at the same time, "move out, we're getting bigger," is a high-wire act of some danger.

What happens when you go to church, and you find that there are fewer people this Sunday than last, and still fewer next Sunday? If what you sell is the Venturi effect of commotion at the door, what happens when the fizz dies down and even turns flat? Clearly, the pastorpreneurs, who, after all, are nothing if not marketing quick studies, know this. So how, with the exception of Haggard, are they coping?

At one extreme is Rick Warren likening his "purpose-driven formula" to an operating chip that can be inserted into the motherboard of any church. He proudly points out that there are more than thirty thousand purpose-driven churches that operate without his hands on the keyboard. They are free to consult his website, which gives one hundred thousand pastors access to email forums and pre-formatted sermons, including over twenty years' worth of Mr. Warren's own.

Or there is Bill Hybels's Willow Creek Association, the consulting arm of the mother church, which has more than twelve thousand member churches. It puts on leadership events, does consulting, and licenses member churches to make mention of their affiliation so that they can use the hook for new members. By so doing, the Association earns the mother church almost $20 million a year. And protects it from the too-close association with the home office.

And then there are the voluntary associations like Calvary Chapel and the Vineyard Christian Fellowship, each of which has several hundred churches affiliated with it (including several other megachurches), many of which were started, or "planted," from within the ministries of these churches. Although the word *franchise* is never used, Saddleback Church has incorporated twenty-seven daughter churches, while Highland Park Baptist Church in Chattanooga, Tennessee, already had in 1983 over sixty chapel ministries.

If this is sounding a bit like the Holiday Inn approach to church as motel with a big sign, it should. In churchspeak, it's called expanding the missionary fields, while in marketing it's brand extension. Ironically, this horizontal expansion is exactly the denominational approach that made the stand-alone megachurch so alluring to begin with. Slowly but surely "this is not your father's church" is well on its way to becoming your father's church.

But becoming exactly what they claim to be opposing—namely, the moribund denomination—is only one of the megas' problems. They face many more hazards, some of their own devising. First, in the heady U.S. presidential election of 2004, many of them eagerly flew into the flypaper of politics. If there is one thing to be learned from history, it is that a church expressing politics is a church about to be embarrassed. And that's not hard to understand. When politics goes punky—and it will, if only because it deals in the world, where heroic promise can be measured—it will disappoint. The so-called red state linkage between low-church megas and the Republican Party is already causing vibrations of disenchantment.

Aligned with this is the inevitable passing of the celebrity pastor either by scandal or retirement. Who's next to take the pulpit? As opposed to the mainline churches that had a bench of eager players down in the minor leagues, the megachurch has to grow its own. There is no replacement for the likes of Rick Warren, Bill Hybels, and Joel Osteen, simply because they are such mavericks, counter programmers, and risk takers. As countless examples in Silicon Valley have shown, it is a rare entrepreneur who makes a good manager.

As I write this, there is an interesting transfer occurring as the Rev. Robert H. Schuller has handed over the leadership of the

Crystal Cathedral to his only son, ending a half century as pastor of a church he started in a drive-in movie theater. "Junior" (as he's unfortunately called) will also take over the popular *Hour of Power*, a religious program broadcast around the world. Chances are that he will fail, and the Crystal Cathedral will end up as Norman Vincent Peale's Marble Collegiate Church did: huge fixed costs now gasping for new membership.

However, Franklin Graham is successfully taking over Billy's place, and he's doing it by asserting exactly the kind of in-your-face Christianity his father studiously avoided. Admittedly, in private, Billy said some rather uncharitable things about minority groups to President Richard Nixon. On the Watergate tapes, Billy opines that the Jews have a "stranglehold" on the media and are responsible for "all the pornography." He went on to add that while the Jews are friendly to him, "they don't know how I really feel about what they are doing to this country." Franklin at least has the gumption to wear his religious prejudices publicly. Islam, he says, is "a very evil and wicked religion." But, as the Grahams illustrate, prejudice is not the enemy of religion, it's the handmaiden. But it may need the illusion of disguise.

The biggest threat to the evangelical megachurch remains that in foregrounding growth as a sign of value, it is asking for trouble down the road. It's a given in megachurch circles that growth slows when the auditorium reaches 80 percent capacity. That's because people have trouble finding seats together. You can split up at the cineplex but not at the sanctuary. But there's a risk of building too far in front of growth. If what you sell is that more and more people are buying whatever it is, then what happens when you go to the store and see the "two for the price of one" sale and then the "moving to smaller quarters" sale? Seeing too many empty seats can panic a congregation. In old-time denominations, growth was not proof of value; stability was. Hence they could ride out the ups and downs of membership. But the megachurch has no cushion to absorb that inevitable day when they have reached the last available seeker, and the balloon deflates.

What's Good about the Megas

Critics of the megachurches miss the point when they allude to them as shopping-mall churches, McChurches, or Wal-Mart churches. Paradoxically, comments like "they offer Ten Commandments–lite—they're less filling, taste great," or "they're discipleship on the cheap—all wrapper, no product" are wrong on two points. First, this really isn't true. These churches generally do hold beliefs, have a clear mission and purpose, and have high expectations for scriptural study, prayer, and tithing. And they say so. The degree of commitment is often deceptive because what is said on Sunday is often less compelling than the community offered throughout the week. In other words, what they may lack in theological rigor they more than make up for in social adaptation.

Critics miss how the megas have co-opted the great marketing developments of the twentieth century. The megas know what customers want. They know because they are, like their colleagues in the commercial world, continually asking. Religious suppliers are no longer living in a world of production but of consumption. In the Land of Plentitude, the customer is king; little comes from On High. Why should religion be different? Consumption, the act of shopping, has become one of the more creative activities of the modern world. Critics don't have to like this inconvenient truth; in fact, from an environmental and historical point of view, it may be nothing short of tragic. But denial of the obvious is worse. Certain churches get to be megas because they know how to sell what people want to buy.

Listen to this indictment of the megas by the general secretary of the World Council of Churches, Samuel Kobia, in 2006. Addressing the council on the threats to its denominational oligopoly, he excoriates the stand-alone big-box church:

> It has no depth, in most cases, theologically speaking, and has no appeal for any commitment . . . The megachurches simply wanted individuals to feel good about themselves. It's a church

being organized on corporate logic. That can be quite dangerous
if we are not very careful, because this may become a Christianity which I describe as "two miles long and one inch deep."

The WCC represents the nearly 350 Protestant and Orthodox
churches that are the very essence of old-line denominationalism.
And what they are seeing in the megas is a much more fearsome
threat than Islam; it is their product in a new, shiny wrapper, with a
few calories subtracted. The mega threatens to disrupt hegemony by
being exactly what Rev. Kobia says it is—"two miles long and one
inch deep." Is there a better characterization of consumer culture?

So while the observation is correct, the deduction is wrong. Yes,
the megas I have seen are mass produced, shallow, self-centered, cor-
poratized, ahistorical, sensational, predictable, ceaselessly energetic,
and a little paranoid. You certainly don't have to carry a cross to be a
member. All you have to do is show up. The rigor is not in the doctrine and theology, it's in the social organization. Over time, the
product has become commodified and predictable, yes, but it is not
boring. Like the repeat-purchase brand, the megas can be counted
on not just for product consistency but dependable effect. How are
you feeling? We can make you feel better. And clearly they do.

It is exactly because the megas are supersensitive to client
needs—forever changing, fickle, impatient, motivated by cutting
margins—that they will continue to do business, at least for a while.
To be sure, the powerhouse brands like Saddleback, Lakewood, and
Willow will atrophy with the passing of Warren, Osteen, and
Hybels, but the marketing plan of self-contained, nondenominational church will out. True, they may not generate the depth of
commitment that small sects do—there are no martyrs for megas—
but they will capture a huge percent of Rev. Kobia's market.

Before all else, the mega is relevant. Like great churches of the
past, it makes itself so by being restlessly exploitative of each new
innovation in delivery. To call it a Wal-Mart church is more than a
backhanded compliment; it is an acknowledgment of the importance of retail. A mega was the first to use JumboTron screens,

acoustical enhancement, satellite relays, comfy seating, video displays, skits, pop music, and near-instantaneous reproductions of the event. It was the first to tie satellite locations together with coaxial cable. In fact, it was the first to use satellites for broadcast. As well, a mega was the first to use video games, blogging, interactive websites, and email blasts.

Consider the future of tithing, which is, after all, the cash register of the endeavor. While the process may be suspect from a doctrinal point of view, it is absolutely central from a business perspective. How do you pay for the service once the golden offering plates of your father's church are shelved? Electronic funds transfer, considered a "killer app" in the banking business, has been eagerly adopted by the megas. In 2000 only 7 percent of mainline churches offered EFT as a means of donating money; in 2005 only 12 percent did. Meanwhile well over half of the megas already have this technology in place. *Ka-ching!*

Or consider the fad du jour in the faith markets, Godcasting. Godcasting is downloading sermons or church messages to the faithful via iPods. Once past the Brave New World overtones, this connection is in many ways more affective (and effective) than the real thing. "Is it real or is it Memorex?" has been replaced by "Am I in church or just pretending to be?" After all, it's just between you and your ears. And you are never "out of church."

While Godcasting may look as if it's Big Brother in your ears, it really puts more control in the hands of the consumer. The mega may generate content, but the consumer determines the time and place. What feeling do I want? asks the modern penitent. And when do I want to have it? "Turn on, tune in, drop out" has become "turn on, tune in, feel connected."

Client-controlled experiences like this may have an impact on the church as profound as that of the printing press. When the first Bibles were printed in the fifteenth century, the monks squawked. No doubt they considered the printed Bible the equivalent of religion "two miles long and one inch deep." And recall that the Reformation that followed resulted in part from the desire to translate those now-available Bibles into the language of the believer, the much feared vulgate. Whatever moves the consumer closer to the unmediated experience is almost always anathema to the entrenched supplier and tonic to the innovator. Grab hold or get Left Behind.

Chances are that if you go to your church and see a hymnal or a pew Bible in the rack in front of you, you are seeing the end of your church in the distance. The hymnal has already been replaced by the bouncing ball on the screen, and the Bible is continuing its never-ending transformation, not only being rewritten but being reformatted. Just as songs are easy to sing, so easy-reading translations like the *Contemporary English Version* (1991) and *The Message: The Bible in Contemporary Language* (1993) have made the sensation of reading the Bible easy. The movement from formal translations, true to the idioms of the original Hebrew and Greek, to modern renditions that are true to the day-to-day experiences of the reader, is an apt analogy of the shift from supplier-centered to client-centered control. Bible publishers actively seek endorsements from pastorpreneurs, well aware that such cross-branding can result in thousands of additional units sold.

Just as the mega has sloughed off heroic lyrics of difficult-to-sing poetry, so too it is moving toward a Bible with no formal language and no verse numbers. It hasn't happened yet, but the King James version is simply too difficult, too reminiscent of the bad old days of Sunday school, too densely textured. If you look at who is most vigorously defending the KJV, you'll see the problem. And what of *The Light Speed Bible* and *The Bible in 90 Days,* aimed at getting the reader through the scriptures as painlessly as possible? When you realize that your handheld device or your cell phone is going to be the venue of Bible reading, you can see the future of church on the fly. Dial it in. "A Mighty Fortress Is Our God" ring tone.

The mega is only one of many institutions that have moved away from print. The euphemism "at a distance" is usually invoked in preference to "dumbed down." We have learning at a distance in higher ed (the electronic class with PowerPoint), and we have art appreciation at a distance (the headphone tour), why not religion?

That's not to say that the difficult museum show does not exist, the hard-to-read book is not assigned, or the King James version will not be read, but only that the movement of retailing experiences has become much more competitive, and the suppliers who seem to do the biggest business are those who pay the most attention to the client as well as to the text.

It's worth remembering how close the academic and religious worlds were once, if only to appreciate their similarities to the commercial world. Until the twentieth century, the academy was run by the very groups it now often holds in contempt: Bible thumpers. Consider Harvard, founded by militant Congregationalists, who asked of its students that they "shall consider the main end of life and studies to know God and Jesus Christ, which is eternal life." The next school founded, the College of William and Mary, insisted that all teachers vow assent to the Church of England's Thirty-nine Articles of Religion and that all students learn the mother church's catechism. At Yale the president or a professor led prayers and Bible readings each morning and evening, and worship on Sundays was mandatory. All the other pre-Revolutionary institutions were founded under church auspices: Princeton (Presbyterian), Brown (Baptist), Rutgers (Reformed Church), and Dartmouth (Congregational), as well as the multidenominational but Protestant University of Pennsylvania and King's College, now Columbia. Such an irony that the oversupplied institutions of church and school are responding in much the same way to much the same market pressures.

The Mega as Harbinger

Although the megas are doing everything the Rev. Dr. Samuel Kobia has indicted them for, much can be said in their defense. First, they are clearly responding to consumer demand. The big-box suppliers are "putting over" nothing on their parishioners. Their target audience is those baby boomers who left the church in adolescence, who do not feel comfortable with reflexive religiosity, who apply the same consumerist mentality to spiritual life that they do to every-thing else. As with the other awakenings, the megachurches are using the tools of American marketing to spread religion not just to where it would not otherwise exist but back over the burned-out areas where it has alternately flourished and faded for generations. That they have repatriated men is no mean feat; in fact, it is a tribute to focused marketing. Can they hold them in place? Who knows?

Second, the megas deliver on their brand promise. They make people feel better. They have hospitality programs, hold orientation classes, encourage participation in fellowship groups or volunteer community service. Ask people who attend, and you hear *joyful*. Of all the words I couldn't imagine hearing on Route 21, this was the missing one. There is an energy to most of the mega services that I found totally lacking in traditional churches. They sing, dance, play electric guitar and drums, and throw their hands in the air—sure it's a bit *American Idol* and *Beach Blanket Bingo*, but let's not forget that all vibrant churches are just on the edge of vulgarity.

Aligned with this, megas are resolutely optimistic, admittedly to the point of jingoism. You never hear a discouraging word. You won't hear much talk of hellfire or such gloomy things. It's the *good news*, dammit! The party line is empowerment and the good life Jesus wants you to have in the here and now: wealth, happiness, and living up to your potential. To a considerable degree, saying it makes it so. The mega is a reality TV show and therapy session all bundled into one. In a way—and this is both its appeal and maybe its dan-ger—it conflates a consumer culture where the individual is empowered to seek happiness through secular success, then return to share it with the church.

Third, why shouldn't churches take back all the stuff they offloaded on the secular world? The megas have restaurants, child care (and that alone might be enough reason to go), gyms, coffee shops, knickknack stores, and basketball courts. Some also have driving ranges, medical facilities, martial-arts classes, music studios, and their own record labels. Putting aside doctrine and politics, it's refreshing to observe community and passionate small-town intimacy. By taking back roles as various as those of the welcome wagon, the USO, the Rotary, the quilting bee, the book club, the coffee shop, and the country-club mixer—and, of course, the traditional family and school—these "next churches" have become the traditional commons/villages that many Americans think they grew up in and can find only on television. The mega, rather like the Starbucks it sometimes resembles, has come to be one of those "third places" we often rhapsodize about. Not home, not work, but that place where we find community.

Finally, the megas are *with it*. The people who put together these churches clearly spent time consuming pop culture. They know that the audience is as much a performer as the headliners and that the entertainment flows not old-style from stage to audience, but new-style with shared performance. To paraphrase Walt Whitman, great rock concerts need great audiences. Ditto megas. Just as clearly, the pastorpreneurs also spent time down at the mall. They know you have to continually shift inventory or lose customer curiosity. They are intensely aware that there's a store next door selling the same stuff. Provide "shopocalypse" or go out of business. Get in the shopper's face.

In many respects the mega is a return to the camp meeting. Maybe the analogy is with the Chautauqua tradition, minus the intellectual component. The megachurch offers a public world, not a private one; a communal display, not a private contemplation; an "I want it now" not a "Let's do it later." Of course, this depends on a level of anonymity, of not being too self-conscious, of being in a crowd.

Who knows where the long and winding road of American Protestantism is going? Certainly not me. But it seems likely that it will retrace the same terrain over and over again, losing steam as it becomes repetitive and then recharging as it gloms on to some new delivery system. When this happens, we'll think we are becoming more religious, but in truth religiosity is simply becoming more compelling as it shifts media to appeal to consumers once again.

Recall that we have been in each other's faces before. From

Roger William's spat with the Massachusetts Bay Colony to John Scopes's monkey trial to Terri Schiavo's feeding tubes, we supercharge some event with religiosity and raise holy hell. At the first session of the Continental Congress, the founding fathers squabbled over religion. A delegate from Boston wanted to open with a prayer. Others objected. After debate, the delegates voted to pray. Sound familiar? But then we go into long periods of lassitude, such as we saw after World War II, in which we seem willing to put aside religious conflict.

No matter how this current tangle works itself out, it probably won't end in the rapture of the Evangelists, the demise of denominations, the gated community of the megas, or in the cosmopolitanism envisioned by the secularists. While it would be nice to think that more and more of the poor and disenfranchised will find their way into a better life thanks to an increase in religiosity, such will probably not happen. Unfortunately, the invocation of an awakened God most likely precedes the drawing of swords and the slaughter of some infidels. As well, it would also be nice to think that commercial secularism could be heroic, self-abnegating, and redemptive, but that too seems doubtful. Alas, a rising standard of living may lift some boats, but it doesn't really increase the amount of shared happiness.

So, it seems as doubtful that we will see the New Jerusalem of the true believers as predicted in the Book of Revelation:

> Then I saw a new heaven and a new earth, for the first heaven and the first earth had passed away, and there was no longer any sea. I saw the Holy City, the new Jerusalem, coming down out of heaven from God, prepared as a bride beautifully dressed for her husband. And I heard a loud voice from the throne saying, "Now the dwelling of God is with men, and he will live with them. They will be his people, and God himself will be with them and be their God. He will wipe every tear from their eyes. There will be no more death or mourning or crying or pain, for the old order of things has passed away."

And it seems equally doubtful we'll see the nonbeliever version predicted by Percy Shelley in *Prometheus Unbound*:

> The loathsome mask has fallen, the man remains
> Sceptreless, free, uncircumscribed, but man
> Equal, unclassed, tribeless, and nationless,
> Exempt from awe, worship, degree, the king
> Over himself; just, gentle, wise; but man
> Passionless—no, yet free from guilt or pain,
> Which were, for his will made or suffered them;
> Nor yet exempt, though ruling them like slaves,
> From chance, and death, and mutability,
> The clogs of that which else might oversoar
> The loftiest star of unascended heaven,
> Pinnacled dim in the intense inane.

Rather, we will continue to vacillate between these two visions as we have since the American religion market opened for business. The preacher (better yet, the teacher) in *Ecclesiastes* had it right.

We have been traversing this middle ground for some time, and it is often a scary and melancholy place to be. Every generation or so we move from Great Awakening to Great Nonchalance and then back to Great Awakening. This is a spiritual world in flux, not wholly driven by the whimsical caprices of the materialists or the unfettered vision of the holy, but always somewhere in between. Speculators on both sides continually scramble to bring new stories to market. As long as the yearning for sensation can be whetted by these stories, and as long as there is a plenitude of suppliers, this market will stay roiled. The only certainty is that the mass-mediated and mass-marketed world of the increasingly powerful Industrial Revolution is drawing us ever closer together. How religion allows us to make either meaning or mincemeat out of this shrinking world remains to be seen.

Endnotes

CHAPTER 1: OH LORD, WHY U.S.? AN OVERVIEW
OF THE SPIRITUAL MARKETPLACE

1 *In 1900 almost everyone:* Noelle Knox, "Religion Takes a Back Seat in
   Western Europe," *USA Today,* August 11, 2005, p. A1.

5 *A generation later, two:* Frank Rich, "The God Racket, from DeMille to
   DeLay," *New York Times,* March 27, 2005, sec. 2, p. 1.

6 *So too the merchandise:* William Neuman, "Jesus Nail Sale—Mel's Deal
   Lets You Buy 'Passion Spikes,'" *New York Post,* February 19, 2004, p. 3.

6 *How powerful was* The Passion: Carol Eisenberg, "America Gets Religion: God Talk Is Everywhere," *Newsday,* April 14, 2004, p. B2.

11 *Christian broadcasters now control:* Sam Husseini, "Religion and Politics: The Media's One-dimensional View," *Extra!,* the magazine of the
   media watch group FAIR, (July/August 1994), www.fair.org/index.
   php?page=2692.

13 *When you go into megachurches:* Jane Lampman, "Megachurches' Way
   of Worship Is on the Rise," *Christian Science Monitor,* February 6, 2006,
   p. 13.

13 *A recent survey by the Pew Research:* Carol Eisenberg, "America's Old-
   time Religious Revival: More People Reaching Out for Spiritual Guid-
   ance," *Washington Post,* April 25, 2004, p. D1. For the most popular
   passwords see: www.foxnews.com/story/0,2933,172014,00.html.

14 *Nearly 6 out of every 10:* these statistics are from the Barna Group website, www.barna.org/FlexPage.aspx?Page=BarnaUpdateNarrow&Barna
   UpdateID=199.

17 *In 2004, books about religious:* Heather Grimshaw, "An Almighty Market: God Is Big Business in the Publishing World," *Denver Post,* July
   10, 2005, p. F1. Also, on the subject of Bible publishing, see Daniel

Radosh, "The Good Book Business," *The New Yorker,* December, 18, 2006, p. 54ff.

19 *In any case, Zondervan:* Cathy Lynn Grossman, "*Rolling Stone* Reverses, Will Accept Bible Ad," *USA Today,* January 24, 2005, p. 8D.

24 *Sixty-four percent of Americans:* And now to really scramble things up here are some more inane figures: $400 million was what Mel Gibson's *The Passion of the Christ* made in the U.S. The Radiant Church in Surprise, Arizona, spends $16,000 per year on Krispy Kreme doughnuts. Outreach Inc. of Vista, California, employs 120 people in equipping more than 20,000 congregations this year with products and advice to raise their local profiles. Life Pointe Christian Church in Charlotte, North Carolina, has given away three thousand water bottles and five thousand Frisbees emblazoned with church contact information and logos. Ten percent of regular attendees say they learned about the church from a Frisbee. The marketing flack for the United Methodist Church claims that if it launches a $4 million four-week campaign integrating TV and other media, the attendance of first-time visitors grows by about 19 percent (when the ads are running). The United Synagogue of Conservative Judaism is urging its 760 affiliated synagogues to establish publicity goals and strategies because "in an age of unlimited choices . . . congregations must enter the world of public relations."

24 *Consider: In 1900 there were 330:* Louis Sahagun, "He Wrote the Book on American Religions" (J. Gordon Melton, obituary), *Los Angeles Times,* April 12, 2006, p. B2.

28 *Observe Sweden and the Lutheran Church:* Noelle Knox, Ibid.

33 *I lift this coinage:* Jonathan Rauch, "Let It Be," *Atlantic Monthly,* May 2003, p. 42.

CHAPTER 2: ANOTHER GREAT AWAKENING?

38 *A few years ago, two churches:* www.churchmarketingsucks.com/archives/2005/05.

39 *The campaign is back again:* Jane Lampman, "On a Billboard Near You: Matters of Faith," *Christian Science Monitor,* April 28, 2005, p. 12.

42 *As an editorial writer for* The Nation: As quoted in Philip B. Kunhardt Jr. Philip B. Kunhardt III, and Peter W. Kunhardt, *P. T. Barnum: America's Greatest Showman* (New York: Knopf, 1995), p. 201.

45 *Like so many pastorpreneurs, Finney:* For more on the extraordinary

Finney, see Keith Hardman, *Charles Grandison Finney, 1792–1875: Revivalist and Reformer* (Syracuse, N.Y.: Syracuse University Press, 1987); Michael Barkun, *Crucible of the Millenium: The Burned-over District of New York in the 1840s* (Syracuse, N.Y.: Syracuse University Press, 1986); Bernard A. Weisberger, *They Gathered at the River: The Story of the Great Revivalists and Their Impact upon Religion in America* (Boston; Little, Brown, 1958); and Whitney R. Cross, *The Burned-over District: The Social and Intellectual History of Enthusiastic Religion in Western New York, 1800–1850* (Ithaca, N.Y.: Cornell University Press, 1950).

48 *These churches, defined by the size:* Michelle Goldberg, *Kingdom Coming: The Rise of Christian Nationalism* (New York: W. W. Norton, 2006), pp. 58–59.

48 *Of 1,004 respondents to a* Newsweek/Beliefnet *poll:* Jerry Adler, "In Search of the Spiritual," *Newsweek,* August 29, 2005, p. 49.

49 *The* Newsweek/Beliefnet *Poll:* Ibid.

50 *As religious historian Martin E. Marty:* As quoted in Jerry Adler, Ibid. p. 58.

51 *According to the* Washington Post: Peter Baker, "Bush Tells Group He Sees a 'Third Awakening,'" *Washington Post,* September 13, 2006, p. A5.

52 *Religion is big news:* Both cities are from Husseini, Ibid.

54 *The mainline suppliers, principally:* Tom W. Smith and Kim Seokho, "The Vanishing Protestant Majority," *Journal for the Scientific Study of Religion,* vol. 44, no. 2 (June 2005): 211–223.

54 *In his 1988 book* Marketing the Church: (Menasha, Wis.: NavPress, 1988), p. 42.

55 *Even though the fraction:* This shift is documented many places, for instance: www.religioustolerance.org/chr_prac2.htm.

55 *In 2005 the 16.4-million-member:* William C. Symonds, "Earthly Empires: How Evangelical Churches Are Borrowing from the Business Playbook," *BusinessWeek,* May 23, 2005, p. 78.

CHAPTER 3: LET'S GO SHOPPING: BROUGHT TO YOU BY GOD®

62 *According to a study by the market research:* Julie Bosman, "Christian Message, Secular Messengers," *New York Times,* April 26, 2006, p. C13.

63 *Pretty soon the Protestants:* See Colleen McDannell, *Material Christianity: Religion and Popular Culture in America* (New Haven, Conn.: Yale

University Press, 1998), and Roy Rivenburg, "Material World of Christianity from Bird Feeders to Bible Games," *Los Angeles Times,* September 24, 1995, p. A1.

64 *According to religious historian:* McDannell, Ibid., p. 43.

65 *Better yet, attend the Christian Booksellers:* Rivenburg, Ibid., and David Gibson, "Religion for Sale: Spreading the Gospel Is Profitable in Booming Christian Market," *The Record* (Bergen County, N.J.), July 25, 1999, p. 1.

66 *When the Style section:* Stephanie Rosenbloom, "A Ring That Says No, Not Yet," *New York Times,* December 8, 2005, p. G1.

66 *If you really want to see:* Cathleen Falsani, "From 'The Passion' to The Purpose-driven Life, Superficial God-Talk," *Chicago Sun-Times,* March 18, 2004, p. 16; and Ruth La Ferla, "Wearing Their Beliefs on Their Chests," *New York Times,* March 29, 2005, p. B1.

71 *Back in the 1970s, Theodore Levitt:* "The Morality of Advertising," *Harvard Business Review,* vol. 48, no. 4 (July–August 1970), p. 88.

72 *But Sheena Iyengar and Mark Lepper:* "When Choice Is Demotivating: Can One Desire Too Much of a Good Thing?" *Journal of Personality and Social Psychology,* vol. 76 (2000): 995–1006.

75 *A study by the retail-industry:* Toni C. Langlinais, "Picking the Right Brand Management Technique," *American Banker*, August 29, 2006, p. 2A. See also James Surowiecki, "The Decline of Brands," *Wired,* November 2004, p. 35.

77 *A few years ago Young & Rubicam:* Richard Tomkins, "Brands Are New Religion, Says Advertising Agency," *Financial Times* (London), March 1, 2001, p. 11.

86 *Climbing rates of church switching:* Michael Hout, Andrew Greeley, and Melissa Wilde, "Birth Dearth: Demographics of Mainline Decline," *The Christian Century,* October 4, 2005, p. 24. See also the many works of cultural geographer Roger W. Stump, such as, "Regional Variations in Denominational Switching among White Protestants," *The Professional Geographer*, vol. 39, no. 4 (1987): 438–49; and Matthew Loveland, "Religious Switching: Preference Development, Maintenance and Change," *Journal for the Scientific Study of Religion*, vol. 41, no. 1 (2003): 147–57.

89 *A USA Today/CNN/Gallup survey:* Roger W. Stump, "Spirituality by Design," *Orlando Sentinel* (Florida), February 13, 2000, p. A1.

91 *I hope this email finds you well:* Email of April 7, 2006.

93 *In August of 2005, speaking:* Shannon Smiley, "Sea of Youth Embraces New Pope," *Washington Post,* August 22, 2005, p. A10.

95 *A recent Gallup survey found:* Bill Broadway, "Poll Finds America 'as Churched as Ever,'" *Washington Post,* May 31, 1997, p. B7; and Jerry Adler, Ibid., p. 48.

CHAPTER 4: HATCH, MATCH, DISPATCH, *OR* BAPTIZED, MARRIED, BURIED: THE WORK OF DENOMINATIONS

101 *The New Testament says nothing:* Dan Barker, "Tithing for Dummies," the Society of Mutual Autopsy on the website: www.somareview.com/tithingfordummies.cfm.

103 *When a cult hits pay dirt:* Lorne Dawson, "Cults, New Religions, Continue to Proliferate," *London Free Press* (London, Ontario, Canada), August 29, 1998, p. F6; as well as Rodney Stark, *The Rise of Christianity: A Sociologist Reconsiders History* (Princeton, N.J.: Princeton University Press, 1996).

104 *Consider the Mormon Church:* Rodney Stark, "The Rise of a New World Faith," *Review of Religious Research,* vol. 26, no. 1 (1984): 18–27.

105 *So Squire Rushnell:* Squire Rushell, *When God Winks at You: How God Speaks Directly to You Through the Power of Confidence* (Nashville, Tenn: Nelson Books, 2006), p. 43.

106 *In 2005 an unprecedented study:* Jane Lampman, "Moments of Truth," *Christian Science Monitor,* December 22, 2005, p. 14.

120 *The teachers of [religion]:* Adam Smith, *The Wealth of Nations,* 1776 repr. (New York: Modern Library, 1965), 740–41.

121 *Why not construct a paradigm:* Economists like Laurence R. Iannaccone at George Mason University, who studied under Becker at Chicago, have helped us understand the metrics of metaphysics. Iannaccone now heads a new academic group, the Association for the Study of Religion, Economics & Culture. This kind of economic interpretation of the faith markets is starting to surface in journals that specialize in economics (*American Economic Review, Economic Inquiry, Journal of Political Economy, Journal of Economic Behavior and Organization, Journal of Institutional and Theoretical Economics,* and *Public Choice*) as well as journals dedicated to the social-scientific, mostly sociological, study of religion (*Journal for the Scientific Study of Religion, Sociology of Religion,* and *Review of Religious Research*).

One of the places to observe academic fashion is not just in what is published but in what is being funded. Relatively few books have been directed toward religious studies. And when you look at the recipients of grants from the National Endowment for the Humanities, American Council of Learned Societies, and Rockefeller and Guggenheim foundations, you'll see why. Very little seed money has flowed into this area. No wonder. Religious studies were thought either too otherworldly or too unrigorous. The John Templeton Foundation changed that, awarding Iannaccone a $500,000 grant in 2005 to support these and other activities over the next three years. Now, thanks to two other large private foundations—the Lilly Endowment and the Pew Charitable Trusts—monies for such economic study of religion are finally appearing.

124 *Finke and Stark's world contains:* "Review of *The Churching of America, 1776–2005: Winners and Losers in Our Religious Economy,*" *The Christian Century,* January 27, 1993, p. 88.

130 *As with any merger:* "Religious Mergers: A Marriage Made in Heaven?" *Economist.com,* February, 21, 2007; and reprinted in the "Informed Reader," *Wall Street Journal,* February 22, 2007, p. B6.

CHAPTER 5: HOLY FRANCHISE: MARKETING RELIGION IN A SCRAMBLE ECONOMY

133 *Mainstream denominations are in deep trouble:* Specific denominational numbers are hard to come by. Like universities submitting data to *U.S. News & World Report,* there is an understandable tendency to fudge. The best source of membership data is Eileen W. Lindner (editor), *Yearbook of American and Canadian Churches* (Nashville, Tenn: Abingdon Press), published yearly and under the auspices of the National Council of Churches. An interesting source for shifting denominations is John C. Green, "The American Religious Landscape and Political Attitudes: A Baseline for 2004," which is based on telephone survey information from a random sample of four thousand adults (www.pewforum.org/publications/surveys/green-full.pdf). More specific is G. Jeffrey MacDonald, "Mainstream Churches Take a Leap of Faith into TV Advertising," *Christian Science Monitor,* March 16, 2004, p. 1; Heather Wilhelm, "Houses of Worship: Anything Goes," *Wall Street Journal,* September 8, 2006, p. W13; and Peter Steinfels, "Under God, but Divisible," *New York Times,* October 9, 2004, p. A17.

135 *The average person now changes houses: Population Bulletin*, vol. 53, no. 3 (September 1998): http://ecp3113-01.fa01.fsu.edu/lively_intro duction/Migration.htm.

135 *With divorce, the child's religious:* Leora E. Lawton and Regina Bures, "Parental Divorce and the Switching of Religious Identity," *Journal for the Scientific Study of Religion*, vol. 40, no. 1 (March 2001): 99–111.

135 *These migration patterns are exaggerated:* Michael Hout, Andrew Greeley, and Melissa J. Wilde, "The Demographic Imperative in Religious Change in the United States," *American Journal of Sociology,* vol. 107, no. 2 (September 2001): 468–500.

136 *A study conducted in 2005:* These data about pastoral migration are from: www.ellisonresearch.com/releases/20051108.htm.

138 *In studies done on apostasy:* Nathan Black, "Survey: Reasons Why Americans Leave the Church," to be found at: www.christianpost. com/article/20061018/22951_Survey%3A_Reasons_Why_Americans_ Leave_the_Church.htm.

138 *In 1958 only 1 in 25:* Richard Cimino and Don Lattin, "Choosing My Religion," *American Demographics,* April 1999, p. 62.

139 *Church literature from one megachurch:* http:hirr.hartsem.edu/bookshelf/ thumma_article2.html.

139 *According to a recent survey:* Unsigned column, "Most Say They Are Religious, Study Finds," *Los Angeles Times,* February 20, 1999, p. 3.

141 *The Church should advertise because:* Charles Stelzle, *Principles of Successful Church Advertising* (New York: Fleming H. Revell Company, 1908), pp. 15–16.

143 *Its public view, expressed in a policy:* Go to: www.vatican.va/roman_ curia/pontifical_councils and search "Ethics in Advertising (February 22, 1997)."

144 *Since 1965 the number of ordinations:* Rachel Zoll, "Vatican Evaluates All U.S. Seminaries," *Detroit News,* October 2, 2005, p. A4.

146 *The Church of England's Sunday attendance:* James Curtis, "Marketing Mix: The Brand of God," *Marketing,* April 17, 1997, p. 22.

147 *One of the biggest suppliers:* Michael Kress, "Marketing Faith: Churches Turn to Advertising," *Newsday,* July 19, 1998, p. G1.

149 *Even the Mormons, who:* Alan Cooperman, "Churches Go Commercial to Spread Their Message," *Washington Post,* July 11, 2004, p. A1.

150 *Well, listen to this:* "Art & Commerce: Selling God," *Adweek,* January 8, 2001, p. 4.

151 *The church attained adman's heaven:* To find Follis's case study of the campaign: www.follisinc.com/casemarble.htm.

151 *So the Church of the Heavenly Rest:* Nadine Brozan, "For the Good Book, a Good Sales Pitch," *New York Times,* October 4, 1998, p. 43.

161 *"The Bouncer" came out:* For more on the controversy, see: Rob Hiaasen, "One House, Many Voices," *Baltimore Sun,* December 11, 2004, p. D1; Waveney Ann Moore, "Inclusive Church Feels the Sting of Exclusion," *St. Petersburg Times,* December 14, 2004, p. 6; Greg Wright, "Churches May Break Away over TV Ad," *Gannett News Service,* November 4, 2005; and Patricia Simms, "Churches Make Pitch on TV," *Wisconsin State Journal* (Madison, Wis.), April 16, 2006, p. D1.

162 *The Mormons and the Lutherans:* Bill Broadway, "Congregations Making a Pitch to Fill the Pews," *Washington Post,* September 2, 1995, p. B6.

164 *For $1,200, any member church:* Lisa Miller, "Religious Advertising Converts, Moving Toward a Tougher Sell," *Wall Street Journal,* February 24, 1998, p. 1.

164 *A generation ago the Episcopal:* Still the best book on this subject is Kit Konolige, *The Power of Their Glory: America's Ruling Class, the Episcopalians* (New York: Wyden Books, 1978).

CHAPTER 6: THE UNITED METHODIST EXAMPLE

167 *Here's the result of their openness:* "Statistics: U.S. Data," United Methodist Church, at www.umc.org.

168 *If ever there was a denomination:* Tribune wire services, "United Methodist Membership Down," *Chicago Tribune,* May 5, 2006, p. 12.

169 *After test-marketing the general concept:* Flo Johnston, "Methodist Launch National Ad Campaign," *Herald-Sun* (Durham, N.C.), July 14, 2001, p. A8.

170 *Here's what they did:* Christopher Schultz, "Ads Aim to Move Viewers from Couch to Church," *Cable World,* September 24, 2001, p. 31.

171 *In a nationwide sample:* Ervin Dyer, "Church Ads Deliver a Message," *Pittsburgh Post-Gazette,* August 6, 2004, p. C1.

172 *The denomination's legislative body voted:* "Campaign Will Help Guide Americans' Search for Spirituality," press release, Business Wire, August 29, 2005.

179 *In 2004, while the campaign:* Sheila Byrd, "Faithful Hands: Churches Reaching Out to Community While Rebuilding Worship Houses," *Topeka Capital-Journal* (Kansas), May 6, 2006, p. 2.

CHAPTER 7: THE CHURCH IMPOTENT:
WHAT'S WRONG WITH THE MAINLINES?

184 *Nationally, the average for Protestant:* www.uscongregations.org/key.htm.

184 *More interesting is that these:* The graying feminity of Protestantism is discussed in chapter 4 of Robert D. Putnam, *Bowling Alone: The Collapse and Revival of American Community* (New York: Simon & Schuster, 2001); and why this is a problem for gathering men in David Morrow, *Why Men Hate Going to Church* (Nashville, Tenn.: Nelson Books, 2005).

184 *I know those women well:* www.bookreporter.com/reviews2/0785260382. asp.

185 *In the mid-nineteenth century:* Fanny Trollope, *Domestic Manners of the Americans,* chapter 8: www.piney.com/AwkTrollope1.html.

185 *Men shy away from commitment:* David Yount, "Men Shying from Commitment in Religion," Scripps Howard News Service, May 22, 2006.

185 *A recent Lutheran-sponsored:* Yount, Ibid.

188 *Of the many insights:* The feminization of denominations is hardly a new thesis. In fact, especially since Ann Douglas's *The Feminization of American Culture* (New York: Knopf, 1977), it has become something of an academic donnée. Consider Barbara Welter, *Dimity Convictions: The American Woman in the Nineteenth Century* (Athens, Ohio: Ohio University Press, 1976); Richard D. Shiels, "The Feminization of American Congregationalism, 1730–1835," *American Quarterly*, vol. 33 (1981): 46–62; Terry Bilhartz, "Sex and the Second Great Awakening: The Feminization of American Religion Reconsidered," in *Belief and Behavior: Essays in the New Religious History,* ed. Philip R. Vandermeer and Robert P. Swierenga (New Brunswick, N.J.: Rutgers University Press, 1991), 117–35; Eugen Schoenfeld and Stjepan Mestrovic, "With Justice and Mercy," *Journal for the Scientific Study of Religion*, vol. 30 (1991): 363–380; W. H. Swatos Jr., "The Feminization of God and the Priesting of Women," in *Twentieth-century World Religious Movements in Neo-Weberian Perspective* (Lewiston, N.Y.: Mellen Press, 1992); Ann Braude, "Women's History Is American Religious History," in *Retelling U.S. Religious History,* ed. Thomas A. Tweed (Berkeley, Calif: University of California Press, 1996), pp. 87–107; and Paula D. Nesbitt, *Feminization of the Clergy in America* (New York: Oxford University Press, 1997).

194 *The preaching was going on:* Chapter 20: www.literature.org/authors/
     twain-mark/huckleberry/chapter-20.html.

196 *He [Slope] is gifted:* Chapter 4: www.cleavebooks.co.uk/grol/trollope/
     barch04.htm.

CHAPTER 8: OUT OF THE IVORY TOWER AND INTO THE MISSIONARY FIELDS

208 *Over 75 percent of these huge congregations:* Unsigned, "Megachurches
     Abound in the South," *Research Alert* (newsletter), February 17, 2006,
     p. 12. See also Charles Trueheart, "Welcome to the Next Church," *The
     Atlantic Monthly,* August 1996, pp. 37–58; and a series on the megas by
     Gustav Niebuhr in the *New York Times:* "Missionaries to Suburbia,"
     April 16, 1995, p. A1; "The Minister as Marketer: Learning from Busi-
     ness," April 18, 1995, p. A1; and "Protestantism Shifts toward a New
     Model of How Church Is Done," April 29, 1995, p. A12. For an
     overview of data: www.hirr.hartsem.edu.

209 *Even in this troubled world:* www.watchtower.org.

221 *Before becoming FaithWorld:* Mark I. Pinsky, "Faith in High Gear:
     Clint Brown Has Brought New Ways of Praise to the Ministry Once
     Led by Televangelist Benny Hinn," *Orlando Sentinel* (Florida), Decem-
     ber 11, 1999, p. E1.

225 *If you google* Clint Brown: Mark I. Pinsky and Linda Shrieves,
     "Singer-Pastor Took Long Road to Prosperity," *Orlando Sentinel*
     (Florida), February 13, 2005, p. A1.

CHAPTER 9: THE MEGACHURCH: "IF YOU ARE CALLING ABOUT A DEATH IN THE FAMILY, PRESS 8."

229 *By definition they have a rather arbitrary:* Bill Broadway, "Services Fit
     for an Arena," *Washington Post,* May 15, 2004, p. B9.

229 *But here's a reasonable guess:* Mark Chavez, "Supersized: Analyzing the
     Trend toward Larger Churches," *The Christian Century,* November 28,
     2006, p. 20.

230 *For a number of reasons:* Malcolm Gladwell, *The Tipping Point: How Lit-
     tle Things Can Make a Big Difference* (New York: Little Brown, 2001).

231 *At the macro level these churches:* Amy Maclachlan, "Megachurches
     Multiply in U.S.," *Presbyterian Record,* July 1, 2005, p. 16.

231 *Little congregations of fewer:* Truehart, Ibid., p. 40.

231 *They have almost no denominational affiliation:* Maclachlan, Ibid., p. 16.

232 *Income at the average:* Scott Thumma, Dave Travis, and Warren Bird, "Megachurches Today 2005: Summary of Research Findings," http://hirr.hartsem.edu/megachurch/megastoday2005_summaryreport.html.

235 *In the 1970s Rev. Robert Schuller:* Paul Goldberger, "The Gospel of Church Architecture, Revised," *New York Times,* April 20, 1995, p. C1.

235 *One week the New Life Church:* Or at least this was before Pastor Haggard went AWOL. The data are from Tom Brokaw in his special "In God They Trust," *Tom Brokaw Reports*, NBC News Transcripts, October 28, 2005.

246 *In the 2004 presidential election:* John C. Green, "Winning Numbers: Religion in the 2004 Election," *The Christian Century,* November 30, 2004, p. 8.

249 *In 1975, as a 23-year-old, Hybels:* Mary Beth Sammons, "Full-service Church: For Willow Creek Faithful, Singular Success Is God's Work," *Chicago Tribune,* April 3, 1994, p. 1.

252 *Sorry for breaking into your day:* Email of October 2, 2002.

253 *Often men would spend:* For an introduction to how men spent their time in the company of other men, see Mark C. Carnes, *Secret Ritual and Manhood in Victorian America* (New Haven, Conn.: Yale University Press, 1989). For instance, almost half the male population in the beginning of the twentieth century belonged to a single-sex fraternal lodge. Clearly the megachurch is currently one of the few places that men can now congregate guilt free with other men. No feminist complains; after all, it's church.

254 *A poster hangs outside:* For more on the consumer-sensitive model, see James Mellado, *Willow Creek Community Church: Harvard Business School Case Study 9-691-102* (Cambridge, Mass: Harvard Business School, 1991); and Fara Warner, "Prepare Thee for Some Serious Marketing," *New York Times,* October 22, 2006, sec. 3, p. 1.

255 *From a first meeting that drew:* Newsmaker of the Week, "Former CU Coach Still Filling Stadiums," *Denver Post,* June 18, 1995, p. C2.

256 *The organization had scaled down:* Eric Gorski, "Adding Politics to Prayer: Reinvented Promise Keepers Seeks a Voice in Social Issues," *Denver Post,* October 25, 2004, p. B1.

257 *The group even has a seven-step:* www.promisekeepers.org/about/7promises.

259 *So who are these meek men:* Joseph P. Shapiro, "Heavenly Promises,"
      U.S. News & World Report, October 2, 1995, p. 68.

260 *You made the team:* Because in my day job I am an English teacher, I
      am always curious about what people read. Assuming that you can
      judge a book a bit by its title, the PK bookshelf is substantial and reve-
      latory. Here's a bit of the Real Men in Spiritual Recovery genre: *With
      God on the Golf Course; Reel Time with God; With God on a Deer Hunt;
      Faith in the Fast Lane; 15 Minutes Alone with God for Men; A Look at
      Life from a Deer Stand; What a Hunter Brings Home; Where the Grass Is
      Always Greener; Every Man's Battle: Meditation for Men; A Man after
      God's Own Heart; The Ultimate Fishing Challenge; The Ultimate Hunt;
      As Iron Sharpens Iron: Building Character in a Mentoring Relationship;
      Wild at Heart: Discovering the Secret of a Man's Soul; With God on the
      Open Road; Fight on Your Knees: Calling Men to Action Through Trans-
      forming Prayer; A Man's Role in the Home; 4th and Goal: Coaching for
      Life's Tough Calls, The Power of a Praying Husband* (Audiobook, Prayer
      Pak and Study Guide); *Real Men Don't Abandon Their Responsibilities;
      What Makes a Man?; Tender Warrior; Locking Arms; A Call to Manhood;
      The Masculine Journey; What God Does When Men Pray*; and for those
      who are too busy to read but still care: *Minute Meditations for Men* and
      Men of Characters—Quotes from Godly Men. There's even a slick
      bimonthly magazine, *New Man,* which features advice on safe sex ("it's
      called *marriage*") and columns on fitness and finances.

260 *All the liberal criticisms:* As quoted by John Leo, "Fairness? Promises,
      Promises," *U.S. News & World Report,* July 28, 1997, p. 18; and feminist
      concerns: www.now.org/issues/right/pk.html.

CHAPTER 10: AND THIS TOO SHALL PASS: THE FUTURE OF MEGAS

266 *An International Monetary Fund:* Marc Gunther, "Will Success Spoil
      Rick Warren?" *Fortune,* October 31, 2005, p. 108.

267 *So, while raising thousands:* Unsigned, "Jesus, CEO; Churches as Busi-
      nesses," *The Economist,* December 24, 2005, p. 60.

267 *For instance, Willow Creek employs two:* Symonds, Ibid., p. 78.

267 *In 2005, both the staid:* Symonds, Ibid., and unsigned, "Onward, Chris-
      tian Shoppers: Religion and Business," *The Economist,* December 3,
      2005, p. 80.

267   *After all, the Lakewood enterprise:* Tara Dooley, "Megahouse of Worship," *Houston Chronicle,* July 10, 2005, p. A1.

267   *And indeed companies:* "Product Placement in the Pews? Microtargeting Meets Megachurches," *Knowledge@Wharton*, November 15, 2006.

268   *At the end of the 1990s:* "Our-Street.com Reveals Kingdom Ventures CEO Puts Christian Speakers & Artists into Bankruptcy Despite Alleged Sale," *Knobias.com*, September 7, 2004. Kingdom Ventures now seems to be a dormant part of Denim Apparel Group, a company that puts logos on sportswear.

269   *The Luis Palau Orlando Festival:* Mark I. Pinsky, "Don't Think Crusade, Think Festival," *Orlando Sentinel* (Florida), November 5, 2005, p. E1.

270   *But, as we learn on page 5: The Shepherd's Guide* (Titusville, FL: 2004/5).

270   *Try the Community Church of Joy:* On their website www.joyonline.org.

272   *In fact, in the 1990s:* Mellado, Ibid.

272   *I am writing this to you:* Email of March 3, 2006.

273   *"I'm an incurable team player":* Russell Chandler, "The Nation's Most Successful Congregations," *Los Angeles Times,* December 11, 1989, p. A1.

274   *But what I find particularly:* Juli Cragg Hilliard, "*Pyro* Goes Ahead; Warren Weighs In," *Publishers Weekly,* August 29, 2005, p. 9.

275   *That's because he's bought:* Richard Vara, "Osteens Want New Lakewood Site to Become a Landmark," *Houston Chronicle,* March 23, 2002, p. 1.

275   *So, for instance, years ago:* Joel Osteen, *Your Best Life Now* (New York: Warner Faith, 2004), p. 46.

275   *What makes this ironically entertaining:* Keith L. Alexander, "Peace on Earth, Not Necessarily aboard Aircraft," *Washington Post,* December 27, 2005, p. D1; and unsigned column, "Wait Your Turn," *Houston Press,* December 29, 2005, no page.

276   *Here are a few tips:* The whole story is told by Michael Roberts, "The Message Prophetable," *Denver Westword* (Colorado), May 26, 2005, p. 1.

278   *Although Haggard's mega:* Patricia Leigh Brown, "Megachurches as Minitowns," *New York Times,* May 9, 2002, p. F1.

280   *At one extreme is Rick:* Unsigned, "Jesus, CEO: Churches as Business," Ibid., p. 61.

280   *Or there is Bill Hybels's:* Cathleen Falsani, "Different Way to 'Do Church' Keeps Growing," *Chicago Sun-Times,* October 23, 2005, p. A9.

282   *"Junior" (as he's unfortunately called):* Unsigned, "Son of Scary," *OC*

Weekly (Orange County, Calif.), November 1, 2002, p. 20.

283 *It has no depth:* As quoted in Anne Buggins, "Evangelical Churches Branded Big Businesses with no Theology," *West Australian* (Perth, Australia), February 23, 2006, p. 1.

285 *Electronic funds transfer:* Greg Latshaw, " 'Godcasts' Spread the Gospel," *Pittsburgh Tribune-Review,* August 13, 2006, unpaged.

285 *Or consider the fad:* Ibid.

290 *Then I saw a new heaven:* Revelation 21:1–4.

291 *The loathsome mask has fallen:* Shelley, *Prometheus Unbound,* act 3, scene 4, lines 193–204.

Index

Page numbers in *italics* refer to illustrations.

307

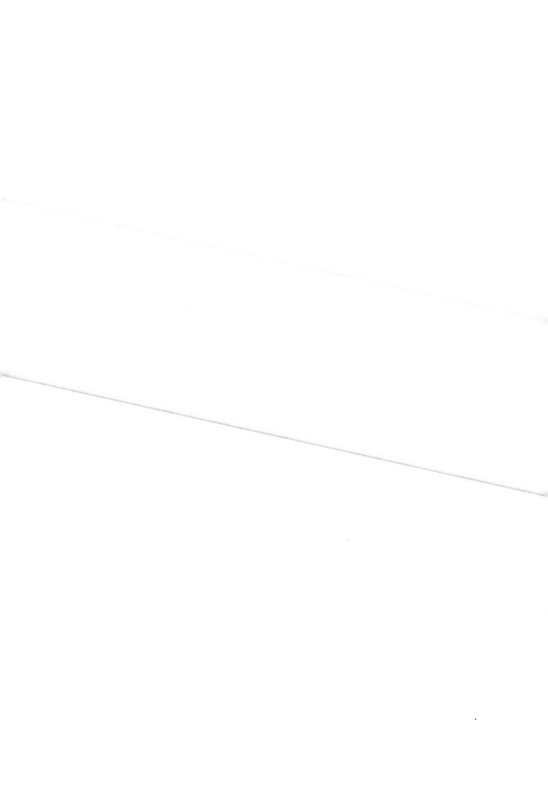

Printed in the United States
By Bookmasters